A Brief Guide
to the Hebrew Bible

A Brief Guide
to the Hebrew Bible

Hans M. Barstad

TRANSLATED BY
Rannfrid Thelle

WESTMINSTER
JOHN KNOX PRESS
LOUISVILLE · KENTUCKY

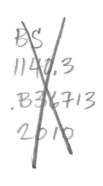

Originally published as *Det gamle testamente. En innføring* in 1993
by Dynamis, Oslo, Norway

Second edition published as *En bok om Det gamle testamente* in 2003
by the University of Oslo

This English edition is translated from the second, Norwegian edition.

First English edition
Published by Westminster John Knox Press
Louisville, Kentucky

10 11 12 13 14 15 16 17 18 19—10 9 8 7 6 5 4 3 2 1

Scripture quotations from the New Revised Standard Version of the Bible are copyright © 1989 by the Division of Christian Education of the National Council of the Churches of Christ in the U.S.A. and are used by permission.

Book design by Sharon Adams
Cover design by Eric Walljasper, Minneapolis, MN

Library of Congress Cataloging-in-Publication Data

Barstad, Hans M.
    [En bok om Det gamle testamente. English]
    A brief guide to the Hebrew Bible / Hans M. Barstad ; translated by Rannfrid Thelle.
        p. cm.
    Includes index.
    ISBN 978-0-664-23325-9 (alk. paper)
    1. Bible. O.T.—Introductions.   I. Title.
    BS1140.3.B36713 2010
    221.6'1—dc22

                                                                            2010003674

Contents

Acknowledgments

I am grateful to Rannfrid Thelle who undertook the difficult task of translating my book from the Norwegian original. At Westminster John Knox Press, Jon Berquist kindly accepted the volume for publication, and Dan Braden very professionally oversaw the production process. I am also very grateful to Gary Lee, whose excellent copyediting contributed enormously toward improving the manuscript. My student Josef Černohous kindly did all the work with the indexes.

Hans M. Barstad
New College, The University of Edinburgh
April 2010

1

Introduction

THE BIBLE IN CULTURAL HISTORY

The Bible is the most important cultural and religious document in the Western world. The three monotheistic faiths—Judaism, Christianity, and Islam—have all grown out of the traditions that we find in the Old Testament, or Hebrew Bible. The Bible therefore has a natural place in a liberal arts curriculum.

But it has not always been this way. Biblical studies do not go back very far, at least not in the Christian cultural sphere. Jewish scholars throughout history have studied the Holy Scriptures and written learned commentaries on the Hebrew Bible. In the Christian tradition, however, the Bible has not had the crucial role that it has for many people today. In the medieval period up to around the year 1000, the learned study of the Bible was all about repeating the interpretations of the early church fathers. Because few people in the medieval period mastered Greek and almost none knew Hebrew, they studied mostly the Latin patristic interpretations. No one studied the biblical texts in their original languages.

In the latter part of the medieval period a few Christian scholars knew Hebrew and were influenced by Jewish scholars and studied the biblical texts in a philological manner (with a focus on the literature and the language). In general, however, the medieval period is not very interesting when it comes to biblical interpretation. This fact was related to the concept of the supernatural authority of the Bible and the view that God had dictated it. Many of these ideas were challenged by the Renaissance and humanism of the fifteenth and sixteenth centuries.

Throughout the medieval period most people did not have access to the Bible. The church did not see it as appropriate that uneducated people should have access to the Holy Scriptures and protected the Vulgate, the Latin Bible, as its own private property. Because of this the Bible did not play a role in the religious lives of ordinary people. The piety of the people was influenced and guided by liturgy, church art, mystery plays, and whatever fragments from the Bible that the priests might happen to quote or comment on.

With Martin Luther and Erasmus the Bible received a central position in theology and church life for the first time in history. With the Reformation and the technology of the printing press, the Bible was translated into the common spoken languages. However, because of the high price of books, it did not become accessible to most people.

Keeping in mind the strong focus on the Bible that we see in many communities today, we need to remember that the Bible did not become a "book of the people" before the founding and growth of the Bible societies around the world (in Europe and America) in the eighteenth and nineteenth centuries. The American Bible Society was established in 1816.

Simultaneously with the establishment of the Bible Societies a change in the intellectual climate took place that was to be of great significance for the exploration of the Bible. Continuing in the spirit of the Renaissance, humanism, and the Reformation, a breakthrough of historical thinking took place in Germany in the nineteenth century. In the wake of this new historical consciousness came the breakthrough for critical, historical biblical science at the German Protestant universities.

When the Reformers rejected church tradition as the norm for teaching, there developed a teaching of the Bible as inspired by the Holy Spirit and therefore inerrant. But as more people read the Bible critically it became increasingly clear that the Bible was a work created by humans and that it had a long and complex history. The attempt to understand this process of the history of the biblical text has dominated biblical studies at the universities all the way up to the present.

THE BIBLE IN ACADEMIA

The study of the Bible in academia has traditionally been historically oriented. In the last few decades it has become more commonplace to supplement or replace a historical approach with a literary approach to biblical study. To say that biblical studies is historical is also to say that there is, in principle, no difference between the methods used in biblical study and the methods used by, for example, philologists, literary studies experts, linguists, historians of ancient times, archaeologists, or others who are concerned with the study of fields such as ancient Norse history, the classical world, or pre-Islamic Arabic culture. Biblical studies rose out of theology but works with historical and literary methods. There is no theological method for biblical scholarship; however, biblical scholarship does influence biblical interpretation, which in turn is central to theological reflection.

THE OLD TESTAMENT AS BACKGROUND FOR THE NEW TESTAMENT

Jesus was a Jew. From what we read about him in the Gospels, we also see that Jesus knew the Law, the Prophets, and the Writings—in other words, what we call the Old Testament. In the preaching of Jesus, the Old Testament was crucial. Old Testament figures, stories, and quotes were common knowledge at the time of Jesus, and it was by using these references that Jesus communicated his new message.

It is perhaps self-evident to some that understanding and knowledge of the Old Testament are prerequisites for understanding the New Testament. I emphasize this point here, however, because history shows us that many have unfortunately forgotten it. After Christians got their own Scripture collection, the New Testament, these texts formed the core of Christian ministry. The ensuing generations of believers in Jesus based their faith on Scriptures written after his death, and the Gospels and Letters became more important to the Christian church than the Old Testament Scriptures. We see this clearly through the study of our church fathers, for example. The church fathers do not question the way in which Paul uses the Old Testament. It is difficult to say whether this is because of the authority that the New Testament acquired, or simply the lack of knowledge about the Old Testament on the part of the church fathers. One thing is certain, however: our knowledge of the texts that Jesus based his preaching on is the foundation for an understanding of the Gospels, and, further, it is decisive for how we experience the church reality that we encounter today.

THE ANCIENT NEAR EAST

Four areas of the world were the scenes of the first civilizations: first, the Middle East; a little later, China and the Indus Valley; and, finally, Central and South America. The scene of the events that unfold in the accounts of the Bible is in the lands of the ancient Near East: Israel, Syria, Mesopotamia, and Egypt. The ancient civilizations of Mesopotamia—Sumer, Babylonia, and Assyria—were all located within the geographical area of what is now Iraq.

In Mesopotamia a gradual transition to a sedentary lifestyle began just after the end of the last Ice Age, around 10,000 BCE. The world's first civilizations arose here, beginning with the Sumerians in the second half of the fourth millennium. Throughout the following centuries, the center of power in Mesopotamia alternated between the great empires of Assyria and Babylonia. Between Egypt and Mesopotamia lay the area that we call Syria-Palestine, which included ancient Israel. Somewhat imprecisely, the terms "Palestine," "Canaan," and "Israel/Judah" are used for the same geographical area.

We will operate with the following chronology: Early Assyrian period, around 1900–1650 BCE; Middle Assyrian period, around 1360–1075 BCE; and Neo-Assyrian period, around 930–612 BCE; Early Babylonian period, around 1850–1600 BCE; Middle Babylonian period, around 1600–1160 BCE; and Neo-Babylonian (Chaldean) period, around 625–539 BCE; Persian (Achaemenid) period, 539–333 BCE; and Hellenistic period, 333–162 BCE. Egypt was at the height of its power in the third millennium BCE and played an intermittent, sometimes dominating political role in the ancient Near East right up to 332 BCE, when Alexander the Great's conquest put an end to three thousand years of political independence.

ANCIENT ISRAEL

Ancient Israel was a late arrival on the scene of the ancient Near Eastern landscape, with its earliest history from the time of the transition from the Late Bronze Age to the Iron Age in the thirteenth century BCE, and with its boom time for a few centuries after the consolidation of the Israelite-Judean kingdom in the tenth century BCE. Later the kingdom was divided into two parts: Israel in the north and Judea in the south. Israel-Judah's political history was not destined to be long. In 721 BCE the Assyrian king Shalmaneser V's siege led to the fall of the royal capital of the northern kingdom, Samaria, and in 586 BCE the Babylonian king Nebuchadnezzar's conquest of Jerusalem led to the downfall of the Judean kingdom.

In scholarly literature one encounters the terms "Israelites," "Hebrews," "Judeans," and "Jews" to name the people who are the subject of the story in the Old Testament. These terms are often used indiscriminately, and this can be quite confusing.

The patriarch Jacob was renamed Israel (Gen. 32:28; 35:10), hence his twelve sons were called "Israelites." Therefore, the term "Israelites" was used as a common term for all of the tribes. This usage is not always simple and clear, because of the division of the kingdom in the tenth century. The term "Israelites" is thus sometimes used to denote the inhabitants of the northern kingdom, Israel. Usage never became consistent, and "Israel" is also used in reference to the southern kingdom of Judah even before the northern kingdom went down with the fall of Samaria in 721. After the northern kingdom Israel ceased to exist, it became quite widespread to use "Israel" also of the southern kingdom of Judah.

The term "Hebrew" is derived from the Biblical Hebrew word *'ibri* (or *'ivri*), which is also a term for an Israelite. From the Old Testament one may get the impression that the term was used most often of Israelites by people of other nations (Gen. 39:14; 41:12), but it is also sometimes used by Israelites themselves. The terms "Hebrews" and "Israelites" are therefore used interchangeably in the Old Testament. The English word "Hebrew" is usually used to designate ancient Israelite language and literature.

The terms "Judeans" and "Jews" both have their origin in the Hebrew word *yehudim*, and were originally used to designate the inhabitants of the kingdom of Judah. After the fall of the northern kingdom in 721 BCE, the term was used for all Israelites.

From the Persian and Hellenistic periods, the term "Jews" came to be a national, ethnic, and religious term for the descendants of the ancient Israelites in Judah, the later province of Judah, or the Diaspora. The use of the term "Jews" presupposes a historical development that enables us to speak of "Judaism" as a religion distinct from Old Testament religion. The term should not be used of anything before the exilic period (i.e., before 586 BCE), and preferably not before the time of the return of the exiles (before 538 BCE). In the New Testament the term "Jews" is used to designate the descendants of the Israelites, as distinct from proselytes, Samaritans, and other peoples.

The term "Israelis" is only used of the inhabitants of the modern state of Israel, which was established May 14, 1948 CE.

THE LANGUAGE OF THE OLD TESTAMENT

The final writing of the Old Testament took place after 586 BCE, in the so-called exilic or postexilic period. The Old Testament is a piece of Near Eastern literature from the ancient period, written mostly in the Hebrew language. Hebrew is a West Semitic language closely related to Phoenician and Aramaic, and was also the spoken language of ancient Israel. From the mid-sixth century BCE, Aramaic was the language of diplomacy in the ancient Near East and was used also by the Jews (it is highly likely that Jesus spoke a West Aramaic dialect). As a result of this development, we also find a few Aramaic texts in the Old Testament (Ezra 4:8–6:18; 7:12–26; Dan. 2:4b–7:28; Jer. 10:10–11; Gen. 31:47).

The two closely related dialects of Assyrian and Babylonian were used in Mesopotamia in the biblical period. These two languages form the Eastern branch of the Semitic language family and are the oldest Semitic languages we know. The study of Assyrian and Babylonian language, history, and literature are called Assyriology, because Assyrian was the first of the two dialects that was deciphered. The term "Akkadian" is often used instead of Assyrian-Babylonian. For a long period the Akkadian language had status as the language of diplomacy, but from about the sixth century BCE Aramaic gradually replaced it, and Aramaic later replaced Hebrew as the primary language of the Jewish people.

BRIEF COMMENTS ABOUT THE CONTENTS

The Hebrew name for the Old Testament is *Tanak*, which is an acronym made from the words *torah* (Law), *nebi'im* or *nevi'im* (Prophets), and *ketubim* or *ketuvim* (Writings). The *Torah* consists of the first five books of the Bible. In our scholarly tradition, these books are called the Pentateuch. The *Nevi'im* is divided into two parts, the "Former Prophets," which consist of the books of Joshua, Judges, 1 and 2 Samuel, and 1 and 2 Kings, and the "Latter Prophets," which encompass the "real" prophets (Isaiah, Jeremiah, Ezekiel, and the Twelve: Hosea, Joel, Amos, Obadiah, Jonah, Micah, Nahum, Habakkuk, Zephaniah, Haggai, Zechariah, and Malachi). All the rest of the books in the Bible are collected under the category *Ketuvim*, consisting of Psalms, Job, Proverbs, the five feast scrolls (or *Megilloth*: Ruth, Song of Songs, Ecclesiastes, Lamentations, Esther), Daniel, Ezra, Nehemiah, and 1 and 2 Chronicles.

CANONIZATION

We know that in the third century BCE the individual books must have looked basically the way that we know them today. The standardization of the whole collection was probably completed around 100 CE. However, there are many uncertainties regarding the canonization process, and we know very little about how it all happened. The Pentateuch may have existed in the form that we know it today as early as in the fifth century BCE. Some have maintained that it was basically finished even as early as the seventh century BCE. The Nevi'im (the books of Joshua, Judges, Samuel, Kings, Isaiah, Jeremiah, Ezekiel, and the Book of the Twelve) may have been known as Holy Scripture almost as early as the Torah in the fifth century, but the latter has always had a higher status. The Ketuvim were canonized last.

THE AUTHORS OF THE BIBLE

Who wrote the Old Testament? The literature of the Bible is tradition literature. This means that it has evolved over a very long period of time, some maintain for as long as a thousand years! Five hundred years is perhaps closer to the truth. Even if the Old Testament was written down in the exilic or postexilic era, the various traditions do not come from this late period, but have gone through a long and complex process of transmission.

It is important to understand that the Old Testament is literature and that most of it is poetry and prose. We find a number of different literary genres represented; the following examples are taken from the German scholar Hermann Gunkel (1862–1932). Gunkel identified the following poetic and prose genres: profane poetry, private poetry, love poetry, funerary lament, wisdom literature, political poetry, war poetry, victory poetry, songs of derision, songs of royal praise, poetry of curses and blessings, religious songs, cult poetry (which is divided into many subgenres), poetic stories, myth, saga, fairytales, fables, historical stories, and laws. We could mention more types than Gunkel, even more informal types, such as drinking songs, riddles, and so on.

Most of this literature is anonymous or "pseudepigraphic," which means that it is accredited to someone without actually stemming from the hand of this person. The best-known example of this phenomenon is the "Psalms of David," which do not come from David at all, and the "Wisdom of Solomon," which does not come from Solomon. This is tradition literature that has been passed on from generation to generation in an oral or written form.

There are many examples of such tradition literature from different ancient cultures. Well-known examples are the *Odyssey* and the *Iliad* from ancient Greece, and the Icelandic sagas from the Norse tradition. The belief held so commonly earlier, that there had been a long period of oral transmission, is gradually losing ground in Homeric research, saga research, and biblical studies. There is, as such, no evidence against the possibility that much of the so-called tradition literature could have been written down in specific periods by individual authors.

THE AGE OF THE TEXTS AND THE MASORETES

The dating of biblical texts is highly controversial. We have to distinguish between when the events being described are supposed to have taken place, and when the writing of these events has taken place. It is important to be aware that the books of the Pentateuch (and the historical accounts in the Old Testament) are not contemporary accounts, but have been written down a long time after the events are purported to have taken place.

The Bible itself has a clear chronology when it comes to the origin stories and the earliest history of the Israelites. The world was created around 3800 BCE. Abraham, who received the promise that he would be the ancestor of the Israelite people, emigrated from southern Mesopotamia around 2000 BCE. The Israelites emigrated from Egypt around 1450 BCE.

When we read an English Bible today we do not usually reflect on the question of text. Which text are we really reading when we deal with the Old Testament texts? Most modern editions of the Old Testament are translations of the Hebrew text of a manuscript called the Leningrad Codex, dated 1009 CE. This is the oldest complete manuscript of the Hebrew Bible known to us.

The rabbis who worked with copying and keeping the Hebrew biblical writings are called Masoretes. The Hebrew word *massorah* means "tradition" and is the term that came to designate the comments in the margins of handwritten scrolls that were supposed to secure the preservation of the reading of the unvocalized text. Because of this, the Hebrew text of the Old Testament is often called the "Masoretic Text" (MT). The Masoretes were very important from the fifth century CE onward.

QUMRAN

The Dead Sea Scrolls, or Qumran Scrolls, is the name of a large collection of texts from the time around the birth of Christ. Most of the texts were discovered in the period 1947–1960 CE in a number of caves by the Dead Sea close to Khirbet Qumran (between Jericho and Ein-Gedi). This location was a main center for groups of Jews who settled in the area between the end of the third century BCE and around 70 CE (when the Romans destroyed the community). After a lot of controversy and drama concerning the publication of some of the texts, an international group is now making sure that all of the texts are being published.

These texts contain a whole range of genres, of which only the most significant can be mentioned here. In a distinct category we find the two scrolls that describe the Qumran community, the *Community Rule* and the *Damascus Scroll*. There are also a number of biblical texts, both complete scrolls and fragments. All of the Old Testament books, with the exception of Esther (and perhaps Nehemiah), are represented. Biblical interpretation is central. One particular genre is the so-called *pesher*, a special form of biblical interpretation that takes an Old Testament text as a point of departure and implements it in the Qumran community's own context. Further, there are a number of psalms, both biblical and nonbiblical, and other liturgical texts. Best known are the *Hodayot* (songs of praise). Wisdom texts are also represented. As the Qumran community was very much characterized by an eschatological self-understanding, it is not strange that there are a number of eschatological and apocalyptic texts. Best known among these is the *War Scroll*. In a category of its own stands the *Temple Scroll*. This is the longest of all of the Qumran texts (about nine yards long), and gives a number of ordinances for the "ideal temple" and comprehensive purity laws.

The significance that the Dead Sea Scrolls have had for the study of the Hebrew text of the Old Testament (the Masoretic Text) can hardly be overestimated. Before the discoveries in Qumran one had access to Hebrew manuscripts only from the medieval period, the most important one dated 1009. With the discovery of a complete Isaiah text in Cave 1 at Qumran one suddenly had access to a text around a thousand years older! By comparing it with the text of the Leningrad Codex, it was confirmed that the Hebrew biblical text had been handed down with amazing accuracy. At the same time textual fragments had been found, for example of the book of Jeremiah, that showed that more than one textual tradition was circulating at Qumran. Thus the study of biblical texts from Qumran also provides an important contribution to the understanding of the standardization of the Masoretic Text and to the growth of the canon. In addition to different versions of one and the same biblical text, a number of psalms that in form and content are very similar to the psalms of the Bible have been found, though these are not found in the canonical book of Psalms. The Dead Sea Scrolls have had great significance also for the study of the development of the Hebrew language.

READING THE TEXTS: THE TASK OF EXEGESIS

Exegesis is the foundation for work with the Old Testament. "Exegesis" means interpretation or commentary and is usually associated with the study of the Bible. The task for the exegete is to understand, in this case to understand the texts of the Bible.

The texts that we encounter are very old, as we well know. The age of the texts alone is a reason why we may experience them as strange. It is therefore important that work with the Bible in an academic context helps us to become competent readers.

In spite of the chronological distance between the text and us as readers, we still experience the biblical texts as meaningful. Even though there are many different and meaningful ways of approaching biblical texts, certain rules are foundational when we begin the task of exegesis. For example, we must clarify what kind of text we have in front of us. Is the text part of a larger story (a larger text), or is it a closed unit? Is it prose or poetry?

Independently of whether it is prose or poetry we are dealing with, it is important to place the text into a context. If we are working with narrative texts, for example the covenant between God and Israel, it is important not to limit oneself to Exodus 24, but also to read what happens before and after this event. We must map out the characters of the story and their significance and function, and we must seek out words and expressions that are important in this text. In Exodus 24 the word "covenant" is of course of central significance, and that God takes the initiative to a committed relationship with Israel is not less important. We would then look up other places in the Bible where the word "covenant" appears, or find places where similar events occur. By introducing the information that other texts give us about covenant and the encounter between God and humans, we would gradually gain an understanding of what the covenant in Exodus 24 might mean. We have now begun the process toward becoming competent readers.

When working with poetry many of the same rules of exegesis apply as when working with narrative texts. But with poetry we do not usually find an outer framework in the way that we do with narratives. We are left with the language of metaphor and symbolism. We know that the development of metaphors is distinctive to each culture. We also know that the Near Eastern culture that the biblical texts originate in is far distant from our own world. In sum, this means that work with biblical poetry can be challenging. That it can be a challenge to find meaning in Old Testament poetry, however, is not a reason to avoid such work. On the contrary, through the process of seeing differences between Near Eastern cultures and our own, we will also discover similarities.

2

The Priestly History

Genesis, Exodus, Leviticus, Numbers

CONTENT AND TERMS

Anyone who opens a Bible will find that it begins with the five books that tradition has ascribed to Moses. These books, called Genesis, Exodus, Leviticus, Numbers, and Deuteronomy, are often referred to as the "Pentateuch" in an academic context. This is a word from Greek meaning "the five scroll (collection)"; it derives from the beginning of the first century, when Jewish scholars in Alexandria, Egypt, used it. Through the Greek translation of the Old Testament, the Septuagint, this term was passed down to posterity.

Among the Jews the Hebrew term *torah* is the most common name for the Bible's first five books. The word means "law," that is, the "law of Moses," which was revealed to the Israelites during their desert wanderings from Egypt. The Jewish term *torah* is very appropriate if we look at the contents of the "five books of Moses." About half of the material in the Pentateuch consists of laws and regulations of different kinds. In terms of narrative, Genesis 1–11 provides us with a description of the creation of the world and human beings, and Genesis 12–50 introduces to us the stories of the ancestors Abraham, Isaac, Jacob, and Joseph. Exodus through Deuteronomy recounts the departure out of Egypt and the wanderings in the desert on the way to the promised land.

Like the term "Pentateuch," the term "Tetrateuch," meaning "the four scroll (collection)," is used in biblical studies; it denotes the four books of Genesis, Exodus, Leviticus, and Numbers. The fifth book, Deuteronomy, does not originally belong together with the first four books, but is an independent work. We will return to Deuteronomy in the next chapter.

The first four books can also be called the "Priestly History." The term "history" as it is used here does not mean the same thing as what most people in modern times associate with "history." The work intends to describe the story of the Israelite ancestors from the creation of the world until the time immediately before the immigration into Canaan.

The Tetrateuch is both a unified work and a work consisting of four individual books, each of them highly problematic as regards their sources and composition. In spite of this, we can regard the work as a compositional unit, "written" by one or more authors. In this context "written" means that one or more persons have contributed to or edited the material in the Tetrateuch to give it the form it has today.

While researchers in the past were most concerned with finding out which sources the author of the work had used and how these had come into existence, scholars today are more interested in seeing the broad lines and connections. What is the message of the Priestly History? Which ideologies are expressed? Even though we cannot know much about how the work developed, and maybe not much about the "historical" past that the authors wished to convey, we can at least learn a good deal about the authors and their work. From the content of the work we are able to designate the authors as "Priestly" (P). Whether this may have been one or more persons, or perhaps even a "school," we cannot know for certain. The work may not even have come into existence on one occasion but may have been the result of several generations of editing.

The Priestly Tetrateuch has been set into a larger context. At a later point in time, the first four books were joined together with the books of Deuteronomy, Joshua, Judges, Samuel, and Kings (the so-called Deuteronomistic History). In this way, we have ended up with one long continuous "history" that tells the story of the Israelite people, God's chosen people, from the creation of the world around 4000 BCE up until the Babylonian exile in 586 BCE.

Another interesting question is who is responsible for this large work that begins with Genesis and ends with 2 Kings. Is the "author" identical with the author of the Priestly History, or does this work come from a later time and the hand of a different "author"? On this issue, we can only guess. Further, redactions and changes have occurred all along, over a very long time. This is apparent from the canonization process and from different ancient Hebrew manuscript variants.

THE PRIESTLY AUTHORS OF THE TETRATEUCH

Together with the "Deuteronomists" (the authors of the Deuteronomistic History) and the "Chroniclers" (the authors of the Chronicler's History: Ezra, Nehemiah, and 1 and 2 Chronicles), the "Priestly writers" make up one of the three major "authors" or "authorial groups" of the Hebrew Bible. The Priestly writers are often abbreviated P. Among the sources of P are the "Yahwist" (J) and the "Elohist" (E). Even though J, E, and P belong to the classic sources of pentateuchal research, their nature is more debated than ever before. The way these terms are used by scholars today is far from accurate. They are, in reality, more practical and descriptive than normative. For these reasons one has to decide in each and every instance how the terms J, E, and P (and also D) are to be understood in contemporary scholarly literature.

When one reads the scholarly literature, one soon discovers that P is not a clear term but is used in different ways. In our context, P refers both to that writer (or group of writers; I use both singular and plural), who in late postexilic times "authored" the four first books of the Bible, and also to one of the four classical sources of the Pentateuch. The other sources are J, E, and D (Deuteronomy). The term "Priestly document" was originally used because of the interest this author shows in everything that has to do with the priesthood, the sacrificial cult, and similar subjects.

When we are identifying different writers in a work such as the Bible, language and vocabulary play a big role. P's phraseology and vocabulary are easily recognizable, as is the characteristic theology that is found in the Priestly work. In the period of classical source criticism, P was recognized as the latest of the four main sources. This had to do, among other things, with the German Protestant view, prevalent in the past, that offerings and cultic acts were expressions of a "deterioration" and "judaization" of "originally" clean and pure religious practice. Today we know that the case is entirely different and that much of the P material most likely goes far back in time. It is therefore only the "historical" frame narrative of the Tetrateuch and the editing of older P material (and other sources) that come from the postexilic P.

Which of the works is older, the "Priestly" or the "Deuteronomistic," is somewhat unclear. Both of these circles could just as well have been responsible for the final redaction of the whole broadly conceived historical-theological work that begins with Genesis and ends with the books of Kings. Perhaps it is most likely that the late P writers were active before the Deuteronomists, and that the D writers, with their work Deuteronomy and the Deuteronomistic History, have attached their work to the Tetrateuch. Perhaps the Deuteronomists are thus responsible for the main redaction of the broadly conceived work Genesis–2 Kings. This major historical work describes the Israelite people's history from the creation of the world until the exile. But here we find ourselves on somewhat uncertain ground.

Regarding the question of which texts come from which author, however, scholarship is less in doubt. Just about all of Leviticus and all of Numbers are pure P material. One extended account in the Deuteronomistic History

(Joshua 13–22) is also often attributed to P, but researchers have not come to an agreement about this. In addition there are significant contributions from P in Genesis and Exodus. P often builds on other sources in these books, primarily those that scholarship has termed J and E, which in later years have been quite controversial. The final redaction of the first four books of the Bible may also be attributed to P.

The outer framework of Genesis, Exodus, Leviticus, and Numbers consists of one long, continuous "story"—a framework that all of the other material is placed within. This is also the case for the great histories of the Deuteronomist and the Chronicler. But whereas the Deuteronomistic History begins with the account of the conquest of the promised land, the Priestly writer (like the Chronicler) begins his story at the beginning of times. The Priestly "history of Israel" is the account of God's chosen people from the time of the creation of the world. Through a number of genealogies Adam, the first human, is connected to Abraham, the father of the Israelites. A keen interest in genealogy and chronology is typical of P.

Thus, when one reads the first four books of the Bible, one should not be misled by a possible first impression of what seems to be an incoherent work. The work is a large and coherent composition. It is a "history" that begins with Genesis 1:1 and ends with Moses giving the law on the plains of Moab by the Jordan River, facing Jericho (Num. 36:13), at the end of the desert wanderings.

Especially in Genesis and parts of Exodus, it is clear that P took his point of departure in old sources when he composed his work of history. Just like the other biblical writers, the Priestly writer is not an author in our understanding of the word. He has quite often left earlier sources in the shape that they were handed down. Instead of rewriting and reworking the sources, P has either woven them together and then placed them into their own account (for example, in the story of the covenant and divine revelation at Mount Sinai in Exodus 19–20), or he has placed his own version next to an older tradition (for example, the creation stories in Genesis 1–2). Even though the material in this way is set into a common frame, it seems very disorganized. Further, there is great disagreement as to the dating of certain parts of the Priestly composition. However, from the content of Genesis–Numbers it is quite clear who stands behind this composition, namely a circle of priests.

Old traditions about the covenant at Sinai and the desert wanderings receive the form of a type of framework story for P's work of religious legislation. In this context the writer presents a number of laws pertaining to the sanctuary, the priests and their duties, holy vessels, the sacrificial altar, and other cultic subjects in Exodus 25–31 and 35–40. In chapters 25–31 the regulations are presented as YHWH's words to Moses on the mountain (YHWH, the Tetragrammaton, is the name of God in Hebrew tradition, sometimes vocalized "Yahweh"). In this way the priestly legislation is connected to Sinai and the desert tradition. In chapters 35–40 the account is given of how Moses communicates the word of YHWH to the people, and how all of the laws and ordinances that have been presented in chapters 25–31 are then carried out. In Leviticus the priestly legislation continues with a number of laws concerning offerings (Leviticus 1–7), the initiation of priests (chaps. 8–10), and purity laws (chaps. 11–15).

In Leviticus 17–26 we find the so-called Holiness Code. This section, which contains a mixture of legislation of various kinds, has played a significant role when it comes to the question of the sources of P. Scholars have maintained that Leviticus 17–26 consists of an older collection of laws that had existed as an independent unit before being incorporated into P, in the same way as the so-called Covenant Code (Exodus 21–23). This is possible. Even though the Tetrateuch in its present shape comes from late, postexilic times, the Priestly circles responsible for it did not take their material out of thin air but built on older traditions. The priests and the cult played a major and significant role in ancient Israelite religion and society.

While Leviticus does not have any narrative framework, we find in Numbers that the priestly laws and regulations, which in many ways give the impression of being an *addition* to the regulations given in Leviticus, are set into a narrative framework. After a miscellaneous mixture of regulations in Numbers 1–9, the story continues in chapters 10–20 with the breaking of camp at Sinai and wanderings through the desert, and in chapters 20–36 with the conquest of the land east of the Jordan. Within this frame, the writer introduces his legal material, which runs through the whole book. This story framework gives the narrative a feeling of coherence, despite Numbers seeming the most disorganized and incoherent of the pentateuchal books. Again, this is due to the Priestly writer's wish to not redact his sources too drastically. While he wishes to express his own view, he simultaneously tries to include as much as possible of the legal tradition. At least this seems to be one explanation for the apparent lack of structure. A further explanation could be the nature of the material. This is, after all, about law, and the legislation had to change as the society changed. It is also possible that in this material we are dealing with additional commentary and additions to the legal regulations, in much the same way we find in any legal corpus.

THE PRIESTLY THEOLOGY

What, then, are the fundamental concepts in the Priestly theology? What ideology is the basis for this version of the history of the Israelite people? And which religious foundational view gives the account its basic colors? It is not easy to answer these questions.

One problem is that the obviously Priestly parts of the Old Testament seem to have come into existence over a relatively long period of time. Nonetheless, it is relatively simple to find major trends in the text in its final form. We are dealing with a story that has been created in late, postexilic times (fifth–fourth century BCE), and that has been tied to and woven into the ancient Israelite traditions about the revelation at Sinai and the wanderings through the desert. We are introduced to the legal material in the Tetrateuch by its association with these events and as a continuation of these events. The legal material is particularly closely connected with the account of the revelation on Mount Sinai (Exodus 19–20). Within the frame that the legal material is placed into, the laws stand out as the expression of the will of YHWH, the God of Israel, toward his chosen people. Be it religious, ethical, or civil legislation, it is connected with the divine revelation and covenant making on Sinai. This particular association between a historical frame narrative and legislation has influenced not only the way that the laws are formed, but also in a fundamental way the whole Old Testament religion and view of God, not least the well-known covenant between YHWH and the people.

If we go to Greek culture, we find a body of legislation that completely lacks a religious aspect. In Roman law there is a religious element, but also here most of the laws come from humans. This is not the case in the ancient Near East. A deity promulgating laws is a well-known trait of Semitic cultures. When Moses receives God's laws on behalf of the people on Mount Sinai, he stands in the same Near Eastern tradition as Hammurabi. The king included Sumerian legal material in his famous Code, but claimed that all of the laws were given to him directly by the sun god Shamash. In our own time we can study in an illuminating way the idea of divine law in Islam.

Even though the exodus and Sinai traditions are not "historical" in a real sense, they come from preexilic material. These traditions were hardly "invented" in postexilic times the way some scholars seem to hold. This view is not consistent with the way that literature was created in the ancient Near East. By setting the appropriate, available P material into an ancient Israelite, salvation-historical tradition, the writer wished to legitimize the Priestly legislation concerning the cult and the priesthood. The writer sought to show that the laws had their origin in YHWH himself, and that they go back to the very beginning of the history of the Israelite people. This legislation, which, just like corresponding legislation in other cultures, had grown gradually over several centuries, is here displayed as the commandments that YHWH gave to Moses during the desert wanderings on the way to the promised land.

At the center of Priestly attention stands the temple and the sacral institutions. Cult and ritual dominate completely. The history of Israel is the history of the chosen people and the covenant that YHWH has set up with them, which secures for them a bright future. Salvation in ancient Israel is always connected to material, social, and political benefits. The outlook is this-worldly, not eschatological.

As with the Deuteronomists, covenant also plays an important role for P. But for the covenant to be upheld, the laws and ordinances of YHWH, primarily the cultic and ritual laws, must be kept. Among these we find regulations concerning the sacrificial cult and the celebration of various feasts, especially Passover. The concept of Moses as the great man of God and leader of the people is also important to P. As opposed to the Deuteronomistic writings, we do not find a negative attitude to the monarchy in P, nor do we find any desire to shut down the local temples and centralize all worship to Jerusalem.

It has been discussed over and over whether the Priestly writers were active in Jerusalem or in Babylon. It follows from the nature of the sources that we cannot give a definitive answer to this kind of question. The majority of scholars today maintain that they were in Babylon, but as the evidence stands, it is just as likely that we might find the authors of the Tetrateuch among priestly circles in Jerusalem.

Even though much of P has a prehistory in preexilic times, we have to seek the explanation for what happens with the creation of the Tetrateuch in the political, religious, and cultural situation in Judah in the postexilic period. The Priestly view dominates completely. In many ways this theological view is the one that through time passed on to develop into early Judaism and that would become one of the primary characteristics of the many-sided phenomenon that Christian scholars, somewhat biased and one-sidedly, have labeled "legal Judaism" (rabbinism, Pharisaism).

Both culturally and politically Judah was at an all-time low during the years after the fall of Jerusalem in 586 BCE. In the preexilic period the power lay with the king and the central administration. After the ruling elite had been brought into exile, a completely new situation arose in the country. For one, the priests gained more power, and the culmination of what we see early signs of in the Tetrateuch can be found in the early Jewish period when the power of the high priest was almost unlimited in Palestine.

GENESIS

The first book of the Bible is Genesis. The Greek word *genesis* means "origin" or "source," and is the title given to the book by those who translated it into Greek, possibly in the third century BCE. In Hebrew the book is called *Bere'shit*, which means "in the beginning," after the opening words of the book. It was common practice in the ancient Near East to call literary works by the opening words of the individual work. In the same way, the Babylonians called their creation epic *Enuma Elish*, "When on high," after the first two words in the account.

Creation in the Hebrew Bible

Concepts of how the universe or world came into existence (cosmogony) are known from most cultures. The idea of creation is central also in the Hebrew Bible, and not just in Genesis. In the following we shall look at some of the fundamental characteristics of Old Testament creation theology. It will become apparent that one should not see the Bible as a type of textbook or reference work for natural science, in the way some people have. The Hebrew Bible is not intellectually but mythically or poetically oriented. As such, we do not find one consistent concept, but a whole range of concepts in the Bible about how the world was created. The two creation accounts in Genesis are well known to most people (Gen. 1:1–2:4a; 2:4b–3:24). In addition, we find concepts about the creation of the earth spread around in other places in the Bible. In the Prophets and in Psalms we find, over and over, expressions that testify to a different concept about how the world was created than that which we find in Genesis. Further, in Proverbs 8:22–31 we find a third creation account.

Before we look more closely at the biblical concepts of creation, it is important to be aware of a significant difference between the Bible's portrayal and the creation accounts that we encounter in, for example, Greek religion and thought. This is important because our culture and thought are strongly influenced by the Greek view of creation. The Christian concept of a *creatio ex nihilo*, "creation out of nothing," was foreign to the ancient Hebrews. Even the expressions we often use when we talk about the concepts of creation in old cultures, such as "cosmogony," or even more broadly conceived, "cosmology," are taken from the Greek world. At the same time it is more correct to talk about cosmology than cosmogony in the Greek world, because matter is conceived as having existed from eternity. Rather than a historical account of the act of creation, we find among the Greeks what we might call "ideal speculation." The Greek word *kosmos* (the ordered world, cosmos) points to the universe as something that exists in itself, independently of everything else.

In Biblical Hebrew language we do not find any word for "cosmos" or "universe" that corresponds to the Greek concept. In later Hebrew thought the word *'olam* came to have this meaning. But in the Bible *'olam* means "eternity," in the sense of an indefinitely long period of time. Another word that is often translated as "world," *tevel*, really means "earth" as opposed to "heaven," and refers to something completely different than the Greek *kosmos*. When the ancient Hebrews felt the need to express something more than *tevel*, they had only the term *hakkol*, "the all," everything. This expression is perhaps the closest we can get to the Greek idea of "cosmos." In late texts, that is, in exilic/postexilic texts, *hakkol* or just *kol* is used in many expressions as a term for everything that is created (Jer. 10:16; 51:19; Isa. 44:24; 45:7; Pss. 8:6; 103:19; 119:91; 1 Chr. 29:14; Job 42:2). From the various contexts it is clear that despite this, *hakkol* is not really equivalent to the cosmogonical/cosmological term "cosmos," "universe," and similar expressions. This tells us something about the essential difference between Greek and Hebrew concepts of creation. The Greek is more speculative, idealistic, descriptive, and rational, whereas the Hebrew is more poetic and mythical.

The difference between the Greek way of seeing the world and the ancient Hebrew way also manifests itself clearly in the overall view of the world. For the Greeks, the world (cosmos, universe) was an organized totality that could be understood and explained. Such an organization of the universe is not found among the Hebrews. For them, creation and the world are important in a theologically comprehensive way and as the background for the relationship between YHWH and the people. By interfering during the course of history, YHWH continues to create also "after creation." Creation, for the Israelite, was just as much about YHWH's action in history as the act of creation or cosmogony itself. Indeed, cosmogony is itself one part of YHWH's historical acts of salvation with his people. However, in wisdom traditions the historical perspective differs. Here God has created the world with its natural laws, and it is up to everyone to try to find out how it functions.

This situation tells us something essential about the way that the Hebrew Bible understands creation. It is important to be aware of this, because when we today use concepts such as "cosmos," "universe," "view of life" and so on, it is due to the influence not of ancient Israelite thought, but of Greek thought. In the same way, the often negative associations that the word "world" has, for example in language such as "worldly," is caused by partly Greek, partly New Testament, and partly early Christian thought. In the Hebrew Bible the created world is viewed positively.

The Creation Accounts in Genesis

Despite the fact that most of us are aware that there are two creation accounts in Genesis, we often hear people referring to "the biblical creation account." From the point of view of the "author logic" sketched out above, this is not wrong. An exaggerated focus on the fact that the two creation accounts in

Genesis 1:1–2:4a and 2:4b–3:24 are clearly distinct from each other regarding style and content would entail that the interest in the author's sources overrides the interest in the author's "real" intentions. This could lead to a violation of the message of the text. In our culture two different accounts about the same event could easily be understood as contradictory. The ancient Israelites had not only two but a number of different creation accounts in the Bible. For them, our comments would be understood as absurd. There was only one God and one creation, but a rich abundance of ways of talking about God and creation.

When we insist on talking about the two creation accounts in Genesis, we do this because the text gives us a good example of just that abundance in the ancient Israelite creation concepts. The different theological profiling in the two accounts may perhaps be expressed by saying that while Genesis 1:1–2:4a asks the question, How has everything come to be? the question in 2:4b–3:24 is, How have humans become the way they are? Because of the succinct style and emphasis on organization with a strict, systematic structure, and because of the distinct vocabulary, scholars have agreed that 1:1–2:4a ought to be attributed to the Priestly writers. The style in 2:4b–3:24 is quite different. The text here does not have Priestly characteristics (e.g., it is not systematic) but is perhaps graphic, bold, and vivid. Scholars have traditionally agreed to attribute this part of the creation account to J, following the use of the divine name YHWH. Regarding date, scholars used to think that J belonged to the oldest of the Bible's sources, but now scholars date also this source later (some have even disregarded J completely as a distinct, separate source).

We notice that P, here as elsewhere, does not make any radical changes in the text. The author has been tolerant and has simply placed the sources he uses next to each other without adapting them to the whole. This is another reason why many scholars have felt that P is incoherent and broken.

The Priestly Creation Account

As mentioned above, P's account of the creation of the world in Genesis 1:1–2:4a is structured in a strictly systematic way. We notice how, after a short introduction in 1:1–2, six days of creation follow. Each section is introduced by the sentence "And God said," and ends with "And it was evening" and so on. At the end of the account we read about how God rested on the seventh day, the *sabbath*, and thus sanctified it. We notice further how the six days of creation are divided into two groups that match each other precisely. On the first day, light is created, and on the fourth day the shining heavenly bodies are created. On the second day the dome that separates the cosmic waters from each other is created, and to match, the birds in the sky and life in the sea are created on the fifth day. On the third day the dry earth comes forth from the water and is clothed with vegetation. To match this, the animals on the earth and humans are created on the sixth day. This systematic monotony and strict framework give an impression of solemnity and an elevated style. This impression is further strengthened by the strict, impersonal, and formal style.

The Priestly creation account demonstrates clear similarities with Meso-potamian material. It is, however, hardly likely that the P writers used this material directly. Rather, this material was widely distributed in the ancient Near East, and most likely came originally from Akkadian prototypes. The account of the creation of the world in Genesis 1:1–2:4a corresponds almost point-by-point to the account of creation in the Babylonian epic *Enuma Elish*. It is not possible to see these similarities as a product of mere chance. The Priestly writers were among the intellectual elite of the day, and the Priestly creation account is the contemporary "scientific" view of how the world came to be. As in a number of other cultural fields, Israel's neighbors to the east were the ones who set the bar also when it came to cosmogony and cosmology. But the Priestly writers did not copy the Mesopotamian models mechanically. Even though the material and the form are identical, the ideol-ogy is characteristic of P. There are striking similarities in the structure and particular details, but the message is different. The most striking difference is that the Babylonian creation account tells of a number of rivaling gods, whereas the biblical creation account is the story of one God. In *Enuma Elish* the name of the primordial waters and the dragon that Marduk kills and parts in two to create heaven and earth is called Tiamat. In Genesis 1:6 YHWH also creates the world from the primordial waters, which in 1:2 is called *tehom*, a word that corresponds to the name Tiamat. But in P the primordial waters are demythologized and are no longer a god.

With P, creation has the clear function of forming the background for YHWH's election of his special people. Through the following genealo-gies the first humans on earth are connected to the Israelite people's ances-tors, the patriarchs. Creation in this way becomes a religious-national affair whose purpose is to underpin the theology about YHWH's chosen people. The genealogies are all from the hand of the Priestly writers and have a clear historical-theological function. We notice the keen interest in order and sys-tem. Abraham's genealogy in Genesis 11 is traced back to Noah and thereby also back to Adam, the first man. If we do not see the connection here, we have lost a significant point about how the creation accounts in Genesis 1–2 should be understood in the Tetrateuch of the Priestly writers. This is not a case of an isolated account; it is part of a larger whole, namely the Priestly presentation of the "history" of Israel from creation to the immigration into the promised land. Only when we see it in this overall perspective can we understand how creation functions in the theology of the Hebrew Bible.

The Yahwist's Creation Account in Genesis 2:4b–3:24

Genesis 2:4b–3:24 is an account about creation and about how sin entered into the world. The style changes all of a sudden here compared to what we find in the Priestly creation account. The difference comes out starkly when we compare the creation process itself in the two accounts. In the Yahwist's version we find no table within which the different days of creation are placed. Instead we are introduced to a vivid and fairly graphic story of creation. A marked difference is that the Yahwist does not see the earth as covered with water, but instead takes as his point of departure an earth that is a dry desert where nothing can grow. After YHWH has let the dry earth be watered by life-giving rain, he shapes the man from clay and blows the spirit of life into his nose. After that he plants a garden in Eden, where the man can live and eat of the fruits of the garden. Then the creation of the animals of the field and birds of the sky follow; finally, while the man is sleeping, YHWH builds the woman from one of the man's ribs. We see that not only does J have a more graphic style than P, but the whole story is also anthropomorphic.

Several scholars have pointed out that the traditions behind this account must come from an area with a scarcity of water, such as Palestine itself. Perhaps this rational explanation is too simplistic. In any case, the J account also takes its model from its neighbors to the east, if not to the same striking degree as P's account. For one, the creation of humans from earth is known from Sumerian texts. Scholars have debated whether P's story might originate in Mesopotamia because the population in this area had experienced the flooding of the Euphrates and Tigris rivers from ancient times. However, concepts about "primordial waters" and "chaos waters" that are commanded to "come to order" are also known from cultures that do not have such natural conditions. This kind of rational explanatory elements in these types of texts should therefore probably not be emphasized too much.

Like P's creation account, the J account is anthropomorphic in character as it continues in Genesis 3:8 and following, which portray YHWH as a man who wanders around in his garden. The account is in the form of a fable. It is late in the evening and it is starting to cool down. The humans have been misled by the snake (also portrayed anthropomorphically) to eat of the forbidden tree. But YHWH calls Adam and forces him to confess. Then all of the actors are punished: the snake must crawl on its belly and eat dust all of its days, the woman must bear her children in pain, and the man is to work the soil to struggle for his daily bread. But YHWH goes back on his earlier word that whoever eats of the forbidden tree shall die. Instead the humans are banished from the garden of Eden. The account here has clear etiological characteristics. It wants to explain why women must bear their children in pain, why humans must struggle so hard, and why the snake crawls on the earth as it does.

Even though, also in this case, we find specific details that seem to have a Mesopotamian model, this account does not show nearly as much dependence on known models as the Priestly account does. The story seems to be put together from a number of different motifs, several of which are known from other cultures' primordial stories. Holy trees are mentioned in several myths and also the motif of a lost paradisiacal state. But also in this case we see that the biblical account has its own message, independently of how the background material is to be understood. All in all it is a characteristic of the biblical creation accounts that they do not appear independently or isolated from the context in which they are set.

We shall now examine a little more closely other forms of creation in the Hebrew Bible. First we shall look at the third creation account, a story that is unknown to many.

The Creation Account in Proverbs 8:22–31

In Proverbs 8:22–31 we find some interesting utterances by Wisdom about herself:

> The LORD created me at the beginning of his work,
> the first of his acts of long ago.
> Ages ago I was set up,
> at the first, before the beginning of the earth.
> When there were no depths I was brought forth,
> when there were no springs abounding with water.
> Before the mountains had been shaped,
> before the hills, I was brought forth—
> when he had not yet made earth and fields,
> or the world's first bits of soil.
>
> When he established the heavens, I was there,
> when he drew a circle on the face of the deep,
> when he made firm the skies above,
> when he established the fountains of the deep,
> when he assigned to the sea its limit,
> so that the waters might not transgress his command,
> when he marked out the foundations of the earth,
> then I was beside him, like a master worker;
> and I was daily his delight,
> rejoicing before him always,
> rejoicing in his inhabited world and delighting in the human race.

Here we have a creation account of a completely different character than that which we find in P in Genesis. The background for thoughts of this type must be sought in, among other places, the ancient Hebrews' thoughts about the consistency of nature and the need for philosophical reflection related to this. It is striking that we do not find these kinds of thoughts put forth systematically in the Hebrew Bible. Rather, they are spread out as small details here and there. Proverbs 8:22–31 is the most comprehensive of these references and has probably been kept because of its context, namely as part of Wisdom's utterances about herself. What makes the portrayal we have in Proverbs 8 special is that Wisdom here plays a major role in the act of creation; the personified Wisdom acts as YHWH's coworker in creation. The details of creation—of the seas, of the mountains, of earth, fields, and sky—remind us of similar descriptions elsewhere in the Hebrew Bible, for example in the book of Job and in some psalms.

Many biblical scholars have pointed to the striking similarities between Proverbs 8 and Egyptian and Babylonian creation hymns. One could go even further and point to similarities in even more distant cultures, for example, the Rig-Veda from India. The philosophical problems implicit in such ponderings on the creation of the world should probably be regarded as being relatively common to all humanity, and there is probably no reason to overdo the hunt for literary models. The people in the ancient Near East lacked completely the scientific worldview that we have today, and when they wished to express themselves about cosmological phenomena they resorted to poetry rather than to scientific terminology. This is perhaps even clearer in the remnants of a fourth creation account that we can find in the Old Testament, the concept of the primordial struggle.

Primordial Struggle as a Creation Motif

In a whole range of poetic texts in the Old Testament we find references to a concept of the origin of the world portrayed as a kind of cosmic battle between different elements. Well known among these are Job 3:8; Isaiah 27:1; 30:7; and 51:9–10. It is, however, first of all in the Psalms that we encounter remnants of this primordial creation battle. A typical example is Psalm 74:13–17:

> You divided the sea by your might;
> you broke the heads of the dragons in the waters.
>
> You crushed the heads of Leviathan;
> you gave him as food for the creatures of the wilderness.
> You cut openings for springs and torrents;
> you dried up ever-flowing streams.
>
> Yours is the day, yours also the night;
> you established the luminaries and the sun.
> You have fixed all the bounds of the earth;
> you made summer and winter.

The main content of this category of creation myth is that YHWH at the beginning of time fought a battle of life and death with a monster-like being. After the Deity comes out of the battle victorious, either by killing or subjugating the monster, the world is created. That this myth has been well known by the ancient Hebrews is clear by the many different names that have been given to this mythic, dragonlike monster: Leviathan, Yam (sea), Nahar (river), Tannin (sea monster, dragon), Rahab (on Tiamat, see above). In several of these names we recognize etymologies for the chaos waters. The primordial waters, or chaos waters, are portrayed as a hostile and life-threatening dragon. By killing chaos, cosmos appears, one might say, using Greek terminology that is not totally adequate.

In the Hebrew Bible we do not find a coherent composition about the primordial battle, only remnants of the myth in different poetic texts. There must have existed larger, comprehensive myths about the chaos battle in ancient Israel; however, because the biblical authors have chosen to make the Priestly version of creation the "official" one, these chaos myths have been forgotten. From extrabiblical texts it appears, however, that we are dealing with a very popular myth. Well known is a Ugaritic myth in which the battle between Baal and Mot is described. Best known to most people, however, is the Babylonian creation epic *Enuma Elish*, which recounts the battle between the god Marduk and the monster-goddess Tiamat. Similar myths may also be found in Sumerian and Hittite texts. Such divine battles are found not only in the Near East but also in a number of ancient cultures, from Greek and Indian culture to Nordic and Chinese.

Adam

Adam is the primordial human according to the Hebrew Bible. In two different versions in Genesis, the Priestly (1:1–2:4a) and the Yahwist (2:4b–4:26), the creation of the first human is narrated. Genesis 2 recounts how God, after he had watered the dry land with life-giving rain, formed the first human out of earth and blew the spirit of life into his nose. After that God planted a garden in Eden where the human could live and eat of the fruits of the garden. Then follows the creation of the animals of the field and the birds of the sky and, finally, while the human is sleeping, God builds the woman, Eve, from the man's rib. According to the Priestly version (Gen. 1:27), humans were created as man and woman in the image of God. Further on, Genesis 3 recounts how the human beings succumbed to the temptations of a snake to eat of the forbidden tree of wisdom. As their punishment the humans were banished from the garden. Humans lost eternal life and must breed to continue their species. The woman must give birth in pain and the man must toil for daily bread. The first human became the father of Cain, Abel, and Seth.

In a history of religions perspective, the account of the creation of human beings in Genesis is related to similar primordial human myths in other cultures. Sacred trees and concepts of a lost paradisiacal state are known also from other cultures. The Hebrew word used in these accounts is not really a proper noun "Adam," but the noun *'adam*, a West Semitic collective word for "human being," "humanity." The word occurs 554 times as a reference to "human being" in the Old Testament. Etymologically we may associate the word with *dam*, "blood," *'adom*, "red," and *'adamah*, "earth," without bringing us closer to a satisfactory explanation. When the text says that God made the human being (Hebrew *ha'adam*) from earth (Hebrew *'adamah*), this is a pun that does not have anything to do with etymology. Only very few times in Genesis 4 and 5 is *'adam* used without the article, as the proper noun, "Adam."

Even though the Adam traditions in the Old Testament are relatively brief, both rabbinic and Christian posterity exhibited great interest in the person Adam and his "fall." A theological authorship was rapidly established and a rich web of legend was created surrounding Adam in pseudepigraphic, rabbinic, Christian, and gnostic literature. Not least, the theories that soon appeared within Christianity about original sin and a negative view of sexuality, which were understood to be results of the fall of Adam, came to play a significant role.

The New Testament emphasizes that all humans are doomed because of the fall of Adam, but that they have been saved through Christ. In Romans 5 and 1 Corinthians 15 Paul emphasizes that while sin and death came into the world through Adam, Christ is victorious, as the second Adam, over the sin and death of the first Adam. Adam is mentioned several times in the Qur'an, and the rich legendary literature in Islam is clearly related to Jewish traditions.

The biblical story of Adam and Eve has been a favorite theme in art and literature throughout history.

Eve

Eve is the name of the first woman according to the creation account in Genesis 2–4. The mother of the sons Cain, Abel, and Seth is, as such, the primordial mother of humankind. Despite numerous attempts to explain the etymology of the name, none has been satisfactory. The speculations that there are ancient mythological concepts of a mother goddess or Mother Earth behind the account about Eve have not enjoyed success either.

After God had created Adam, the first human, he realized that the man was lonely and created the woman from the man's side (traditionally, "one of his ribs"). The woman was tempted by a snake to eat fruit of the forbidden tree and also led the man to eat. One of the punishments for this was that the woman must bear her children with pain and that she must be subordinate to the man. From Genesis 2:20 it is clear that Eve is created to be a helper (Hebrew *'ezer*) for the man. Together with the argument that the woman was created after the man, and from his rib, these texts have been used throughout time to legitimize the subordinate position of women in society (compare the New Testament, 2 Cor. 11:3 and 1 Tim. 2:13–14). Seen in relation to the great significance that the story of Eve came to have in postbiblical literature and in Christian culture, it is striking that she is not mentioned elsewhere in the biblical writings at all.

Noah and the Flood

In Genesis we read about how all living things are devastated by a great flood after it has rained for forty days and forty nights. Only Noah and his family survive. In addition, all the animals that Noah brought with him onto the ark survive. This vessel was built on God's command. After the flood is over, the earth is again populated when God repeats the words of the creation account to Noah and his sons, "Go forth, increase, and multiply!"

Mythical flood disasters, such as the one we find in the account of Noah's ark in Genesis 6–9, are known to us from other cultures. As in the Old Testament, it is most often the wickedness of humankind that leads to the catastrophe.

From ancient Mesopotamia we know of a similar flood account, handed down to us in the Gilgamesh Epic. The Babylonian Noah is called Utnapishtim. Both the wise man and his wife receive eternal life from the gods after the floodwaters have receded.

Deukalion and his wife Pyrrha are the main characters in a Greek flood legend. The two of them escape the wrath of Zeus by building a boat and drifting around the oceans for nine days.

In Greek there is also a flood account that has been transmitted through the account of Lucian of Samothrace called *The Syrian Goddess*. This story, it turns out, has more characteristics in common with the biblical story of Noah and the flood in Genesis 6–9 (and with the Mesopotamian account of the flood in tablet 11 of the Gilgamesh Epic) than with the Greek story of Deukalion.

The Tower of Babel

In Genesis 11:1–9 we read the mythical account of the tower of Babel. After the flood had receded, the human generations came to the plain of Shinar. There they built a tower that was to reach into the heavens. God stepped down on earth to see what the human beings were up to. He confused their language so that they no longer could understand one another and spread them out across the earth. The city and the tower are named using a pun on the Hebrew verb *balal*, "to mix," "to confuse," and "Babel," that is, Babylon. Some have claimed that the background of the account is the temple of Marduk in Babylon, known for its enormous staircase tower (ziggurat), but we might also be dealing with much older mythical ideas.

Few biblical accounts with connections to ancient Mesopotamia have had the influence on the Western world that the legend of the tower of Babel has had. Early on, the tower of Babel became a symbol of human curiosity and quest for knowledge, but also of the human arrogance that leads to chaos and confusion (cf. the English word "babble"). In early linguistic research the legend played a large role, and up until the nineteenth century the biblical accounts remained the foundation for scientific views on how languages had developed.

There are countless portrayals of the tower of Babel in literature and art. The image that gradually became the standard in the West builds partly on images from antiquity (Herodotus), but also shows striking similarity with the minarets of the Abbasids from the eighth and ninth centuries CE (e.g., the mosque of Samarra). Particularly famous is Pieter Brueghel the Elder's painting from the 1560s CE.

The Patriarchal Accounts in Genesis

The patriarchal accounts, the stories of the fathers, take up most of Genesis. We can divide them into three main groups: the story of Abraham (12:1–25:18), the story of Jacob (25:19–37:1), and the story of Joseph and his brothers (37:2–50:26). As a literary genre, the patriarchal accounts can perhaps best be classified as *saga*. In their present form, the stories of the fathers are an account of one family through three generations. It is possible, and even likely, that this "family saga" has been transmitted and shaped over a long period of time through a complicated tradition process. At several points the Hebrew text reveals what seem to be stages of development in its own history. For pragmatic reasons, however, what matters to us is the text in its present, final form.

As texts that have been written down in a late period, the ideology and socioeconomic conditions in the patriarchal stories primarily reflect the period of the author rather than the ancient past that the story is projected into. In other words, we cannot expect to learn anything about the Middle Bronze period (1900–1550 BCE) from these accounts, whereas we may learn a good deal about the conditions of the Israelites during and after the exile. However, we must not disregard the possibility that there may be ancient traditions in the accounts.

The sagas of Abraham, Isaac, Jacob, and Joseph are ancestor stories that serve to underpin and legitimize important, contemporary ideologies. By virtue of being a national epic the accounts legitimize national, religious, and cultural identity. The patriarchal and matriarchal stories tell of a wealthy herding family's experiences and their relationship to the family Deity. This is a frame story about the "pious Israelites" Abraham and Sarah, Isaac and Rebekah, Jacob and Leah and Rachel, Joseph and Asenath. In the account of their many wanderings and experiences, the promises from God stand out clearly. The promises from YHWH play an extremely important role in the Hebrew Bible. The difference between the promises in Genesis and other promises in the Old Testament is that in the patriarchal stories nothing is demanded in return. We find ourselves in another context than that of the covenant (Gen. 22:16–18). An overview of the promises in Genesis 12–50 shows that the clearest promise is the promise of descendants. YHWH has elected for himself a people that will grow and become large. We find the promise of descendants in 12:1–3; 13:16; 15:15; 16:10; 17:2, 5, 6, 16, 20; 18:18; 22:17, 18; 26:2–5, 24–25; 28:3, 14; 32:12; 35:11; 46:3; 48:4, 16, 19. After that follows the promise of land.

Because the concept of election and the land ideology are so central in the patriarchal and matriarchal stories, they also have a larger biblical context. In Exodus the promises are tied in with the calling of Moses and the charge to lead the people out of Egypt and to the promised land. The promise of land runs like a connecting thread through the whole Pentateuch and makes it possible for the Israelites to endure the many trials through the "forty years in the desert." We find the promise of land in Genesis 12:7; 13:14–15, 17; 15:7–21; 24:7; 26:3, 4; 28:4, 13; 35:12; 48:4; 50:24.

There are also a number of other types of promises in Genesis 12–50. These include the promise of a son, which is related to the promise of descendants, the promise of God's presence, the promise of blessing and progress, and the promise of covenant. All in all, the promises from the Deity to the patriarch, and first and foremost to Abraham, stand very strongly in Genesis 12–50. In an even larger theological context, the promises in many ways make up the fundamental element in the whole of the Hebrew Bible, the message of which in reality can be summed up as one single, extended salvation-historical act by YHWH with his chosen people, from creation up until the rebuilding of Jerusalem under the leadership of Ezra and Nehemiah. If we imagine that this work was written down in the period of the exile, we understand how important it was for the authors of this national epic to tie their contemporary period to the past. Only by holding up the past as an ideal could the cultural elite provide hope also for the future. Times could seem dark, but God, people, and land had a history that went back in time. God's promises had been given for all time and he did not let his people down. Thus one is not surprised to find the promises to the patriarchs mentioned also outside Genesis. In the New Testament we find a resonance and a development of this important theme in Matthew 3:9; Luke 13:16; 16:24; 19:9; Acts 7; 13:26.

Abraham

Biblical research has been intensely preoccupied with the character of Abraham, but is not unified in its view on the question of the historicity of Abraham. Some scholars suppose that Abraham is a historical person, that he has connections to the Amorites, and that he can be dated to around 2000–1800 BCE (Early Middle Bronze). Others maintain that he is a purely literary character. Most scholars take a middle position and think that the Abraham narratives contain a historical core, but that through time it has been modified and expanded before the narratives received their final form in postexilic times. In the wake of the ongoing change of climate in biblical research, the purely historical views are under criticism, giving way to more literary approaches. Many now claim that this unhelpful, exaggerated focus on historicity has led to a situation in which the most significant theological and literary points of the Abraham narrative have receded into the background.

In later Jewish tradition Abraham appears as the major exemplary figure for piety and obedience, who even went so far as to be willing to sacrifice his own son Isaac when God asked him to (see below on Aqedah). As the founder of a religion only Moses surpasses him. In the *Haggadah* Abraham is mentioned as the one who kept all of God's commandments, even those that had not yet been revealed. In early Jewish philosophy he appears as the great righteous one, as prophet, and as philosopher. In more recent times the promise of land to Abraham's descendants has received renewed interest with the rise of Zionism.

In the New Testament, Abraham is mentioned more than any other Old Testament figure (72 times) except Moses. Also in the New Testament Abraham's pious obedience is emphasized. Abraham also becomes the model for justification through faith, and Christians are considered to be the real children of Abraham and the heirs of the Abrahamic promises. The promise to Abraham, that in him all generations on earth shall be blessed, is understood in the New Testament to be a foretelling of the Christian gospel (Gal. 3:8).

The biblical Abraham traditions are important also in Islam. Through his son Ishmael, whom he had with Hagar, Abraham became the founding father of the Arabs. Abraham was Muhammad's favorite prophet and is mentioned in 25 of the Qur'an's 114 suras (75 times by name). Sura 14 is dedicated to Abraham, and in sura 4 Abraham is mentioned as one of those who received God's revelation before Muhammad.

Aqedah

Aqedah ("binding," that is, the binding of Isaac) is a central theological motif in Judaism. As the most prominent representative of pious obedience, Abraham went so far as to be willing to sacrifice his son Isaac when God asked him to (Genesis 22). This story, known as the Aqedah (from Gen. 22:9), was the subject of much legend, especially in Judaism but also in Christianity and Islam. In Targum, Midrash, and later rabbinic philosophy the sacrifice of Isaac is seen as a voluntary self-sacrifice that atones for the sins of the descendants, and the Aqedah thus represents a rabbinical parallel to the sacrificial death of Christ. The Aqedah has always been a popular theme in Jewish art. Also the liturgy of the synagogue refers to the tradition at several points. The Aqedah has continued to play a major role in art and literature also in more recent times, for example, in Thomas Mann's novel *Joseph and His Brothers*.

EXODUS

After Genesis comes Exodus. The name is a latinization of Greek *exodos*, the name in the Septuagint, the Greek translation of the Old Testament, and it means "exit," or "going out." The word refers to the most central event in the book, the Israelites' departure out of Egypt. In Hebrew the book is called *We'elleh shemot*, "and these are the names of" (that is, of Jacob's sons in Egypt), after the opening words of the book. It is usually shortened to simply *Shemot*, "names."

Moses, Exodus, and Sinai

In the Priestly History we are introduced to a story about the twelve Israelite tribes. They descend from the twelve sons of Jacob and are therefore descendants of Abraham and Isaac. The Priestly History continues on to tell the story of these tribes and their sojourn in Egypt, where they live under extremely difficult conditions. Finally, the Israelites succeed in escaping from Egypt with Moses as their leader. As one collective contingent they wander to Mount Sinai. Here the Israelites enter into a covenant with YHWH, the God who by miraculous means had allowed them to flee from the slavery of Egypt. The sojourn in the desert lasts for forty years before the people finally reach the promised land.

The key themes in the Priestly History are the promises to the patriarchs, the exodus, YHWH's revelation and the covenant on Mount Sinai, the desert wanderings, the allotment of the land, and the conquest of Canaan. Exodus deals first of all with two of these key themes: the exodus out of Egypt and the covenant on Mount Sinai.

In the Priestly History the charismatic, prophetic lawgiver Moses plays a major role. It is Moses who liberates his people from the slavery of Egypt and who leads the Israelites through the desert for forty years, all the way to the land that YHWH, their God, has promised them. On the way he receives the laws and regulations from YHWH that the people are to keep, after they have settled in the promised land. This legislation fills most of the Priestly History.

The story of Moses and the events at Sinai is not historical but builds on old traditions that have developed over a long period of time. Moses is mentioned only in the Bible, and we have no other sources that can shed light on Moses as a historical person. We have no choice but to accept that the sources we have at our disposal are not of such a character that they allow us to draw conclusions of a historical nature.

The figure of Moses dominates the narratives of the Pentateuch completely. According to the biblical account, Moses is born in Egypt of the Levitical couple Amram and Jochebed. However, we know very little about what role Moses actually may have played in the early history of the Israelite people.

The approaches to Moses within biblical scholarship have varied widely. Some have held that Moses is completely unhistorical, that he is a pure literary fiction. However, it is just as likely that Moses existed as that he did not. If Moses did exist, we can unfortunately not know much about him. The many legendary characteristics that tradition has come to attach to the figure of Moses have led to the disappearance of any historical Moses, and he is no longer available to us.

This is clear already in the dramatic account of his birth. Because Pharaoh wants to kill all male children of Hebrew descent, Moses is first kept hidden by his mother and then set out on the Nile in a waterproof container. He is found by Pharaoh's daughter, who hires his real mother as a wet nurse. Finally, he is adopted by Pharaoh's daughter, who gives him the name Moses and raises him in Pharaoh's household. Paradoxically Moses is thus saved by the daughter of the pharaoh who oppresses his people and whom Moses later opposes.

However, this account is clearly popular and traditional, not historical. We find similar accounts in many cultures. Closely related to the story of Moses is, for example, the Sargon Legend, an Akkadian text that recounts the birth of Sargon of Akkad. According to this text Sargon's mother took him secretly and placed him in a reed basket that floated down the Euphrates. Finally, he was found by the water-drawer Akki, who raised the child as his own. Sargon was protected by the goddess Ishtar and grew up to be a famous king.

The enormous significance of Moses in later Judaism and Christianity cannot be overestimated. His significance is naturally first of all related to his role as the great lawgiver. The extent of Moses' influence in early Christianity is seen in the New Testament, which mentions Moses more than any other Old Testament figure (79 times) and in which central texts point to Moses as announcing the coming of Jesus (Luke 24:27, 44; John 5:39, 46; Acts 26:22–23).

The heritage of the Hebrew Bible lives on also in our day. Hardly any Old Testament text is as vivid in people's awareness as the Ten Commandments. Because the Ten Commandments have been part of the fundamental education of children in the popular catechisms in Catholic and Lutheran traditions and in the teachings of the various Reformed traditions, they have become part of a common cultural heritage. The Ten Commandments, or the Decalogue (Greek for the "ten words"), appear in the Hebrew Bible in Exodus 20:2–17 and also in Deuteronomy 5:6–21 (with some differences). In Deuteronomy they are part of Moses' long speech, in which he points to YHWH's saving deeds with his people in history before they are to go in and take possession of the promised land. In addition, we find quotes from and allusions to the Decalogue in a number of places in the rest of the Old Testament.

It is important to be aware, however, that the Decalogue makes up only a very small part of the extensive legal material in the Priestly History. In the biblical tradition, Mount Sinai is the place that the whole law was revealed to Moses, and the Sinai legislation occupies most of Exodus, Leviticus, and Numbers (see Exod. 31:18; 34:29; Lev. 26:46; 27:34; Num. 10:33; Deut. 33:2).

Religious Feasts

Various festive occasions play a large role in the Hebrew Bible. Even though there were many different religious feasts in ancient Israel, it has not always been easy to understand how they were celebrated or what their significance was. There are few or no rules for the feasts, and their content is lacking. We are therefore left to reconstruct the feasts from the texts in the Bible where they are discussed.

What is common to all the ancient Israelite feasts is that they are religious institutions that regulate the relationship between God and humans. In addition, they were occasions of great social significance, which included meals, among other things. The most important feasts in ancient Israel are the Passover (Pesach), the Feast of Weeks (Shavuot), and the Feast of Booths (Sukkot).

Passover

The Passover stands in our day as one of the most important feasts of Judaism. Passover is also one of the greatest feasts of Christianity. Yet there are a lot

of uncertainties as to the question of the origin of this feast and its development and significance in ancient Israel. Again, we see that it is not easy to
put together the jigsaw puzzle, with the pieces being spread out in the whole
Bible. It does not get any less confusing when it becomes apparent that we
may not be dealing with just one feast, but two different feasts, *chag happesach*,
"the feast of Passover," and *chag hammatsot*, "the feast of cakes," or, as it is
also called, "the feast of unleavened bread." In several of our sources these
terms seem to be used indistinguishably. In contemporary Judaism, the term
pesach is used for all rituals associated with Passover as well as the Feast of
Unleavened Bread. Josephus (Jewish historian in the first century CE) refers
in several instances to the "feast of unleavened bread" as the correct title of
the whole festival complex, but refers in a couple of places to the feast "that
is called Passover." From this we see that the term "Passover" was probably
a popular term for this feast, though originally there had probably been two
feasts.

The Feast of Weeks

The next great feast that we shall examine a little more closely is the so-called
Feast of Weeks, *chag shavuot*, also called *chag haqqatsir*, "the feast of reaping." Crop gathering in ancient Israel could last from the end of April to the
beginning of June. From the beginning of the cutting of the crop until the
gathering was finished, around seven weeks usually passed. *Shavuot*, "weeks,"
is therefore meant as a reference to the whole period. In later sources the last
day of the feast, the day of the feast itself, was also called *yom chamishim*, "the
fiftieth day." From this derives the Greek term *pentēkostē*, Pentecost. Another
term for this feast is *chag habbikkurim* "the festival of the first fruits."

The Feast of Weeks was primarily a harvest festival, and has not undergone
any essential historical development as, for example, Passover has. It is somewhat uncertain what it was originally known as. The term *chag haqqatsir*, "the
feast of reaping" or "the festival of harvest," as it is called in Exodus 23:16, is
perhaps the oldest term for the feast. The feast itself lasted only one day (in
the Diaspora it lasted for two days, to be sure that one did not celebrate the
feast on the wrong day). The fixing of the time for the feast is discussed in the
regulations in Leviticus 23 (cf. Exodus 23; Numbers 28). In Leviticus 23:15–
16 we read: "And from the day after the sabbath, from the day on which you
bring the sheaf of the elevation offering [see vv. 10–11, where the Israelites
are commanded to bring the first sheaf of the harvest before the priest, who
will raise it before the presence of YHWH on the day after the Sabbath], you
shall count off seven weeks; they shall be complete. You shall count until the
day after the seventh sabbath, fifty days; then you shall present an offering of
new grain to the LORD."

It seems clear that the feast referred to as the "Feast of Weeks" did not have as its function to commemorate specific historical events in the history of the Israelite people. It was basically a feast of reaping. On this point, all biblical sources agree. It is only in the late book of *Jubilees* that this feast is understood as a feast to commemorate the covenant of Noah, which was supposedly made on this day.

The Feast of Booths

We find the legislation for the Feast of Booths in Leviticus 23:39–43. The Feast of Booths, *chag hassukkot*, is the third of the great feasts in ancient Israel. The feast began on the fifteenth day of the seventh month, Tishri. In the Jewish calendar this month falls in the last half of September and first half of October. Tishri is the postexilic, Babylonian name for the month that in Hebrew was called *Ethanim*. Tishri is a busy month of festivities, with *Rosh Hashanah* (New Year) on the first day in the month (originally on the tenth), followed by the solemn "great day of atonement," *Yom Kippur*, on the tenth day, before joy can finally be released for eight days during *Sukkot* (the Feast of Booths). As the day of the new year was originally celebrated on the tenth day, that is, on the same day as Yom Kippur, it is possible that what we have is later specializations of what originally was one festal complex. Sukkot was celebrated in autumn with a lot of joyful activities. The feast was partly celebrated as an end of the agricultural year and partly as a commemoration of the wanderings in the desert.

It is possible that the feast functioned to renew the covenant, and it is this feast that Sigmund Mowinckel has in mind when he talks about the great autumn and New Year feast, with the celebration of YHWH as king and his rising to the throne. The feast is also called *chag YHWH*, "YHWH's feast," or simply *hachag*, "the feast," which clearly signals its significance in ancient Israel.

In the Priestly rules about the feast in Leviticus all people in Israel are commanded to build and live in huts made of leafy branches for seven days. In Deuteronomy 16:13–15 the aspect of joy is more at the forefront, and everyone, even the servants and sojourners, are to rejoice. Further, it is emphasized that the feast must be celebrated in the temple and that offerings must be brought to the temple on that occasion. There is no command to build leafy huts and live in them. We see here, as in a number of other cases, a difference between the Deuteronomist and the Priestly writer in their understanding of the religious feasts. In line with the demand about the centralization of worship to the temple, the Deuteronomist demanded that "all male Israelites must appear before YHWH three times a year." These three times were at Passover, the Feast of Weeks, and the Feast of Booths.

It follows from the biblical material, however, that the Feast of Booths was originally a *pilgrimage feast*. In the fall perhaps a special sacrifice took place out in the fields. This is possibly what 1 Samuel 1:21 describes in the account of how Samuel's father, Elkanah, set out for Shiloh to take part in the yearly sacrifice. The huts that were set up at this feast and that later were to recall the wanderings in the desert and the simple conditions the people had to live under probably have their origin in the primitive sheds that were set up in the vineyards in the fall. These were to give the workers protection from the harsh sun in the day and perhaps for staying overnight, so that they could start their work early in the morning. Probably watchmen also stayed in the huts to prevent theft of the harvest. All of this shows that we are dealing with a typical agricultural feast, a feast of reaping that has been practiced in ancient Canaan. Eventually, the Israelites tied traditions about the desert wanderings to this feast.

In early Judaism the Feast of Booths became very popular. It was then celebrated as a pilgrimage feast in which thousands of Jews from outside Jerusalem and even from the Diaspora flocked to Jerusalem to participate. In Josephus we can read about how the looting of pilgrims on their way to Sukkot in Jerusalem was a big problem in his time. In the eschatological literature it is Sukkot that is the model for the image of the nations flocking to Jerusalem to worship YHWH (Zech. 14:16ff.; Isa. 2:2ff; 56:6ff.).

The Great Day of Atonement

Most significant among the lesser feasts was the great Day of Atonement, *Yom Kippur*. Originally the day was part of the New Year festival cycle, but gradually it came to be a separate holiday, a day of fasting that was highly solemn. We find the ordinances about this fast in Leviticus 16 and 23:27–32. On this day it was important to refrain from eating and working. Further, it included an offering by fire to YHWH (23:27). In Leviticus 16 we read that this day is the only day in the year that the high priest can enter the Holy of Holies, the innermost chamber of the temple. The same chapter describes the ritual of the two rams. One ram is slaughtered and sacrificed as a sin offering to atone for impurity, sin, and guilt. In the story, there is also a ritual of sprinkling blood that commemorates Passover. When this part of the rite is over, a living ram is brought forward. The high priest lays his hands on the head of the ram and confesses the sins of the people. In this way the sins are transferred to the ram. After this the ram is sent out into the desert. Even though the details of the ritual may not be well known to most people, the expression it has created, "scapegoat," is well known. The fast on Yom Kippur is the only fast that is prescribed in the Old Testament. It probably developed at a late stage. The details of the conditions surrounding the growth of this particular day of fasting are not known to us. In Judaism this day came to acquire a very particular significance, not least in later times when questions regarding the sin and guilt of human beings and the holiness of YHWH came more and more to the forefront.

The Sabbath

In ancient Israelite and Jewish religious practice the seventh day, the Sabbath, stands at the center. The word "sabbath" itself may derive from the Hebrew word *shabbat*, which means "to cease," "to come to an end," but this is contested. The origin of the Sabbath has been explained in several different ways. The question makes up part of a very complicated set of questions about calendars and ways of measuring time. A week in ancient Israel lasted for seven days. In general a week is a middle measure between the astronomically based units of time, "day" and "month." As the English word "month" indicates, this unit of time is calculated from the movements of the moon. Different types of "weeks" are known to us from different cultures, in which the length of the week has been four, six, eight, ten, or fifteen days. The seven-day week is known only from ancient Israel. The length of these weeks could have depended on the phases of the moon, or they could have been associated with the time for market days.

Regarding the origin of the ancient Israelite seven-day week, scholars have not been able to agree. Here we must also take into account the great significance that the number seven had all over the ancient Near East as a special, symbolic number. The ancient Israelite seven-day week continued throughout the whole year, independently of what otherwise happened in the lunar year or the solar year. We may therefore assume that the seven-day week in ancient Israel was an additional calendar. The same goes for the seven-year sabbath and the Jubilee (every fiftieth year). The strength of the position of the seven-day week can be seen, for example, by the fact that it passed on from Judaism to the Christian calendar.

In early Judaism controversy over the correct calendar ran high. Since YHWH had declared that particular feasts should be celebrated on particular days, it would be tantamount to blasphemy to celebrate the feast on the wrong date. In the strict Qumran community an alternative calendar was being used, the so-called Sectarian Calendar. This calendar is known also from the pseudepigraphic books of *1 Enoch* 72–75 and *Jubilees* 6:29–38. But this alternative calendar did not have any kind of influence on the celebration of the Sabbath, which followed its familiar pattern of the seven-day week system.

If we look to the neighbors of ancient Israel to the east, we find that Assyria and Babylonia divided the lunar month into two parts, separated from each other by the fifteenth day (*shapattu*), which was the day of the full moon. According to some, the etymology of this term has links to the Hebrew word for the seventh day (*shabbat*). Nevertheless, it is not a simple issue to find the explanation for the origin of the Sabbath. We have to accept that the attempts that have been made to explain it are highly hypothetical and that none of them has been completely convincing.

Let us look a little more closely at how the Sabbath may have functioned in ancient Israel. In a text such as Exodus 34, the Sabbath appears to be more of a practical than a religious or cultic event. In verse 21 we read, "Six days you shall work, but on the seventh day you shall rest; even in plowing time and harvest time you shall rest." And in Exodus 23:12 we find the following humane reason for the Sabbath, "Six days you shall do your work, but on the seventh day you shall rest, so that your ox and your donkey may have relief, and your homeborn slave and the resident alien may be refreshed."

We see that the two texts presuppose an agricultural society. The same regards the rationale given for the Sabbath by the Deuteronomist (Deut. 5:12–15). It is therefore possible that the Sabbath developed in an agricultural society and had its place in pastoral life. It is perhaps less likely that such a day of rest suited transhumant societies the same way, whose primary task was to herd their animals. It is the nature of flocks of sheep to demand daily care.

A separate question is whether the Sabbath was purely a day of rest, or whether from the beginning there had already been certain rites associated with the day. The regulations about the Sabbath in Leviticus 19:30, "You shall keep my sabbaths, . . ." may indicate that the Sabbath was not only a practical arrangement but that it also had a cultic element. In Numbers 28:9–10, for example, the cultic content is very clear: "On the sabbath day: two male lambs a year old without blemish, and two-tenths of an ephah of choice flour for a grain offering, mixed with oil, and its drink offering—this is the burnt offering for every sabbath, in addition to the regular burnt offering and its drink offering." In late biblical times the cultic element came to be the most important content of the Sabbath. For that reason the rationale given for keeping the Sabbath also changed over time. This development is perhaps most clearly expressed in the Decalogue in Exodus 20:8–11. In verse 11 we find a purely theological argument for the Sabbath, "For in six days the LORD made heaven and earth, the sea, and all that is in them, but rested the seventh day; therefore the LORD blessed the sabbath day and consecrated it."

That the Sabbath in preexilic Israel was not always celebrated the way the Yahwist prophets wanted it to be celebrated is seen from some texts in the prophetic writings. In Hosea 2:11 we read, "I will put an end to all her [Israel's] mirth, her festivals, her new moons, her sabbaths, and all her appointed festivals." This oracle of doom must be seen in association with other cult-critical expressions in the Prophets. The same negative view of the Sabbath is found in the cult-critical passage of Isaiah 1:13: "bringing offerings is futile; incense is an abomination to me. New moon and sabbath and calling of convocation—I cannot endure solemn assemblies with iniquity." Another prophetic text, Jeremiah 17:21–27, on the other hand, contains one single, long prohibition against carrying goods through the gates of Jerusalem on the Sabbath, followed by the threat of Jerusalem's destruction should this Sabbath command not be kept and a bright oracle of salvation for Judah and the future of its kings should they keep this command. The dating of this passage in Jeremiah is contested, but it seems undeniably priestly. The existence of similar expressions in the priestly oriented prophet Ezekiel should not surprise anyone, however. In a long range of accusations against the Jewish people in chapter 22, accusations for not having kept the Sabbath claim an important place (vv. 8 and 26). In Ezekiel 45 and 46 the sacrificial cult of the Sabbath is discussed as just as important as the sacrificial cult of the other feasts.

One of the texts in Ezekiel that mentions the Sabbath is 20:12: "Moreover, I gave them my sabbaths, as a sign between me and them, so that they might know that I the LORD sanctify them." This text is late but it is also important because it shows a clear development in the direction of the Sabbath becoming an identifying mark for the holy people. When Nehemiah came to Jerusalem in the postexilic period he found, according to Nehemiah 13, that the celebration of the Sabbath had ceased. He therefore had to reinstate both the cultic content as well as the command not to work on the Sabbath.

In the centuries that followed, the Sabbath became increasingly significant in Judaism. Gradually, the Sabbath came to express the essence of Judaism, and a comprehensive legislation about the Sabbath developed that became more and more extensive. In early Judaism the Sabbath was a source of huge controversies among different parties who wanted to go in different directions. A reflection of this phenomenon can be found in the New Testament accounts of controversy between Jesus and the Pharisees about the correct honoring of the Sabbath. But at this stage in the history of Judaism we have ended up far away from the ancient Israelite concept of Sabbath, not just in time, but also as regards content and the purpose of this institution.

LEVITICUS

The next book in the Bible is called by a latinized Greek word, "Leviticus." The Greek word, *Levitikon*, "Levite," and the presupposed *biblion*, that is, "the Levite's book," are easy to misunderstand. The laws and regulations that we find in Leviticus are *not* dedicated to the Levite priesthood. The Levites are only mentioned in a minor context in Leviticus 25:32–34. All the regulations regarding the Levites are to be found in Numbers, and we should perhaps have expected this book to have received the name "the Levite's book." But this is not the way it is.

Among the Jews, Leviticus is called *Wayyiqra'*, "and he called," after the first words of the Hebrew text. In the period around the beginning of the Common Era, Jewish scholars referred to Leviticus as the "Priestly Law." This name is also what best characterizes the content of the book. The whole of Leviticus is concerned with priestly cultic laws and regulations.

Leviticus is the only one of the five books of the Pentateuch that does not contain narrative traditions (with the exception of the story about Nadab and Abihu in chap. 10). The legal material bears the mark of having developed over a long period of time. We can see this from the many repetitions and seemingly scattered arrangement of the material. With his introductory formulae the redactor has placed all of the legal material of the Tetrateuch into the Sinai tradition, "These are the commandments that the LORD gave Moses for the people of Israel on Mount Sinai" (27:34).

Sacrifice

The sacrificial cult is central in the Hebrew Bible and ancient Israelite religion. The sacrifices are the most prominent feature of worship. Accompanied by different rites, slaughtered animals and other provisions were presented to the Deity or consumed in the presence of the Deity in a communal meal. Sacrifice is a religious and social act known from most cultures. Many attempts have been made to explain the phenomenon. One of the most common explanations for the sacrificial cult is that its function is to please the deity. A sacrifice such as the sacrifice of atonement can also be explained as arising from a fundamental need among humans in general to atone. In some cases it seems that sacrifices were meant as food for the deity. In other cases the communal meal had as its function to give food to the poor and needy. Sacrifices can also be understood as something that the deity could demand as a privilege of being a god. This could entail a pledge of duty or of honoring or a worship offering. One can also imagine that sacrifices create a psychological feeling of a change in the subjects who are offering the sacrifice themselves so that their status changes, and that this type of status improvement feels necessary.

We must also imagine a series of combinations of the possible explanations of sacrifice mentioned above. What is most certain is that sacred rites such as sacrifices in no way can be set to one formula and can definitely not be explained rationally. No matter which explanation we espouse, it is undoubtedly clear that the need to communicate with the powers above seems to belong to human nature. It definitely does not show much understanding for the complex religious phenomenon that sacrifice is if one simply points to one of the types of models briefly mentioned above. In previous research it has been customary to explain all sacrifice in so-called primitive societies as solely motivated from the *do ut des* model. (This refers to the concept that in order for the gods to react to human pleas, humans must offer them something.) In societies that were on a higher level of development this "primitive" concept of sacrifice was substituted with another that understood sacrifices as a type of worship or symbolic act, without underlying motives of benefit. Today we know that this analysis is too simple and does not come close to giving a satisfactory explanation of the religious phenomenon of sacrifice. Today we are also very much aware that cultures do not develop from lower to higher stages as presupposed in the past.

Concerning sacrifices that are described in the Hebrew Bible, it is worth noting that both regarding technical terminology and content they exhibit striking similarities with extrabiblical sacrifices, for example from Mesopotamia, Syria, and the Phoenician colonies, and also from Arabic and Hittite documents.

The Burnt Offering

The most extensive sacrificial legislation in the Hebrew Bible can be found in Leviticus 1–16. Here the priestly sacrificial practice is described in detail. The first three chapters deal with the sacrificial cult from the point of view of the participant. In chapter 1 we find regulations about the burnt offering. Because this was the only form of sacrifice that was consumed at the altar in its entirety, in Hebrew it is called '*olah*, which means "whole offering" (compare Deut. 33:10 and 1 Sam. 7:9). From Leviticus 1:4 it is explicit that the burnt offering also had the function of atonement. The same is clear from 9:7 and 14:20. In other contexts it is not stated that this type is a sacrifice of atonement. In those contexts the sacrifice seems to represent a spontaneous offering, an expression of joy (Lev. 22:17–18; Num. 15:1–3). The main purpose of the sacrifice seems to be to give YHWH honor. This offering is probably the oldest type of sacrifice in ancient Israel. It is also possibly the sacrificial type that was most widespread.

Clearly, the regulations in Leviticus 1 emphasize that the sacrificial animal had to be without blemish. Further, they had to be taken only from the "herd and the flock," or it could also be a pigeon. Wild animals could not be sacrificed, not could domestic animals such as camels or donkeys. It is further emphasized that only male animals could be used as sacrifices.

Food Offering

In Leviticus 2 the regulations for the food offering (grain offering), the *minchah*, are given. The Hebrew word *minchah* is used in the Bible also as a noncultic term for "gift." In the Priestly literature *minchah* is always a term for different grain products: fine flour (2:1–3), baked goods (2:4–10), or toasted grain (2:14–16). Leviticus makes a point that all of these products must have salt added to them and that leavened dough must not be used. From the regulations about the food offering it is apparent that not all of the sacrifice was burnt at the altar (as opposed to the whole offering or burnt offering discussed above). The food offering played an important social role in ancient Israel, for it would not be possible for everyone to sacrifice bulls or sheep as burnt offerings. Even pigeons could entail a large expense for someone who was poor. The food offering in this case served as the poor person's *'olah*, "whole offering" or "burnt offering."

Peace Offering

The third chapter of Leviticus gives the regulations for the "peace offering" or "sacrifice of well-being/peace" (Hebrew *shelamim*). As opposed to the two types of sacrifice described above, *'olah* and *minchah*, the *shelamim* offering has no function of atonement but is primarily a communal meal where the people who are making the sacrifice eat of the sacrificial gifts in the temple or in the home. Therefore this sacrifice is also called "slaughter sacrifice" or "meal sacrifice" (Hebrew *zevach*). Apart from this the regulations are identical to those of the burnt offering, with the exception that pigeons are not mentioned and that both male and female animals may be offered. The peace offering is a less solemn sacrifice than the two previous ones.

Guilt and Atonement Offering

While Leviticus 1–3 deals with regulations regarding the individual who is making the sacrifice, chapters 4–5 treat the sin or purification offering and the guilt or atonement offering, in Hebrew *chatta't* and *'asham*, respectively. The purpose of these sacrifices was to remove cultic impurity that might have come into the sanctuary through breaches of the cultic laws and regulations. It is important to note that we are dealing solely with impurity as a result of unawareness or carelessness, not with conscious breaches of cultic, religious, or moral commandments. Chapter 4 treats the sin offering, *chatta't*, which is divided into four categories. There are regulations for how the sanctions should be for the different breaches according to whom the perpetrator is, whether it is the anointed priest (high priest), the whole congregation, a ruler, or one of the people. Cultic rank and economic capability thus contribute to determining the size of the different sacrifices. The high priest must sacrifice a young bull; the same goes for the congregation. A ruler must sacrifice a male goat, while an ordinary person must sacrifice a female goat. Regulations for this sacrifice are also found in Leviticus 5:1–13, which discusses certain special cases. Here the economic capability of the perpetrator is primarily considered. In 5:14–26 a sacrifice that is related to the sin offering is discussed, the "guilt offering" or "atonement offering," 'asham.

In chapters 6–7 we are introduced to further sacrificial legislation. Here all the types of sacrifice that are mentioned in chapters 1–5 are discussed anew. The exposition, which is organized systematically according to the significance of each sacrifice, touches on a number of details that were not mentioned earlier.

About the Priests

In Leviticus 8–10 a number of regulations about the priests follow. Leviticus 8 deals with the initiation of the priests. The chapter should be seen in association with Exodus 29. To simplify somewhat, what is commanded in Exodus 29 is put into action in Leviticus 8. The connection with Exodus 29 becomes clear with the set formula that completes each section of the initiation ceremony, "as the LORD (YHWH) commanded Moses." Through each part of the initiation ceremony, the washing, dressing, anointing, sin offering, burnt offering, and initiation sacrifice, the priests are initiated into their office as cultic servants. They are also given the right to their portion of the tithes and offerings that are brought to the sanctuary.

Leviticus 9 recounts the appointment of the priests to their office and details the various offerings associated with this duty. On the eighth day after the initiation ceremony the priests' official duties begin. These are mainly concerned with carrying out various sacrificial rituals. From 9:6 it follows that the purpose of all offerings is to make YHWH reveal himself.

In 10:1–7 we find the story of the priests Nadab and Abihu, who must die because they do not fulfill the requirements of cultic service that are demanded. The episode shows how strictly the correct keeping of the cultic regulations was judged. Verses 8–20 give further rules about the behavior of the priests during the cultic acts, for example, about the consumption of those parts of the sacrifice that were allotted them (10:12–15).

Purity Laws

In Leviticus 11–16 the famous regulations of purity and impurity appear. In Leviticus 11 the clean and unclean animals are described. With this text we are very likely dealing with concepts that go far back in time. Because these are regulations about what the Israelites can and cannot eat, and not about cultic acts, no penalties are detailed should these regulations be broken. Regardless of what the origin might be of the different rules about clean and unclean animals, Leviticus gives only one reason for why the commandments should be kept—holiness (vv. 44–47). The Israelites are commanded to strive toward holiness because YHWH, their God, is holy (v. 44).

For the priests, cultic holiness entails a type of anthropological purity, a condition that humans can attain by following the rules that count: offer the required sacrifices, eat the correct things, and in general behave in the right way. This view is different from what we find in Deuteronomy. For the Deuteronomists holiness is not a state one can choose to set oneself in; rather, the people are in a state of holiness because YHWH has chosen them, and not by their own merit. Something similar is found also in the Deuteronomists' view of the sacrificial cult. For the Deuteronomists the sacrificial cult is not strictly necessary. Its major function is social and for the common good, not least because the poor and needy could take part in the meal and enjoy it and benefit from it.

Few texts in the Hebrew Bible have been as mind-boggling as the regulations about clean and unclean animals. For example, contemporary people find it difficult to grasp that sea creatures with fins and shells should be "clean," while every other sea creature should be "unclean" and thus forbidden to eat. Or why are the rabbit and the pig unclean, whereas cattle and sheep can be eaten? And why can some species of grasshoppers be eaten and others not? Biblical scholars have through the ages attempted to explain the purity laws by various theories. Some have wanted to explain them as rules that take medical knowledge as their point of departure. The explanation that the ban on pork is based on the danger of disease in this meat is well known. Yet others have seen the proscriptions against the background of foreign cultic practice. The unclean animals were used in non-Israelite sacrificial cult and should therefore not be eaten by worshipers of YHWH.

None of these rational explanations is satisfactory. At least they do not give plausible explanations for all the different regulations of all the different types of animals. The explanation that the cultural anthropologist Mary Douglas has put forth seems far more likely. She considers first of all the texts themselves and sets all the purity laws in the Hebrew Bible into a larger context, using the explanation in Leviticus 11:44–47 as a point of departure. According to Douglas we are dealing with the general need for us as humans to classify the world around us in ordered/safe and destructive categories. Based on the knowledge we have of such phenomena also in other cultures and, not least, from psychiatry, this model of understanding seems to take us a long way.

NUMBERS

The English title of Numbers is a translation of the Greek *Arithmoi*, and derives from the content of the first chapter, where we find a population census. The most common Hebrew term for the book, *Bammidbar*, "in the desert," comes from the fact that most of the story in Numbers takes place in the desert. In line with Jewish practice the book is also called after the opening words in Hebrew, *Wayedabber*, "and he (YHWH) spoke."

The composition of Numbers seems incoherent and unstructured. The Priestly author has clearly used a great deal of older sources in his exposition, though we are not able to say much about how old these sources are. The author is, nevertheless, fairly easily recognizable with his typically Priestly style.

We find the following main themes in Numbers: like Exodus 19ff., Numbers 1–10 relates episodes in the Israelite camp in the wilderness of Sinai. Numbers 11–12 narrates the complaints of the people in the desert and their rebellion. A major part of Numbers consists of accounts of the allotment and taking of land. These begin already in chapters 13–14 with the account of the twelve spies, continue on sketchily in chapters 20–21 and claim most of chapters 31–36. Unmistakably Priestly material is found mainly in the genealogies of chapters 1 and 26, the camp arrangement in chapters 2–3, the travel itinerary of chapter 33, the border lists of chapters 33–34, and the various juridical and cultic regulations that we find spread out in the whole book. The tradition about the prophet Balaam in chapters 22–24 occupies a position of its own.

The Levites

The picture that we get of the Levites in Numbers 3–4 and 16 is not representative of the Hebrew Bible. According to the Priestly description in Numbers, the Levites belong to the lowest rank of the priesthood; it is in reality only the priests, the descendants of Aaron, who are allowed to carry out the true priestly duties. The Levites were comparable to a type of lower laborer or servant rather than to the priests. For example, the Levites could not even touch the cultic objects in the temple, as these would become unclean through their touch.

With the Deuteronomists the case differs. From Deuteronomy 33:8–11 we get the impression that the duties accorded the Levites are much more in line with the regular priestly duties.

The Chronicler (the collector, or collectors, of the books of Chronicles and, as some claim, the books of Ezra and Nehemiah) also places the Levites on a much higher social plane. According to 1 Chronicles 9:28 and 23:28 the Levites were to assist the priests in worship and help them to carry and clean the holy vessels and other cultic objects. This is radically different than what we find in Numbers 4:15–20 and 18:3, which state that the Levites would die if they did anything like that. In a number of other places the Chronicler values the Levites highly. Accordingly, some of them were to have been prophets, scribes, instructors, and judges. Others were to have played significant roles during the appointment of kings. The Chronicler even goes so far as to say, "for the Levites were more conscientious than the priests in sanctifying themselves" (2 Chr. 29:34). In the books of Chronicles we also find several places that describe how the Levites conduct ritual functions that were exclusively the domain of the priests according to the Priestly writers themselves. Examples of such functions are law instructors and officiators in the Passover celebration.

The view of the Levites in the Bible is thus fairly nuanced. This could be the case because the sources derive from different historical periods, but it could also reflect a conflict of interest between different power groups. In many ways, the Chronicler's account should probably be seen more as propaganda for the Levites' position than as any real description of contemporary conditions. However one chooses to view this material, it is nevertheless clear that the significance and influence of the group must have changed over the centuries. In some contexts they seem to have stood at the bottom of the cultic rank, and at other times they were seen as belonging to the same status group as the ordinary priests.

Balaam

One text from Numbers that is interesting to study a little more closely is the story of the prophet Balaam in Numbers 22–24. The account is not only interesting in itself but also throws light on the prophetic movement in ancient Israel and in the ancient Near East. Further, it contributes to the knowledge of how biblical traditions may have developed.

Many characterize the account as a legend or even as a fable (not least because of Balaam's conversations with the donkey he is riding). In sum, when the Israelites during their desert wanderings from Egypt to Canaan draw near Moab, the tiny state east of the southern half of the Dead Sea, the Moabite king Balak is overcome by fear and calls upon the "seer" Balaam in order that he may curse the Israelites. After the intervention of YHWH Balaam ends up blessing the Israelites instead of cursing them, and cursing Israel's enemies.

It is of interest here that in other parts of the Old Testament and also in the New Testament we find other Balaam traditions than the positive version in Numbers. In Deuteronomy 23:4–5 it is stated that YHWH did not want to listen to Balaam when he came to curse the Israelites. In Joshua 13:22 we read about how the Israelites kill Balaam together with the enemies of Israel. That same tradition can be found in Numbers 31:8. In Numbers 31:16 Balaam is portrayed as the one who led the Israelites to worship Baal of Peor in Moab (Numbers 25). In Joshua 24:9–10 YHWH does not want to listen to Balaam, but rather he saves the Israelites from him. In Nehemiah 13:2 the expression is more neutral (see also Mic. 6:5).

Via early Judaism the Balaam traditions were transmitted also to the New Testament. Second Peter 2:15 refers to Balaam as he "who loved the wages of doing wrong." In Jude 11 Balaam is placed next to evildoers such as Cain and Korah with the mention of "Balaam's error for the sake of gain." Revelation 2:14 speaks of "the teaching of Balaam, who taught Balak to put a stumbling block before the people of Israel, so that they would eat food sacrificed to idols and practice fornication."

We see that the Balaam traditions in the Bible are far from uniform: from the very positive reference to Balaam, the "worshiper of YHWH" in Numbers 22–24, to the concept of the great crook and deceiver of the people in the New Testament. This richness shows us that we are dealing with traditions that have been transmitted, changed, and written down over a very long period of time. Through the short notes about the Israelites' slaying of Balaam we thus come to know a tiny shred of a much larger, and more comprehensive, negative Balaam tradition. This tradition has been lost to posterity. Again we are reminded that what we find in the Hebrew Bible represents only a selection of an indefinitely much larger pool of different traditions that we no longer know.

What makes the Balaam traditions particularly interesting is an archaeological discovery at Tell Deir Alla in the Jordan valley (in present-day Jordan). Dutch archaeologists started digging the site in 1960. In 1967 they discovered an ink text on a mural wall of a building that had been destroyed by fire, possibly in relation to an Assyrian campaign around 700 BCE. The dating, however, is much debated, and many prefer a much later date. Some also think that an earthquake destroyed the site.

The text is written in a local West Semitic dialect (related to epigraphic Hebrew), and discussions took place concerning the language. Was it Ammonite, Aramaic, or some other vernacular? The language question has not really been settled.

The text has been greatly restored to a great extent, and the putting together of the fragments is also debated. Nevertheless, what we may read of the text is rather exciting to anyone interested in ancient Israel. The text tells of a prophet Balaam who received a message from the gods. The deities, who appear to have assembled for a kind of divine council, seem to be discontent with things on earth.

Some rituals may refer to a cult of the dead. What is sensational in the Deir Alla texts are the several similarities between these texts and the biblical

Balaam stories. The geographical location is the same in the two traditions. The name Balaam son of Beor appears to be similar. Not a few of the West Semitic words that appear in the text are found also in Numbers. Through the discovery of the extrabiblical Balaam we have, so to speak, reached "behind" the Hebrew Bible, and we are witnessing a stage in the very formation history of the text. We may assume that the Balaam traditions were strong in the East Jordan area in antiquity. The Deir Alla text shows us that the biblical writers must have had ancient traditions at their disposal. They also show how changeable these traditions were.

SOME ASPECTS OF THE HISTORY OF PENTATEUCHAL RESEARCH

That the Pentateuch has been referred to as "the books of Moses" in Jewish as well as in Christian tradition is due to the earlier belief that the five books had been written by Moses. Gradually, however, scholars began to ask questions about this understanding. This happened already in antiquity, but in a more reflective way for the first time in the medieval period, by Jewish scholars.

Today we are quite confident that Moses is not the author of the Pentateuch. We now know that most of the legal material that we find in the "books of Moses" reflects conditions from later periods and therefore cannot be as old as intended by the historical framework that it is set into. Any reading through the text soon reveals the state of the "authorship" of Moses. In Genesis 12:6 and 13:7 we find the small note, "at that time the Canaanites were in the land." It is clear that whoever is telling this story is looking back from the time of writing to the past that the text is narrating. Here the redactor or author has revealed himself. Another example is the account of Moses' death in Deuteronomy 34. It is illogical to assume that Moses should have written the story of his own death and burial! It is these types of simple observations that contained the first seeds of critical pentateuchal research.

Most biblical scholars today assume that the Pentateuch does not display a "natural unity," but that we are dealing with an extremely diverse web of the most disparate types of traditions. These traditions grew together over the centuries before finding their final shape in late, postexilic times. We are dealing with a piece of ancient Near Eastern tradition literature without any real "author" in our modern sense of the word. As with all tradition literature, special rules apply for how the biblical traditions have developed.

In recent years, however, more and more scholars have voiced a healthy skepticism toward the feasibility of discovering which traditions and sources were the basis for the authors of the final fixed text. Recent research has therefore shifted more toward the actual text as we have it. In the past, one could easily get the impression that the final product itself represented the least interesting stage in the wanderings of the traditions toward a "finished Bible." Often, the message of the texts did not seem to be of any interest to scholars either. Today these tendencies of earlier times seem to be in the process of disappearing. Recently some have gone so far as to claim that the Pentateuch is the work of a single author from the postexilic period. No matter what one's attitude is toward these questions, it will always be one of the main tasks of biblical research to try to gain insight into how the Bible has come into existence.

As mentioned above, we find the first seeds of critical reflection on the composition and development of the Pentateuch quite far back in time. In spite of this, it was not until the seventeenth century that the first truly historically grounded work on biblical writings appeared. In a history of ideas perspective, this is associated with the dawn of historical thinking in the Western world following the Renaissance and the Enlightenment.

Richard Simon is regarded by many as the founding father of historical biblical research. In 1678 this Catholic priest published a "critical history of the Old Testament." Among other things, he discussed the composite character of the Pentateuch. Simon was viciously attacked for his views, both by Catholics and Protestants. His books soon ended up on the Catholic Church's Index of Prohibited Books.

After Simon, many years passed before anyone discussed the "books of Moses" through a historical approach. This was probably due to the turmoil and public offense that had been caused by the publications of Simon's books. In 1753 the French doctor Jean Astruc, also a Catholic, published a literary analysis of Genesis. Astruc attempted to prove the existence of two sources for Genesis, and through his work laid the foundation for the modern source hypothesis. He arrived at his views by distinguishing between texts that use the divine name YHWH and texts that use the name Elohim. On the basis of this distinction he was able to present two parallel main accounts in Genesis.

The strong reactions to Astruc's theories from the Catholic Church perhaps led a Protestant to pick up the work of Astruc and refine the so-called source hypothesis. The German scholar Johann Gottfried Eichhorn, with a three-volume introduction to the Old Testament (1780–1783), has received the honor of having founded critical biblical scholarship as a distinct discipline. Eichhorn was the first scholar to reflect truly methodically on the character and essence of biblical scholarship itself. Through his work he laid the foundation for all future pentateuchal research.

Around the beginning of the nineteenth century the so-called literary-critical method had its final breakthrough. Different ways of conceiving the growth of the Pentateuch saw the light of day. Roughly speaking, one main concept saw the work as composed of several fragments (the fragment hypothesis), and another that a core text had later been supplemented and expanded (the supplementary hypothesis).

The nineteenth century experienced several great names in the area of biblical research. All of them were preoccupied with further developing the literary-critical work of dividing the Pentateuch, "the five books of Moses," into different sources. The breakthrough finally came with the greatest pioneer of them all, Julius Wellhausen (1844–1918).

Wellhausen took as his point of departure the research results of Karl Heinrich Graf (1815–1869) and Abraham Kuenen (1828–1891). Graf has primarily received the honor of having proven in a convincing way that the legal material in the source that scholars gave the name P (the Priestly Source or Priestly Code), and that they found richly represented in Exodus, Leviticus, and Numbers, was of a much later date than the rest of the sources of the Pentateuch. Kuenen, on the other hand, gave the whole of the Priestly Source a late date. On this background Wellhausen developed his classical thesis about the sources of the Pentateuch that came to be widely accepted, and that in its main outline has stayed intact until recently, when the thesis has received so many attacks that it no longer seems viable.

The classical source hypothesis maintains that the Pentateuch is composed of four distinct main sources:

1. The Yahwist Source (often abbreviated J), which uses the divine name YHWH.
2. The Elohist Source (often referred to as E), which uses the divine name Elohim.
3. Deuteronomy (or simply D).
4. The Priestly Source or the Priestly Code (abbreviated P).

The dating of these sources has varied, but scholars have generally agreed on dating the Yahwist to the tenth century BCE, the Elohist to the eighth–seventh century BCE, Deuteronomy to the seventh century BCE, and the Priestly Source to the sixth century BCE.

Pentateuchal research achieved an important supplement to source criticism through form-critical and tradition-critical research, represented first of all by Hermann Gunkel (1862–1932), Albrecht Alt (1883–1956), Martin Noth (1902–1968), and Gerhard von Rad (1901–1971). Based on the observation that a particular historical context or occasion has its correlate in specific literary forms, tradition-historical research has tried to find out how the rich Old Testament traditions circulated and changed through the centuries until they received their final shape in the Hebrew Bible we have today.

Within Scandinavian research the term "tradition history" came to be used about studies of the oral transmission of biblical material before it was written down. Well-known Scandinavian scholars who have had a major influence are the Swede Ivan Engnell (1907–1964), the Dane Johannes Pedersen (1883–1977), and the Norwegian Sigmund Mowinckel (1884–1966).

To illustrate how the Scandinavian tradition-historical research has worked with the material, we may briefly mention Pedersen's work with Exodus 1–15. In the first fifteen chapters of Exodus we find the story of how Moses is called by YHWH to lead the people out of Egypt, about the plagues that he sends on the Egyptians because they refuse to let the Israelites go, a number of laws regarding the Passover, and the account of the Red Sea crossing. What Pedersen found most conspicuous about these accounts was the clear cultic context they seemed to be situated in. He took particular note of the accounts about the Passover and claimed to be able to show that with these texts we are dealing with material that had been in use at the annual Passover feast in Palestine from the time after the conquest around 1200 BCE. The texts were thus not as old as the account gave the impression of being. Exodus 1–15 was used as the Israelite Passover liturgy. When the Israelites' old "history" was to be written down, this Passover legend was projected back into history. We are thus not speaking of historical texts that have been "ritualized" at a late stage, as some scholars had thought. According to Pedersen it was rather the opposite; it was all about the historicizing of a cultic legend or ritual.

For a long time the traditional Old Testament research methods of literary criticism, source criticism, form criticism, tradition-historical criticism, and redaction-historical methods ruled the field. But in the course of the last few decades we have seen a significant reaction against the traditional ways of working with the Pentateuch. This reaction has probably primarily been brought about by the dissatisfaction caused by the many and often contradictory hypotheses that followed in the wake of literary criticism and tradition history. Research had gotten stuck in a positivist and historicist blind alley and needed radical renewal.

Among the more recent directions within pentateuchal research, we can particularly highlight those that have sailed under the banner of "the Bible as literature." This has had its impact mainly in the United States, but has gradually increased its influence also in Europe. "The Bible as literature" movement attacked traditional research for being one-sidedly focused on pushing back behind the text. Instead of being interested in texts in their final form, that is, the way they are available to us in the Bible, historical-critical research had only been interested in the compositional history of the text. In that way, the traditional method of research contributed to a development where scholars missed the important fact that the texts after all do have a message to convey.

To read the Bible as literature entails that biblical texts be read in the same way as other texts that we call "literary," and that methods from modern literary study be applied to the Bible. In the United States we therefore find scholars of the Bible not only at theological seminaries but just as often in the departments of literature and cultural studies of liberal arts colleges. This way of approaching the Bible has represented an important challenge to the somewhat tedious enterprise that traditional historical-critical research gradually developed into. It has also contributed to the rediscovery of the Bible as a powerful, ancient Near Eastern literary masterpiece, where the most beautiful poetry appears side by side with the most blood-curdling dramatic accounts of war, and where all of this is set into the framework of a deep religious message.

Even more serious is the criticism that has been voiced against traditional research in the wake of, among other trends, "the Bible as literature" movement and that has led to major changes in the traditional learned exegesis itself. While it was still possible to see traditional biblical research and modern literary methods as mutually supplementary, the latest development within pentateuchal studies has all but undermined the foundation of traditional source criticism itself. While the status of the E source as an independent, coherent source has long been under attack, scholars have recently attacked the very foundation of the source hypothesis, the J source. Scholars like John Van Seters in North America, Rolf Rendtorff in Germany, and Hans H. Schmid in Switzerland have all in convincing ways argued that it is either meaningless to talk of an independent J source at all, or have dated it so late that the classical four-source hypothesis can no longer be upheld. The British scholar Roger Norman Whybray (1923–1998) published *The Making of the Pentateuch* (1987), in which he argues that the whole Pentateuch was written by one person in the sixth century BCE who partly invented the stories and partly used traditions from his own time, none of them very old.

At the present time classical pentateuchal studies seem to be facing great changes. The old theories have (rightly so) been thrown back into the pot, and it is difficult to say what the future will bring. We see that important impulses for new ideas within this exegetical field are coming not only from the "old" fields within biblical scholarship but to a large degree from "new" academic disciplines such as tradition studies, folklore studies, sociology, and cultural anthropology. The field of research on the Hebrew Bible is embarking on an exciting time.

3

The Deuteronomistic History

*Deuteronomy, Joshua, Judges,
1 and 2 Samuel, 1 and 2 Kings*

The next major work for our attention is the Deuteronomistic History. The work consists of the biblical books of Deuteronomy, Joshua, Judges, 1–2 Samuel, and 1–2 Kings. Within the Hebrew Bible the Deuteronomistic History is a very important work. But the influence of the Deuteronomists extends far beyond this. It is possible that the Deuteronomists are the ones who have joined their own work of history together with the Priestly History (Genesis, Exodus, Leviticus, Numbers). If this is the case, these authors are responsible for the whole major work that begins with the creation of the world in Genesis and ends with the fall of Judah and the exile in 2 Kings. We also find clear traces of Deuteronomistic influence in a number of other biblical books, for example, in the Prophets and Psalms. As such, the Deuteronomists have had a significant role in the final shaping of large parts of the Hebrew Bible.

THE DEUTERONOMISTIC HISTORY

A reason that Deuteronomy, the last book of the Torah, stands so much in the center of biblical research today is because the theology that we find in this work has had an influence on the development of the Hebrew Bible that extends way beyond Deuteronomy itself. The covenant and covenant theology do play an important role for a number of other Old Testament writers. However, it is no exaggeration to claim that the covenant in no other place plays a role anywhere close to what it does in Deuteronomy and in the circle of writers who work in the spirit of this book and who are responsible for the so-called Deuteronomistic History. For lack of any knowledge about their true identity we call these writers the "Deuteronomists," or sometimes using the collective singular, the "Deuteronomist" (D). The name "Deuteronomistic History" has been given to the work because research showed early on that there were striking similarities in the historical-theological view that one found in Deuteronomy (with a clear emphasis on election and covenant) and the ideology that saturates the books of Joshua, Judges, Samuel, and Kings.

As the last of the five books of the Pentateuch, Deuteronomy's position is strategic. At the same time Deuteronomy also belongs to another and greater context. There is a large degree of consensus among scholars today to see Deuteronomy, Joshua, Judges, Samuel, and Kings as an independent and coherent literary work. The many and difficult questions associated with dating, size, composition, and origin cannot be discussed in much detail here. Unfortunately, little agreement has been reached on these issues, and scholarly views vary greatly. The size of the Deuteronomistic History is about one-fourth the text of the whole Hebrew Bible. It aspires to tell the story of the history of Israel from the time of the conquest around 1200 BCE to the final destruction of Jerusalem in 586 BCE, a period of around six hundred years. And this is not just any six hundred years. The Deuteronomistic History wishes to tell the story of the people of Israel through its entire existence in Canaan, in the land that YHWH, their God, gave them. The Deuteronomistic History is the story about a people and their land from the time that the nation came into existence to the time that Judah ceased to exist as an independent nation.

If we compare the Deuteronomists' view of central religious questions with that of other biblical writers, we will often find that the Deuteronomists represent a somewhat more abstract and theoretical view. In many areas the Deuteronomists might also give a more secular or demythologized impression. This becomes even clearer particularly if we compare the Deuteronomists' work with the Tetrateuch, the Priestly History (P). As an example we can mention the view of the sacrificial cult. As opposed to the Priestly view of sacrifice, particularly as we find it portrayed in Leviticus, the Deuteronomists think that sacrifice should not be practiced for its own sake. YHWH does not need offerings. Further, we do not find any trace of the types of sacrifice such as the sin offering and the guilt offering, that is, lesser offerings that have as their purpose to atone for unintentional sins, impurity, theft, and so on. According to Deuteronomy it seems that a more "spiritual" atonement can atone for sins, with a confession of the sins, expression of regret, and prayer. Deuteronomy's legislation regarding the sacrificial cult seems to restrict itself to sacrifices that were to be consumed by the sacrificing subjects in the temple and are meant to be shared by the poor, the Levites, the strangers, the widows, and the orphans. The continuous emphasis that the sacrificial meal should be shared between those participating shows that the primary purpose was charitable, as well as "religious."

It is striking that the sacrificial cult is not further discussed in Deuter-onomy. Why is this? It could be that knowledge of the sacrificial cult is assumed, or that the writers simply are not interested in the sacrificial cult. For the Deuteronomists the sacrificial cult is obviously not a joint institu-tional responsibility. Besides the humanitarian aspect of providing food for the poor and needy, the sacrifices are an expression of the subject's gratitude to the Deity. When without further ado the Deuteronomists decided to close down the many sanctuaries in rural areas where the sacrificial cult has been going on through the years, this entailed a low evaluation of the priesthood and of the significance of the sacrificial cult.

The same "desacralized" view that we find in the Deuteronomists' writ-ing regarding the sacrificial cult is also evident in other areas of religion, for example in their view of the tithe. The tithe is not, as with the Priestly writers, "sanctified to YHWH" but remains the property of the giver and can even be secularized and used for profane purposes (if an equal amount of money is paid and without the extra fee of one-fifth that is required in Leviticus 27). Also the various feasts and holy days are seen somewhat differently in Deuter-onomy than what we know from P. The most striking difference, however, is probably the view of the Passover sacrifice.

Well known from Exodus is the account of the Passover sacrifice as a cel-ebration in the home. The Passover celebration was accompanied by rites with the brushing of blood on the doorposts and above the door, and there were specific regulations for the preparation of the sacrificial animal (Exodus 12). With the Deuteronomists we find nothing of this. Here the Passover sac-rifice is portrayed as a sacrificial meal in the central sanctuary in line with all other offerings. The Deuteronomists have similar views regarding the other feasts, differing from the Priestly tradition. For example, the Feast of Booths is portrayed as stripped of its sacral content and can no longer be separated from the Feast of Weeks.

One can see a similar situation with the Sabbath. The Priestly rationale for keeping the Sabbath is well known: the Sabbath shall be kept sacred because YHWH rested on this day after he had created the world (Exod. 20:8–10). But in Deuteronomy 5:12–14 the rationale for keeping the Sabbath is that all humans need a day of rest after a week of work. Again, the sacral attitude is replaced with a humanitarian one.

Corresponding departures from the Priestly tradition can be found also when it comes to the concepts of "clean" and "unclean." The phenomenon of "holy," "cultic impurity" is interesting the way we find it described in P. The concept that certain persons, certain clearly marked areas, and other things are "sacred," "separated" in an almost magical way, is well known especially from Leviticus and Numbers. These books describe in detail a whole array of regulations pertaining to the clean and unclean. We can read here about how "holiness" is a state that can be attained by following specific ritual acts concerning what one can eat, how one should wash, and so on. In Deuteronomy this is quite different. Holiness is not a state one can or cannot attain, but it is a state that one is in as a consequence of belonging to the chosen people. Because YHWH has chosen a people, this people are holy. For that reason the people must not do such and such; therefore the people must act in a particular way. A "holy people," 'am qadosh, is a key concept in Deuteronomy. With P it is the individual or the land that is holy.

In many ways we can say that the Deuteronomists represent a "process of secularization." Again, this is associated with their view of the centralization of the temple cult. There was only supposed to be one temple—in Jerusalem. But the many local sanctuaries out in the countryside and in other cities naturally had their functions to keep. With a centralization of the cult many of these functions were released from their sacral context. This had consequences for the justice system with the secular magistrates besides the priests. The cult centralization also had consequences for the right to asylum.

The laws about warfare have also lost much of their sacral tone in Deuteronomy. Warfare in the Old Testament is always "holy war." Israel's wars are YHWH's wars. This is particularly clear in the Priestly account of the desert wanderings. But again, the difference between P and Deuteronomy is striking. According to P (Num. 10:9), the task of the priests was to go out among the soldiers before the battle and blow the sacred horn to get YHWH's attention. According to the Deuteronomistic view, the task of the priests associated with war was limited to going out and talking to the soldiers in order to comfort them. Again we have a clear example of how Deuteronomy moves things from the sacral sphere into the human sphere.

DEUTERONOMY

The name of the fifth and last book of the Torah, "Deuteronomy," is a Greek word that means "the second law." The word comes from the Greek translation of the Old Testament, the Septuagint. The term is taken from Deuteronomy 17:18 and is actually a mistranslation. In the Jewish tradition Deuteronomy is usually called *Devarim*, "words," or *'Elleh haddevarim* after the opening words of the book, "These are the words. . . ."

According to its form, Deuteronomy consists of one long speech held by Moses in the land on the east side of the river Jordan. The time of the desert wanderings is past, and the Israelites are about to start the conquest of the promised land. The content of the speech, which for the most part consists of laws and regulations that the Israelites must keep when they enter their new land, clearly reflects a later time. This shows that the "speech" with its rules and regulations in no way goes as far back in time as the impression that the writers wish to create. In certain ways Deuteronomy is therefore "pseudepi-graphic," that is, it is a piece of writing that is ascribed to someone other than the real writer. The Deuteronomists wish to legitimize their contemporary religious legislation. Therefore the laws are put in the mouth of Moses, the great lawgiver and man of God in ancient Israelite tradition. The Deuterono-mists certainly did not invent this way of writing and editing law material; P utilizes the same principle of legitimization. In a larger context we are talking about a Near Eastern convention, well known not only from the Bible.

Deuteronomy is easily recognizable by its language, even in translation. What characterizes the narrative is the admonishing rhetoric and artistic prose style, with the repetition of certain key words. The main theological points can be found in cliché-like formulas that are continuously repeated.

The Content of Deuteronomy

The content of Deuteronomy consists largely of legal material. Most of this is known also from other parts of the Pentateuch, but some of it represents material peculiar to Deuteronomy. We can divide Deuteronomy into roughly three parts. Chapters 1–11 contain a mixture of "historical" reviews look-ing back to the desert wanderings and the making of the covenant on Sinai; the promises to the ancestors Abraham, Isaac, and Jacob; and a number of admonitions to the audience of Moses. At the center of the presentations stands the salvation history of Israel, their history with the God YHWH, who has chosen for himself the people of Israel among all the nations of the world to be his special people, and he their special God. The relationship between YHWH and the people was regulated through a particular treaty. YHWH had set up a covenant (*berit*) with his people. The historical context that Moses' speech is set into presupposes a situation just before the crossing of the river Jordan and the conquest of Canaan, the land that YHWH had promised to his people. If the people will worship YHWH as their God and keep his laws, they will fare well in the land they are about to possess. In the opposite case curses will strike and evil will come over them. Elements such as blessings and curses play a very important role in Deuteronomy.

The next part of Deuteronomy, chapters 12–26, contains a sequence of laws and regulations. It is natural to set up a dividing line here because chap-ters 12–26 depart from the previous section in both form and content. While chapters 1–11 deal with more general matters, the texts starting with chapter 12 give much more concrete and individual regulations about, among other things, idolatry, feasts, and marriage. It is here that we find the famous commandment about the centralization of the cult to one place (chap. 12).

The last part of Deuteronomy, chapters 27–34, do not essentially depart from the previous chapters 12–26, but because the text itself provides a dividing mark with 26:17–19, it has been customary to view chapters 27–34 separately. As is so often the case when we read the laws in the Pentateuch, we are struck by what to us seems like a lack of structure in the rather haphazard presentation. Such a style could be the result of a redaction of a mixture of legal material that bears the mark of having come into existence over a long period of time and that therefore also reflects the differing needs of different periods. Yet Deuteronomy may seem more coherent and structured than, for example, Exodus or Numbers.

Just like Deuteronomy 12–26, chapters 27–34 also contain a mixture of laws and regulations, admonitions, promises, and threats. These are addressed to the people who are about to enter the promised land. In the text the Israelites are commanded by Moses to keep the laws and commandments of YHWH also after they have entered the promised land. Then a number of curses are set forth that will come upon the people if they do not keep the laws and commandments of YHWH. Just as important as the statutes and ordinances are the promises of blessing and the threats of punishment. The exposition reminds us of what we find in the early chapters of Deuteronomy: if the people keep the laws of YHWH and worship him as their only God, they will fare well. If they do not keep the laws and worship other gods, the curses will come on them. The punishment is described in great detail: disease, bad harvests, defeat in war, siege, invasions, looting, and deportations. In chapter 30 we read that it is up to the Israelites themselves to make the choice between YHWH and the benefits that he brings with him, and the other gods with the punishment that following them would entail. There is, as such, a special treaty, a covenant, between the Deity YHWH and the people Israel.

The Covenant

At the very center of Deuteronomistic theology stands the covenant between YHWH and the Israelites. When we use the expression "covenant," Hebrew *berit*, we are referring to a very specific concept. The concept of covenant is of key importance not only to the Deuteronomists but also elsewhere in the Bible. A covenant is basically a juridical treaty. An example is the covenant between Laban and Jacob in Genesis 31. Another example of a mutual covenant between two equals is the covenant between David and Jonathan in 1 Samuel 18. In Genesis 21 we can read about the covenant between Abraham and the Amorites. Here we are dealing with another type of covenant, a mutual treaty between two political subjects. Similar covenants are the treaties between Abraham and Abimelech, the king of Gerar (Genesis 21), between Israel and the Gibeonites (Joshua 9), between Abner and David (2 Samuel 3), between David and the people (2 Samuel 5), between Solomon and Hiram, the king of Tyre (2 Samuel 5), and between the Judean king Asa and Ben-hadad, king of Damascus (1 Kings 15). Also the marriage between man and woman is referred to as a covenant (Ezekiel 16; Malachi 2). To fully understand the relationship between the Israelite people and their God it is a prerequisite to understand the role that the covenant played in the ancient Near East. In Deuteronomy the covenant becomes the core of the religion itself.

The covenant was an important and comprehensive political, social, cultural, and religious institution all across the ancient Near East. The covenant was the institution that had to guarantee justice in a society that did not know the type of system of rules and laws that we have in modern societies. From the ancient Near East we know about a whole array of examples of covenants. Most famous are perhaps the type of agreements that were set up between the Hittite kings and their vassal princes in the second millennium BCE. We owe the fame of these covenants to the fact that scholars at an early stage thought that there was a direct influence from the Hittite vassal treaties to the biblical concept of covenant between YHWH and his people. Such a direct influence is hardly the case, however. Such covenants, or treaties, are known also from other cultures in the ancient Near East, for example, from Syria (in Aramaic) and from Assyria-Babylonia (in Akkadian).

An interesting characteristic of the Near Eastern covenants or agreements is that they seem to be constructed according to a specific literary form. For example, if we look at the Hittite vassal treaties, we find the following literary form:

1. Introduction. The Hittite king, who is the initiator of the covenant, identifies himself.
2. Historical review. The previous connections between the two parties are identified.
3. Stipulations. Certain conditions must be met in order for the treaty to be ratified. In the case of the Hittite vassal treaties, the vassal has a heavy burden of duties, whereas the Hittite king's duty in return is relatively modest. He need only guarantee that the vassal's family remains on the throne when there is a change of throne. Such a downplaying of the weak party's rights would hardly be considered fair in our day.
4. Agreements concerning the treaty document itself. The clay tablets that the contract is written on shall be kept in a temple and read out loud at regular intervals.
5. List of deities. Contains a list of all the deities that witness the covenant.
6. A list of the various curses and blessings that will come over whoever, respectively, breaks or keeps the contract.

When we read through Deuteronomy with this pattern in mind, there can be little doubt that we seem to be dealing with a common cultural institution in the ancient Near East. For the author of Deuteronomy the concept of covenant stood out as the most central element of the Israelite people's understanding of God and, as a consequence, also of their own identity.

THE BOOK OF JOSHUA

The book of Joshua takes its name from the most significant character in the book, the warrior Joshua, who took over as the leader of the Israelites after Moses (Num. 27:18–23; Deut. 31:7–29). In Hebrew the book is simply called *Yehoshua*, and in Greek, *Iēsous*.

Like the other "historical" books, the book of Joshua gives a motley and incoherent impression. The book is divided into three parts: chapters 1–12 recount the conquest of the promised land under the leadership of Joshua; in chapters 13–21 the land is divided among the various tribes; and chapters 22–24 relate the last days of Joshua. As with traditions about other great characters in the Bible, the Joshua traditions also seem to have gone through extensive development. The reworking of traditions begins already in the Hebrew Bible itself, increases in early Judaism, and eventually many legendary traditions are associated with the figure of Joshua. One indication that the Joshua traditions stand strong in the later Jewish tradition is seen from the opening words of *Pirqe Avot* (a tractate in the Mishnah, one of the founding documents of Judaism): Joshua received the law from Moses and passed it on to the elders. Just as the Deuteronomists wanted to legitimize the "lawbook," Deuteronomy, by conceiving it as a "testament" from Moses to the Israelites (see, e.g., Deut. 31:26), a lawbook appears also in Joshua (Josh. 24:26). In a larger historical context the book of Joshua represents one stage in YHWH's story of salvation with his chosen people, a kind of middle station, before the chosen people can end their long wandering through the desert and possess the land that YHWH had promised them.

Holy War

One of the phenomena that we encounter in the book of Joshua is that of so-called holy war. It does not show up here for the first time, however. Already in the victory song of Moses after the miraculous crossing of the Red Sea (Exod. 15:3), YHWH is called an *'ish milchamah*, a "man of war." A striking characteristic of the whole narration of the desert wanderings is that the people are portrayed as a field unit on the move, with a strict military organization of the Israelite tribes, led by YHWH himself as the divine warrior.

In a way that might be difficult for us to imagine in our day, war was part of everyday life in the ancient Near East. The language of war, the psychology of war, and the metaphors of war saturate all of the Old Testament literature in a way that few today realize. In our day most consider war negatively. This was often not the case in ancient societies. Although the horrors of war were well known, so were the glorifications of the victories in the field, the celebration over the complete destruction of the enemy, the joyful rush to the booty, and the devotion to heroes of war. Also, the nationalism that is associated with the ideology of war in the Hebrew Bible, where territorial claims to land inhabited by others are made as a matter of course, shows us how far from our way of life the ancient Near East and the Old Testament stand.

As with all wars in the ancient Near East, every war of the Israelites was also a "holy war," from the most ancient times up until the time that Judah ceased to exist as a nation in 586 BCE. In these holy wars YHWH plays the part of the god of war, the divine warrior at the head of his troops. In the narratives of the Hebrew Bible the enemy has no chance. If the Israelites choose to put their trust in YHWH, on their behalf he will put an end to the enemy with miraculous acts. It was therefore important to consult the Deity before engaging in battle. In the Old Testament stories it was YHWH who, in a sense, gave the signal before the battle could begin. In a society where war was just as natural a part of existence as growing food in fields and gardens, it was only natural that this also made its mark on religion.

The Bible and Archaeology

As mentioned earlier, the Old Testament accounts are not "historical" in our sense of the word. We are dealing with ancient traditions that were transmitted through numerous generations and that have been subjected to continuous changes and development. What at one time might have been a "historical core" has through the tradition process been expanded, among other things, with a whole array of descriptions of a supernatural character, of saga and legend. An important question is therefore how we can control any supposed historicity in these accounts. In this context, archaeology has come to play an increasingly bigger role.

Views on the earliest history of Israel have varied considerably in biblical research, especially with regard to the stories of the patriarchs, the twelve tribes, the rise of the monarchy, and perhaps most of all the settling of the land. The discussion in the post–World War II era first took the form of a debate between what has been called the Alt-Noth school on one side and the Albright school on the other.

It is customary to trace the Alt-Noth school's view of the origin of Israel back to the Old Testament scholar Albrecht Alt's epochal book on the settlement of the Israelites in Palestine (1929). In this small booklet of only thirty-five pages Alt put forth his hypothesis that the Israelite settlement of Palestine could not have taken place the way the Deuteronomistic historians would have us believe, and that Joshua's descriptions of the massive conquests and destructions of Canaanite towns could not be historically correct. Alt's point of departure is that the central highlands of Palestine were sparsely populated in the Late Bronze Age, and that this opened up the opportunity for nomadic or seminomadic tribes to push farther and farther into the land each summer, in search of grazing lands.

As these groups pushed farther west, they came to settle down more and more, taking on the agricultural way of life and forming villages. This is how ancient Israel became a nation. It all took place peacefully, over a very long period of time. Only later, according to Alt, did Saul and David come into conflict with Canaanite city-states, and these conflicts resulted in military battles.

On the other hand, the well-known American archaeologist, orientalist, and biblical scholar William Foxwell Albright attempted to show through the use of archaeology that the impression that the book of Joshua gives of a total Israelite military occupation of Palestine is overall historically correct. Albright wrote his most significant contributions in several short articles in the 1920s, '30s, and '40s.

In the 1950s the debate between the two schools was at its peak. As mature fruits of the two schools, the Alt student Martin Noth presented his history of Israel in 1950 (Eng. trans. 1958) and the Albright student John Bright his *History of Israel* in 1959. Both works have been published in several later editions.

As time passed it became apparent that both Alt's and Albright's original theories were burdened by a number of weaknesses. Alt's greatest weakness was perhaps his lack of knowledge about the nomadic system. In part he lacked practical knowledge about nomadism as a phenomenon, and in part he was influenced by the contemporary view of nomadism as one step in the evolutionary process of development. Regarding Albright, it has turned out that his main ally, archaeology, has now made his views difficult, if not impossible, to uphold. However, even though Albright today probably has the majority of scholars against him, some individuals have lately attempted to deal with the archaeological facts by dating the Israelite settlement to an earlier time. Yet another variant is represented by the Israeli archaeologist Yohanan Aharoni, who attempts to argue that the Bible has combined conquest accounts from a time long before the settlement with social conditions from a time long afterward into one long epic. According to him, this has happened consciously and with the purpose of justifying the monarchy.

The positions of Alt and Noth have also been modified and improved over the years. A number of scholars, particularly in Europe, have worked within the framework that had been set up by the Alt-Noth school. A representative scholar in the spirit of Noth is Manfred Weippert. Despite the fact that his book about the settlement (1967; Eng. trans. 1971) is excellent in many ways, it came to signify the summing up and end of an epoch. While the 1960s were still dominated by the debate and the tensions between the followers of Alt and those of Albright, the discussion in the 1970s would take new directions. This is, not least, due to the views that George E. Mendenhall had put forth in an article on "Covenant" in the *Interpreter's Dictionary of the Bible* (1962). After Mendenhall's thesis had been picked up and developed further by Norman K. Gottwald, in particular in his monumental work *The Tribes of Israel* (1979), the so-called Mendenhall/Gottwald thesis came to be a new fad in the 1980s. What characterized this new direction in biblical research of the early history of Israel was primarily the claim that Israel had come into existence neither as the result of a peaceful settlement nor though any military conquest, but as a result of internal socioeconomic change within the borders of Canaan. But before we look at these new points of view more closely, it is necessary to comment a bit on the role of the archaeology of Palestine in all of this.

In his work on the settlement of the ancient Israelites, Alt's claim that the central highlands of Palestine were sparsely populated in the Late Bronze Age was made on the basis of detailed study of Egyptian texts. Only later has archaeological exploration proven him right in his claim. On the whole, the archaeological exploration of Palestine plays a highly significant role in the reconstruction of ancient Israelite history. And if the difference between Alt and Albright on the one hand and the scholars of the 1980s on the other may seem significant, this difference is nothing at all compared to the vast difference in archaeological knowledge in the 1920s and '30s and what we know today. This knowledge becomes even more relevant when we consider that most of the debate between the two schools took place before 1970. The significance of Palestinian archaeology for the reconstruction of the history of early Israel became truly apparent only after 1970, and above all from the 1980s on.

It is customary to trace the history of the archaeology of Palestine back to W. M. F. Petrie's excavation of Tell el-Hesi in 1890, when Petrie made the first pioneering stratigraphic observations and discovered that typological differences in the ceramics were associated with the different stratigraphic layers. The earliest methods were further improved through G. A. Reisner's excavations in Samaria/Sebaste in 1908–1910. Reisner was able to make significant contributions to the development of stratigraphic analysis, architectural studies, mapping, and finalizing of reports, among other things. But despite the attempts of Petrie, Reisner, and other pioneers, the period up to the First World War must be characterized as not very fruitful for the archaeology of Palestine. As is always the case with pioneering projects, the period was characterized by inadequate techniques and seriously flawed interpretations of the material.

The first real breakthrough in the long journey of archaeology on its way to becoming a science came with Albright's development of a typology for ceramic ware in the 1930s. With this, the foundation was laid for the establishment of a proper chronology. In the time between the two World Wars a number of tells (mounds) were excavated, and the archaeological techniques were improved.

After the Second World War, digging was quickly resumed. What particularly characterizes this period, and was to be of great influence later, is the growth of the national archaeological schools in both Israel and Jordan. In the same period indigenous museums also started to develop.

In the 1950s a new golden age began for the archaeology of Palestine. This was due, not least, to an event that can be characterized as the second breakthrough in the field (after Albright's typology of ceramic ware in the 1930s): the British archaeologist Kathleen Kenyon's three-dimensional technique, called the "balk-debris" method. This entailed digging in small grids, usually 5 × 5 meters, where the emphasis was on following the natural stratigraphy of the tell. The method, which was invented by R. E. Mortimer Wheeler, was used by Kenyon in Jericho in 1952–1958, and in Jerusalem in 1961–1967. The Wheeler-Kenyon method soon came to be used by almost all British and American archaeologists who worked in the Middle East. Through a combination of Albright's ceramic typology and Wheeler-Kenyon's stratigraphy the Americans were to radically improve the archaeological methods and techniques in the 1960s.

The Israelis, who after the establishment of the state of Israel in 1948 were concerned with laying the basis for a national archaeological policy, began with more interest in re-creating their national identity and therefore concentrated primarily on large projects associated with areas not previously excavated. But in this way they soon came to isolate themselves from the scientific development of Anglo-Saxon archaeological research. This situation started to change only toward the end of the 1960s when a younger generation of Israeli archaeologists began to make their mark. Today there is significant archaeological work going on in Israel, where Israeli archaeologists often work in close cooperation with foreign institutions. From the end of the 1970s hardly any difference can be seen between American and Israeli methods within archaeology.

In the 1970s further improvements took place in archaeological techniques and methods. But lately the picture has changed completely. After having gone through a long and cumbersome development, the archaeology of Palestine became an independent discipline at the end of the 1970s. From its frail beginnings as a sideline for biblical scholars, archaeology, like Semitic philology before it, has liberated itself from its role as *ancilla theologiae*, the "handmaid of theology." It is no longer possible to do serious archaeology as an amateur. Today archaeologists must be full-time professionals. Stated somewhat simply, the time that one could do archaeology in the Middle East with the Bible in one hand and the trowel in the other definitely belongs to the past.

One characteristic of the radical development that has taken place is the great cross-disciplinary aspect. Associated with a dig today we find not only archaeologists but also geologists, physical anthropologists, cultural anthropologists, paleobotanists, paleozoologists, paleontologists, zooarchaeologists, osteologists, geographers, architects, technical drawers, photographers, ceramicists, historians of technology, nuclear physicists, and a variety of other experts. The earth and sand that earlier generations saw as irritating obstacles on the way to their goal can today be sent to research labs across the world, where highly specialized personnel go through the material on a constant hunt for pollen or other particles that can reveal more knowledge about our past. The disadvantage of this impressive cross-discipline is that it makes it difficult to keep track of all the data.

While the most difficult problem of earlier times was associated with field reports that either never came or were delayed before being published, many of the present-day results are published in highly specialized journals within a variety of different fields.

Several characteristics distinguish the so-called new archaeology from the previous kind. The tendency today goes more and more in the direction of turning away from the individual tells and more toward digs targeting a certain issue, such as one-period settlements, surface surveys, and regional surveys. Research of the relationship between the city and its surroundings (villages), the mapping of changes in the pattern of settlement, and so on, are seen as more important than the concentration of earlier times on temples and other monumental architecture. Here we clearly see the influence of the social sciences. If one wishes to characterize these tendencies more precisely, one could say that while the "old" archaeology was more inductive, idiographic, particularistic, classificatory, historical, and descriptive, the "new" archaeology is more deductive, anthropological, explanatory, and nomothetic.

Another characteristic to note is the relatively large amount of material and the precise description and the conclusions it has been possible to draw on the basis of this archaeological material, particularly in the last few years.

Today we know far, far more about the archaeology of Palestine than what was known only a few years ago. As a result, we can no longer ignore archaeology in our reconstruction of the history of ancient Israel. To do that would be to stick our heads in the sand.

The question, then, is what can contemporary archaeology tell us about the conditions in ancient Israel at the end of the Late Bronze Age? This is the period during which the exodus and settlement of the land supposedly took place. One thing is clear: the archaeological material points unilaterally toward the conclusion that the portrayal of the Israelite conquest of Canaan as it is described in the book of Joshua cannot have taken place. A number of the cities that Joshua is supposed to have conquered, as described in detail in the book of Joshua, simply did not exist at the end of the Late Bronze Age but had been destroyed at a much earlier point in time. Among these are Heshbon, Arad, Jericho, and Ai.

Other towns were indeed destroyed in the period we are talking about, but not in the way described in the Bible. Their destruction did not happen suddenly but through a long period of decay, often spanning several generations. Such towns are Hazor, finally destroyed around 1275 BCE, and Lachish, finally destroyed around 1160 BCE. Yet other sites have so few Late Bronze remains that it hardly can be maintained that they were much more than small villages or even only cemeteries in the designated period. Among these we find Dan (Laish), Gibeon, and Jarmuth (Yarmut).

Now, an essential change did certainly take place in Palestine in the transition from Late Bronze to Early Iron Age. This did not, however, have anything to do with a sudden breakdown in the Canaanite city-state civilization, which in some places continued also through the transitional period of Late Bronze/Early Iron. The changes occurred in the settlement pattern in the countryside. Throughout the whole Late Bronze Age, and definitively at the end of this period, we do not know of any small settlements without city walls in this area. Then suddenly, with the dawn of the Iron Age (ca. 1200 BCE), hundreds of them show up. In modern archaeological research many scholars equate the study of these villages, their form, economy, and social structures, with the study of the first Israelite settlements in Canaan. The settlements began in the central highlands and subsequently spread to other parts of the country.

THE BOOK OF JUDGES

The part of the Deuteronomistic History that goes by the name of "the book of Judges" takes its title from the content of the book, which deals largely with the so-called judges and their activity in Israel. In the Deuteronomistic History this period in the history of the people of Israel corresponds to the transitional period between the conquest of Canaan and the establishment of the monarchy around 1000 BCE. In Greek the book of Judges bears the title *Kritai*, and in Hebrew, *Shophetim*. As with the book of Joshua, the book of Judges takes its name in Hebrew not from the opening words but from the content.

We find a number of literary genres in the book of Judges: legends and folk traditions and historical sagas mixed with the redactor's own historical and theological views. We notice in particular several beautiful poetic compositions. These give an impression of antiquity, and can more or less, even in their present form, go back to the preexilic period. Here we may mention in particular the Song of Deborah (Judges 5), Jotham's fable (9:7–21), and the riddle of Samson (14:8–20). We also find a number of poetic fragments. The dating of these pieces is very controversial, however, and lately many scholars have argued that they cannot date back as far in time as had been maintained earlier.

The term "judges" itself is subject to misunderstanding. When we use the noun "judge" (which in Hebrew would be *shophet*), we immediately think of a courtroom. But this is not the setting for the biblical "judges." Indeed, no one is called "judge" directly in the book of Judges. It is said about eight people that they "judged" Israel. But when we examine what it was that these eight "judges" did, we see that they were chosen leaders rather than someone performing a juridical function. Only the colorful woman judge Deborah is described as having judged in judicial affairs (Judg. 4:4–5). The "charismatic" judges of the book of Judges were appointed by YHWH and were in close contact with him. They combined various functions, such as political and military leadership, with the practice of judicial roles and, not least, prophetic roles.

When we read the colorful narrations in the book of Judges, we immediately recognize the Deuteronomists' portrayal of the people of Israel as a mass without a will, with a strong need for a leader figure. Under good judges the people follow YHWH as their God and keep to his laws and regulations. When the leader dies, the Israelites go astray and worship the Baals, the Canaanite gods. When this happens, YHWH punishes his chosen people and allows the enemy to be victorious in battle. The people regret their sins and pray to YHWH that he may save them. YHWH answers the prayers of the Israelites and sends them a new judge to save them from the enemy. After the death of the leader the same story repeats itself, in a cyclical pattern: the people fall from YHWH and begin to worship other gods and so on. Here we have, in a nutshell, the Deuteronomists' view of history. As we can see, we are dealing with a theological interpretation of history rather than an account of it. The history of the Israelite people is primarily the history of a single, continuous breach of the covenant. All history writing is, so to speak, an interpretation of history. Nevertheless, it is clear that we will not get very far if we wish to use these kinds of texts at face value to find out "what really happened."

THE BOOKS OF SAMUEL

The books of Samuel, which are divided into two books in the Bible, were originally one book. The division came about with the Greek translation, the Septuagint, in the third century BCE, which called the books of Samuel *Basileion alpha* and *beta*, and the books of Kings *Basileion gamma* and *delta* (the books of the monarchy 1, 2, 3, and 4). Even though this division was introduced already before the Common Era, it does not appear in the Jewish/ Hebrew tradition until 1448, in a manuscript of the Bible. The view that Samuel was the author of the books of Samuel is also late and comes from talmudic times (*Baba Bathra* 14b). In the same source (15a), we can read that the accounts following the death of Samuel were written down by the prophets Gad and Nathan. This talmudic tradition is probably based on 1 Chronicles 29:29, "Now the acts of King David, from the first to last, are written in the records of the seer Samuel, and in the records of the prophet Nathan, and in the records of the seer Gad. . . ."

According to the biblical tradition the great prophet and judge Samuel lived in Israel in the last half of the eleventh century BCE. First Samuel contains a description of his life and work. The importance of Samuel is seen in particular through his task, laid on him by YHWH himself, of anointing both Saul and David as kings of Israel. Samuel was a charismatic leader. He was also the last of the great judges. With him, Israel passes from the time of the judges to the time of the monarchy.

Second Samuel is the story of King David. David was the greatest of all the kings in ancient Israel. The accounts of the growing hostility toward King Saul and his own way to the throne are very dramatic. Contrary to the later David traditions (especially in Chronicles), however, there is no ideal image of King David in the Deuteronomistic writings.

The stories about the kings Saul and David are the accounts of how YHWH takes his blessing away from one and gives it to another. While the kings of the Davidic dynasty would sit on the throne until the catastrophe hit them in 586 BCE, Saul was left with curse and disaster. The ancient Israelite traditions about the Davidic dynasty continued for a long time. In the messianic prophecies of later and worse times about the great king who was coming (*messiah* means "anointed," i.e., king), the Davidic traditions bloomed in a new and different way and brought hope for the future. When we come to the ages of early Judaism and Christianity, the Jewish expectations are expanded in the New Testament to include also Jesus of Nazareth, who was considered a descendant of David (Matt. 21:9; Luke 2:4; 3:31; 18:38).

Another David tradition that was to gain significance was the tradition about the king as a poet. This tradition led to much of the poetry of the Bible in later times being attributed to David.

To us, the composition of the books of Samuel seems incoherent. Reading through the narratives gives the impression that the author, here as in other biblical books, has used a number of sources for this composition. To mention just one example, in 1 Samuel 8–12 we find the account of Saul's way to the throne. The different "sources" that have contributed to this composition make Samuel on the one hand protest violently against establishing the monarchy and on the other hand act vigorously to have it established. We read in 1 Samuel 8:6–7: "But the thing displeased Samuel when they said, 'Give us a king to govern us.' Samuel prayed to the LORD, and the LORD said to Samuel, 'Listen to the voice of the people in all that they say to you; for they have not rejected you, but they have rejected me from being king over them.'"

This negative view of the monarchy, so typical of the Deuteronomist, stands in clear contrast to the following account in the story about Saul, which obviously must come from a different source. In this story, there is no end to the appreciation Samuel shows for having Saul elected king.

In a larger context the books of Samuel are part of the broadly conceived salvation-historical epic, Genesis through Kings, that stretches from creation and ends with the exile in 586 BCE. We find ourselves in a time of transition: the time between the charismatic "judges" and the establishment of the monarchy. The Deuteronomists' negative view of the monarchy is a theme that permeates the Deuteronomistic History—it is the kings who have brought Israel to the brink of disaster. In the end, the kings are responsible for YHWH's wrath and punishment, which culminates with the destruction of Jerusalem and the temple and the deportation into exile.

THE BOOKS OF KINGS

The books of Kings originally consisted of one book, but were divided in the Greek translation of the Septuagint, where the books are given the names *Basileion gamma* and *basileion delta*, "3 and 4 books of the monarchy" (the first two "books of the monarchy" are the two books of Samuel). Just as with the books of Samuel, it was only in a Hebrew manuscript from 1448 that the Jewish manuscript tradition divided the book of Kings for the first time. The English term "Kings" derives from the church father Jerome, who in the fourth century CE published the Latin translation, the Vulgate, and who, in line with the Hebrew term *Melakim*, "kings," preferred the Latin term *Regum* for these books. In late talmudic tradition (*Baba Bathra* 15a), the authorship of the books of Kings is attributed to the prophet Jeremiah. This tradition is completely unknown in the Bible and owes its existence to the later Jewish tradition of wishing to attribute all of the biblical books to prophetic authors.

The books of Kings portray the Israelite people's history over a period of around four hundred years, from the time that David's son Solomon inherits his father's throne to the destruction of Jerusalem and the exile to Babylon in 586 BCE. The work is highly eclectic and seemingly builds on a number of different sources that to us appear more or less arbitrary. The books of Kings themselves mention other sources, such as "the Book of the Acts of Solomon" (1 Kgs. 11:41), "the Book of the Annals of the Kings of Israel" (14:19; 15:31; 16:5; etc.), and "the Book of the Annals of the Kings of Judah" (14:29; 15:7, 23; etc.).

The particular view of the Deuteronomists characterizes the two books. Emphasis is on the major tragedies in the history of the Israelite people: the partition of the monarchy after the death of Solomon in 922 BCE (into the northern kingdom of Israel and the southern kingdom of Judah), the fall of Samaria in 721 BCE, and finally the big catastrophe in 586 BCE, when Judah ceased to exist as a nation. The slant on the account is highly theological; all the tragedies occur because the people have not kept the covenant, have not worshiped YHWH as their only God, and have not kept his laws and ordinances. The strong theological overtones appear in a narrative pattern that is highly stylized. The kings are characterized as good or bad (usually bad) with the characteristic phrase, "King X did what was evil/good in the sight of the LORD (YHWH)" or "X departed from the LORD (YHWH) and followed other gods." A good king was one who worshiped YHWH as his only God and kept his laws and ordinances. The kings of the northern kingdom, those who had rebelled first against the Davidic dynasty, are all considered bad kings. The punishment also hits them early. The ungodly northern kingdom is destroyed already in 721 BCE when the Assyrians conquer Samaria.

Such an idealized and schematic portrayal makes it very difficult to use this work as a historical source. In addition, we do not have any relevant extra-biblical sources before the time of Omri (ninth century BCE). Neither David nor Solomon is mentioned in any source outside the Bible, except for the Tell Dan Inscription (ninth–eighth century BCE), which seems to refer to "the house of David."

The story of King Solomon stands in a category of its own (1 Kings 1–11). The reason for this is obviously Solomon's building of the temple. The Deuteronomists portray it as a demand from YHWH that all cultic activity should be centralized in Jerusalem and the temple there. By building the temple Solomon has shown the biggest possible faithfulness to YHWH. Because of this, he is somehow excused even though his thousand wives seduced him to be unfaithful against YHWH and to follow other gods. He is, however, punished for this, and most of his great kingdom is taken away from him. For posterity Solomon's kingdom stands as the golden age. Solomon's power and wealth were widely known, and the tradition about his wisdom led to the attribution of almost all of Israel's wisdom literature to him.

THE DEUTERONOMISTIC HISTORY AND HISTORY

Above we touched on the major significance of the covenant, or contract, in Deuteronomistic theology. In the Deuteronomistic History we read about how this special treaty between YHWH and his chosen people functioned throughout history, from the time of the settlement of the land up to the invasion of the Babylonians and the destruction of Jerusalem in 586 BCE. The way that the Deuteronomists tell the story it comes across as one long story of a people who, in every way and on every possible occasion, broke this contract with their God. If we look at Deuteronomy and the structure of this book compared to the conventional way of setting up a covenant in the ancient Near East—for example, the way we find it in the Hittite vassal treaties—we will find clear and striking similarities with the whole Deuteronomistic History. The "history" of the Israelite people is really a covenant history, and the telling of the story bears the marks of the covenant pattern. What characterizes the Deuteronomistic view of the relationship between the two parties in the deal, YHWH and his people, is that the "historical review" is seen as a theological salvation history, where *election* is made the central point. The famous scholar Gerhard von Rad has used the term "the short historical creed" about the texts of Deuteronomy 6:20–25 and 26:2–9 (see Josh. 24:2–13). Deuteronomy 6:20–25 reads,

> When your children ask you in time to come, "What is the meaning of the decrees and the statutes and the ordinances that the LORD our God has commanded you?" then you shall say to your children, "We were Pharaoh's slaves in Egypt, but the LORD brought us out of Egypt with a mighty hand. The LORD displayed before our eyes great and awesome signs and wonders against Egypt, against Pharaoh and all his household. He brought us out from there in order to bring us in, to give us the land that he promised on oath to our ancestors. Then the LORD commanded us to observe all these statues, to fear the LORD our God, for our lasting good, so as to keep us alive, as is now the case. If we diligently observe this entire commandment before the LORD our God, as he has commanded us, we will be in the right."

It is doubtful that von Rad is right when he claims that these texts are pre-Deuteronomistic and represent ancient confessionary formulae. However this might be, these textual fragments do give an excellent impression, in concentrated form, of the historical-theological, Deuteronomistic covenant and election concept that forms the basis for the whole Deuteronomistic History. We are not dealing with a work of history in our sense of the word, but rather with an ideological or theological work of history, a "salvation history." Now we must not be led to think that the Deuteronomists were pure "storytellers" who "invented" their material as they wrote. The Deuteronomists were bearers of tradition who built on those traditions they had at their disposal. What these traditions may have looked like prior to the Deuteronomists we cannot say much about. On the other hand, many historical facts are to be found in the Deuteronomistic History (and in other books of the Hebrew Bible). Every single historical event, however, has to be investigated separately and cannot be taken at face value.

No other writers have put their mark on the Old Testament literature to the extent that the Deuteronomists have. Their view of history is clearly expressed in the so-called Deuteronomistic History (Deuteronomy, Joshua, Judges, Samuel, and Kings). We see here how the history of Israel from the settlement up to the exile is portrayed in light of the same overall view that we find in Deuteronomy. In this way the portrayal is not really of the history of the Israelite people but of their relationship to YHWH and the covenant, with the consequences this has had for history. The whole account of the history of Israel, from the settlement to the doom of 586 BCE, is an account of the chosen people that does not keep its part of the covenant. From beginning to end, the story from Deuteronomy via Joshua, Judges, Samuel to Kings is a story of apostasy and a people that did not follow YHWH as its God. The catastrophes that hit Israel in 721 BCE and Judah in 586 BCE are explained as the high price the people themselves must pay for breaking YHWH's laws and ordinances. In the Deuteronomistic History the kings are given the main blame for the catastrophes. The books of Kings are not about kings per se, but about good and bad kings. Kings are either faithful to YHWH or not faithful to YHWH. As it is the kings who are given the blame for the destruction of Israel and Judah, it is not strange that we find a very negative view of the monarchy throughout the Deuteronomistic History.

Realizing that we are dealing with a strongly ideological and idealizing work, we understand that we face great problems if we attempt to use the Deuteronomistic History as a source for the reconstruction of the history of Israel, of "what really happened." Even though the Deuteronomistic History contains many individual historical pieces of information (for example, historical events and the names of kings), we cannot write the history of ancient

Israel on the basis of this work. The history of ancient Israel in the period from 1000 to 586 BCE is lost to us. The work of the Deuteronomists was probably written in exilic or postexilic times, with the primary aim of accounting for the status quo of the Israelite people. The work primarily wishes to explain why things happened as they did when the catastrophes struck.

The German scholar Martin Noth has claimed that one person, the Deuteronomist, was responsible for the whole Deuteronomistic History, and that this person wrote his work in Palestine in the mid-sixth century BCE. Noth's thesis has been heavily contested. It is, however, difficult to see that the arguments that have been brought against Noth's classical theory are any more convincing than Noth's own view. We can hardly expect to reach any final answer to the question. But perhaps we should talk about the Deuteronomists in the plural, rather than about one Deuteronomist. Possibly we are dealing with a circle of scholars rather than with one individual. Perhaps the term "school" is more adequate. But again, we are left to speculate.

The Deuteronomists themselves try to give Deuteronomy the appearance of great age. They have done this by incorporating the story of King Josiah's religious and political reform in 622 BCE, mentioned in 2 Kings 22–23. The account of finding a lawbook in the temple has worked so well that, up until our time, many have been convinced that this lawbook was Deuteronomy. However, we are probably dealing with literary conventions that are supposed to legitimize the authority of Deuteronomy, perhaps at the expense of the Priestly circles. But the episode in 2 Kings 22–23 is still interesting. If we look more closely at the account, we get the impression that King Josiah has not been aware of the content of the "law of Moses" before the finding of the scroll. If we look even more closely at the text, we see that the scribe Shaphan plays a major role in the events surrounding the discovery of the lawbook (2 Kgs. 22:8–20). He is the first one to read it, and he is also the one to get in touch with the king. Perhaps it was a scribe who was responsible for the Deuteronomistic History?

Some of the disagreements between the theology of the Tetrateuch and that of Deuteronomy may be explained by the background of ideological tensions between priests and scribes in the time after the fall of Jerusalem. Also, that the Deuteronomistic History is strongly critical of the prophets can point in the direction of scribes, or learned men in Jerusalem, as authors of the Deuteronomistic History, and may reflect ideological tensions between different groups, different "parties," in the ancient Israelite society in the sixth century BCE.

To sum up this overview of the Deuteronomistic History, it is not a work that tells history as it was, but that interprets history in its own very special way. The work is not "historical" in our sense of the word but "theological," and we have briefly touched on the difficulties this entails for those who wish to reconstruct the history of ancient Israel. That the Deuteronomistic History contains some historical information is clear, as we can see from the few extrabiblical sources that mention Israel and Judah.

An important part of ancient Israelite history is the history of its religion. The Deuteronomists' view of ancient Israelite religion is clear: the Israelites were considered orthodox YHWH worshipers already from the time of Abraham. Through its long history they continuously kept falling away from the right faith and following other gods. But this is not a historically correct portrayal of the religious situation in preexilic Israel.

The traditional image of ancient Israelite religion is probably well known to many: the Israelites who settled in the land had had little experience with agriculture; in their new situation they turned to the Canaanite gods of fertility in the hope of attaining good harvests. The result was a type of syncretism, where Israel's God YHWH was worshiped side by side with the Canaanite gods El and Baal. After a while this syncretism developed, and when we reach the time of the monarchy YHWH and El have become fully assimilated, while Baal stands as the great competitor of YHWH. This is the way that we find the history of ancient Israelite religion described in most introductory literature. Deities other than YHWH were understood to be "Canaanite," non-Israelite. All in all, the ancient Israelites were seen as monolatrists, while the Canaanites were polytheists. This monolatry developed into monotheism in the exilic period. If the worship of other gods did exist in the monarchic period, scholars understood this as the survival of Canaanite cults at "the popular level" and could not be considered representative of the "official" ancient Israelite religion. The foreign gods were seen as threats from the outside, a danger to the pure YHWH religion. Even though a careful blending together of certain more acceptable elements of native religion may have occurred, the most important thing remained the rejection of the foreign elements. Specific gods such as Asherah, Astarte, El, or Baal had rarely been the object of Israelite worship. The Israelites worshiped YHWH and YHWH alone.

However, the religion of ancient Israel was far from static; it underwent a continuous development. By comparing the biblical texts with available archaeological material and extrabiblical sources we can today say with certainty that the religion of Israel did not distinguish itself very much from the religion of the surrounding cultures. We are dealing with a variant of traditional West Semitic religion, in which the God YHWH was worshiped as the national God of Israel, but also other gods were worshiped. The ancient Israelite YHWH religion was therefore quite different from the late description that we find in the Bible, which is a product of postexilic developments.

YHWH AND THE GODDESS ASHERAH:
A GLIMPSE BEHIND THE CURTAIN
OF PRE-DEUTERONOMISTIC RELIGION

In the ancient Near East deity couples were well known: Baal and Anat from the Ugaritic Ras Shamra texts, Isis and Osiris from Egyptian religion, An and Urash in ancient Sumerian religion, and Telipinu and Hatepinu in Hittite religion. A marriage ritual has been handed down in association with the main deity, Attar, of pre-Islamic, South Arabian religion. In the Syrian/Hellenistic domain the deity couple Hadad and Atargatis was prominent in several regions. Many other examples could be mentioned from the colorful and rich, but often somewhat disparate, world of Near Eastern gods.

One distinctive exception in this impressive collection of more or less successful divine marriage alliances is apparently the ancient Israelite Deity, YHWH. The strict and jealous Old Testament God YHWH knows no female deity by his side, at least not if we are to believe the Hebrew Bible. And that is what most of us have done.

We know now that ancient Israelite religion is not identical to Old Testament religion. We do not know the pre-Deuteronomistic ancient Israelite religion as such—we know only reconstructions of it. It might seem clear that Yahwism was not the only religion in ancient Israel, the way the Deuteronomists would have us believe. Yahwism was possibly one of several religious cults that competed for the favor of the Israelites, though Yahwism was the national, royal religion. Moreover, early Yahwism was quite different from the Yahwism that the Deuteronomists and other biblical writers describe to us. "Classical Yahwism," the way it is described in the Bible, is a result of a long development. The earlier Yahwism was not as uniform; rather, it was often syncretistic, and it was far more similar to the Canaanite cults than most have been willing to admit. We are here going to examine only one detail of pre-Deuteronomistic YHWH religion: whether YHWH may have had a female deity by his side.

The suspicion that YHWH might not always have been as alone as the Hebrew Bible would have us believe goes back some time. In the Persian period a colony of Jews lived on the island of Elephantine in the Nile. From this site derive the famous Elephantine papyri, parts of which were published in 1906, 1911, and 1953. These papyri are extremely important documents for our knowledge about the Israelite-Judean Diaspora in early times. They are also very interesting for the history of ancient Israelite religion. The religion that we gain acquaintance with at Elephantine is not at all the orthodox Yahwism that we know from the Old Testament. In addition to Yahu, the Old

Testament's YHWH, we know that the inhabitants of the island worshiped gods with the (to us) strange-sounding names of Ashim (or Eshem)-Bethel and Anat-Bethel. The goddess Anat-Bethel is known in the texts also as Anat-Yahu. Much acumen has been applied in attempting to sort out the different divine names from Elephantine, without reaching any consensus. It seems clear, nevertheless, that the divine name Anat-Yahu must be interpreted in the direction of "YHWH's Anat." Should this be correct, we have support at Elephantine for the Israelite God YHWH having a female deity by his side, at least in one local expression. The ordinary explanation for this phenomenon is that we are dealing with a highly extraordinary deviation from the religion of the homeland, and that such a syncretistic cult could hardly have been the norm in Judah/Israel. But the question is whether the evidence from Elephantine might rather give us a glimpse of the traditional, pre–Old Testament religion of Israel. Recent research seems to support this view.

Two texts in particular, found in Israeli territory, merit attention: a funerary inscription from Khirbet el-Qom and an inscription on a jar from Kuntillet Ajrud. The funerary inscription no. 3 from grave II is one of several epigraphic texts published by William G. Dever in 1969/1970 from his excavation in the area of Khirbet el-Qom, around 14 kilometers west of the city of Hebron. The dating varies somewhat, but a date of sometime in the eighth century BCE seems probable. In terms of the Old Testament literature, we are in a time that traditionally has been associated with the prophets Amos, Micah, and Isaiah. Even though the text had been known to scholars for some time, only after the French epigraphist André Lemaire had given his interpretation of the text in 1977 did researchers take seriously its significance for the history of ancient Israelite religion. The inscription in question has been on the tomb of a person named Uriyahu. The reading of line 2 as ". . . blessed be Uriyahu for YHWH . . ." has not been controversial. Line 3 has been a major problem. Here Lemaire reads, as a continuation of line 2, ". . . and for his [that is, YHWH's] *asherah* . . ." If Lemaire's reading is correct, this is nothing less than sensational.

Now, the reading of line 3 is highly problematic, and able scholars after Lemaire have read the line differently. Nevertheless, Lemaire's reading remains the most probable. This has interesting consequences for our view of pre-Deuteronomistic Yahwistic religion. The term *'asherah* occurs about forty times in the Hebrew Bible, but its sense is debated: is it the name of a goddess or just a symbol of the goddess? Clearly, however, in at least some of the Hebrew Bible texts, *'asherah* is the name of a goddess.

The question is then how we are to understand Lemaire's reading of line 3. Does the expression "YHWH and his *'asherah*" refer to the goddess Asherah, or does it refer to the symbol of her? Naturally, the answer is not possible to determine with certainty. There is, however, a great probability that it refers to the goddess. Asherah was well known as a divine name in the Old Testament world. That in this inscription it should refer to YHWH and the symbol of the goddess seems labored. That the Hebrew Bible seems to give the impression that the term *'asherah* refers not to a goddess but to a divine symbol could be explained by the intention of the Deuteronomists and other authors to give the purest possible impression of ancient Israelite religion.

The distinction is actually quite academic. What difference does it really make to our understanding of line 3 in Uriyahu's inscription whether it refers to YHWH's Asherah as a goddess or YHWH's Asherah as a symbol of the goddess Asherah? In both cases we have proof that the Deity YHWH was worshiped alongside the goddess Asherah, who is well known from the Hebrew Bible. If Lemaire's reading is correct, we have evidence indicating that the Old Testament God YHWH was worshiped with a female god by his side. Another point worth mentioning is that the formula "YHWH and his Asherah" is roughly parallel to the divine name Anat-Yahu from Elephantine.

In 1975–1976 the Israeli archaeologist Ze'ev Meshel directed the excavation of an Israelite caravanserai, dated 800–700 BCE, at Kuntillet Ajrud in the eastern part of the Sinai desert, around seventy kilometers south of Kadesh-barnea. In association with the temple several Hebrew and Phoenician inscriptions were found on brick walls, on large storage jars, and on stone jars. In addition to the divine names El and YHWH, the names Baal and Asherah are also attested. The people who lived in this caravanserai had obviously worshiped several gods. Since Phoenician inscriptions were among the findings, the appearance of several divine names might be explained as the remains of different groups of people who had stayed at Kuntillet Ajrud, and that they had worshiped their respective gods. The explanation cannot be that simple, however. The most interesting texts were found on two large pithoi, storage jars, richly decorated with drawings as well as inscriptions, written in red ink, in ancient Hebrew script. Above one of the drawings, which shows three deities, there is a text that can be read in the following way, ". . . may you be blessed by YHWH of Samaria and his Asherah. . . ." On the other pithos we find a text with similar content, part of which reads, ". . . may you be blessed by YHWH and by his Asherah. . . ."

Again, one aspect of the discussion among scholars that followed after these sensational texts became known was concerned with whether YHWH's *'asherah* referred to the goddess or to the cultic symbol of this goddess. While Meshel himself has opposed the identification of YHWH's *'asherah* with the Old Testament's Asherah, a scholar like William G. Dever sees *'asherah* in Kuntillet Ajrud as a female deity by YHWH's side and as identical with the goddess Asherah in the Hebrew Bible. He is probably right. Other scholars have been more reticent in their interpretation of the material and think that *'asherah* probably refers to the wooden symbol of the goddess and that these texts do not prove that Asherah was worshiped as a female god at YHWH's side. Again, the discussion seems moot. Whether YHWH is associated with a goddess by the name of Asherah or the symbol of this goddess that is called *'asherah* amounts to nearly the same thing. It is difficult to see what practical significance this distinction would have for the view of the YHWH cult in ancient times.

Further, I find it hard to believe that we are dealing with the symbol of the goddess rather than the deity herself. Such an interpretation is naturally due to the Old Testament's, that is, the Deuteronomists', conscious effort to play down the pre-Deuteronomistic lack of orthodoxy. It is quite revealing that the tendency to interpret a term as a reference to a symbol rather than a goddess pertains, on the whole, only to *'asherah*. When other divine names appear, scholars have not regarded them as referring to a symbol of the deity rather than the deity itself. In light of the texts we have explored above it is clear that the whole *'asherah* question in the Hebrew Bible is in need of a total reevaluation, and more and more scholars are now convinced that YHWH in ancient times was worshiped with a female deity Asherah at his side.

The examples referred to above from extrabiblical texts are interesting on their own account, but it is primarily as the background of, and in combination with, the biblical material that they really generate interest. The biblical writers were in part determined by ancient Israelite tradition, and in part they were dependent on their religious, cultural, and political contemporary society. It is precisely this ideological structure that gives us the key to understanding the Old Testament and how it developed. The liberty that these writers felt toward their material was not imaginative but was based on their ideological metastructure and the comprehensive will to express their message. For that reason their exposition is full of disturbing "noise." And it is precisely this noise that interests the scholar who wishes to reconstruct the pre-Deuteronomistic, pre-Priestly, or pre-Chronistic religion in ancient Israel. The discovery of extrabiblical texts has contributed significantly to filling in the holes in our knowledge about this very interesting period in the history of religion in the ancient Near East. We can today say with certainty that YHWH, like Baal, was worshiped in ancient Israel with a female deity at his side. When it comes to the question of how widespread this particular type of YHWH cult was, we know too little at present to be able to say. I still think we should be prepared to say that it was fairly extensive.

4

The Chronicler's History

Ezra, Nehemiah, 1 and 2 Chronicles

In the present chapter we are, for pragmatic reasons, treating Ezra, Nehemiah, and 1 and 2 Chronicles as one work, the Chronicler's History. However, the relationship between the books of Chronicles on the one side and Ezra and Nehemiah on the other is ambiguous. In previous research, the common authorship of the books of Ezra and Nehemiah was much debated. Even though some scholars express other views, the trend today seems to be that Ezra and Nehemiah make up two distinct works that should be dated to different periods. As always, exact dating is problematic when it comes to individual biblical books. Moreover, the relative chronological order of Ezra and Nehemiah still seems as difficult as ever to fathom. Which book was produced first? What is the relationship between the two works? There appears to be no consensus in these matters. Nevertheless, research in Ezra, Nehemiah, and Chronicles has made vast progress in recent years thanks to important studies by scholars like Sara Japhet, Isaac Kalimi, Gary Knoppers, Thomas Willi, and Hugh Williamson.

For several reasons the Chronicler's History cannot have been a unified work from the outset. For example, there are a number of differing perspectives in Ezra and Nehemiah on one side and Chronicles on the other. A main issue would be that while the focus on the temple is at the very center of Chronicles, less weight is accorded the temple in Ezra and Nehemiah. From the textual history of the Hebrew Bible, we note that Ezra and Nehemiah and 1 and 2 Chronicles seldom appear in order in the ancient manuscript traditions in the same way as in English Bible translations. In the Hebrew Bible, Ezra, Nehemiah, and Chronicles are placed at the very end, in that order. Western Bible translations, however, follow the order of the Septuagint and place these books after the books of Kings, and with Ezra and Nehemiah (treated as one book) placed after Chronicles. In all likelihood, what we find in the Hebrew Bible reflects the original chronological order of the two corpuses, implying that Chronicles is the latest of the three books.

In relation to the period dealt with, the Chronicler's History (Ezra, Nehemiah, 1 and 2 Chronicles) is the most comprehensive of the historiographical works of the Old Testament. The Chroniclers (it is probable that there were more than one, but sometimes I will use the singular for convenience) want to tell the story of the Israelite people from the time of the creation of the world until the restoration of the land in the postexilic period. The writers (editors) of the work, the Chroniclers, were perhaps also active through more than one generation. The group responsible for the final form of the text was possibly active as late as around the mid-fourth century BCE.

Formerly, interest in the Chroniclers was quite subdued among biblical scholars, who were struggling with the legacy of the pioneering historical biblical research in the late nineteenth century. At that time, the prophetic movement was seen as the peak of ancient Israelite religion. After the "golden age," things just went downhill. The reason for this skewed understanding has partly been sought in the romanticist love of the "original," and partly in a Hegelian view of history. It can also, to a certain extent, be explained by anti-Jewish attitudes that were prevalent at some of the Protestant universities where biblical research made its first breakthrough.

Interest in the postexilic period was traditionally low. The books that had been written during this late stage belonged clearly to Judaism and represented a decline from the pure prophetic religion. This trend has had unfortunate consequences for biblical study in that scholars have ignored this late period in many ways. The period between ancient Israelite religion and culture and the New Testament era is crucial for understanding the historical processes that led to the formation and growth of both Christianity and Judaism. In recent times, however, we have fortunately experienced a change in this field, with a greater and increasing interest in the late biblical periods.

The Chroniclers were possibly active around 350 BCE. They were thus writing their work toward the end of the Persian period, just before Hellenism made its arrival in the Near East. The use of the term "Hellenism" is here purely conventional. In reality, Greek influence on the Levant, and Near Eastern influence on the Greek world, had been ongoing for at least a couple of centuries before Alexander made his arrival on the international scene. According to the inner chronology of the Hebrew Bible, the temple in Jerusalem was rebuilt sometime before 500 BCE. The Chroniclers, therefore, belong to the environment of the Second Temple period.

The books of Chronicles, which cover all of the history of the Israelite people from creation to the exile, present their own distinct outlook of the history of the chosen people. As we shall see, the Chronistic view of history distinguishes itself in a number of ways from the Priestly and Deuteronomistic ideas on the history of the Israelite people. However, the Chroniclers clearly stand in the tradition from both of these "predecessors." Their theological and ideological foundation is in some ways a variant of the Deuteronomistic view of history. Above all, this applies to the way in which the history of Israel is seen as the history of a people who constantly broke the covenant that they had set up with their God. At the same time, the Chroniclers espouse a view of purity and holiness that reminds us of what we find in the Priestly History and in Ezekiel.

The Chroniclers represent a major historical source to an important period in the history of ancient Israel. Other important sources of knowledge about the history of Judaism in the late postexilic period are the four postexilic prophetic books of Trito-Isaiah (Isaiah 56–66), Haggai, Proto-Zechariah (Zechariah 1–8), and Malachi. Also some of the Old Testament psalms (e.g., Psalm 85) come from this late period and bear testimony to the spiritual climate of the time. As our sources are limited, the books of Ezra, Nehemiah, and Chronicles become even more important in our attempts to acquire information about this decisive period when so much was happening, and so many of the traits that would later become characteristic of Judaism were being formed.

NAMES, TERMS, AND LANGUAGES

In our modern Bible translations, Ezra and Nehemiah are two separate books. This was not always the case. In the various stages of the process of collecting and editing that led to the canonization of the Hebrew Bible, Ezra and Nehemiah had grown into one book. The first time that we find the two books separated again appears to be in a Hebrew manuscript from 1448. In the Greek translation of the Hebrew Bible, the Septuagint, the division has happened much earlier. It seems that both Origen (died 254) and Jerome (died 420) knew manuscripts in which the separation was already a fact.

In Hebrew the book of Ezra is called simply "*Ezra*," while the book of Nehemiah is called *Divre nechemyah ben-chakalyah*, "the words of Nehemiah son of Hacaliah" or *Sepher nechemyah*, "the book of Nehemiah." The language of the books of Ezra and Nehemiah is of the same type that we find in the books of Chronicles, Late Biblical Hebrew. In addition, we find pieces that are written not in Hebrew but in Aramaic (Ezra 4:8–6:18 and 7:12–26). This type of Aramaic is referred to as Imperial Aramaic. The same language is found also in the book of Daniel (Dan. 2:4–7:28).

THE BOOK OF EZRA

We can divide the book of Ezra into two main parts. Ezra 1:1–6:22 describes the return of the Israelites from the exile in Babylon. The rest of the book, 7:1–10:44, gives an overview of the work of Ezra.

In Ezra 2 we find a list of those families who, according to the Chronicler, returned to Judah. We read about how the priests and the Levites and some of the people settled in Jerusalem, while the rest of the people returned to their respective hometowns. A complete exile of the whole population to Babylon is presupposed. This does not correspond to historical reality. We know that large parts of the inhabitants continued to live in Judah and Jerusalem after the invasion of Nebuchadnezzar. Ezra 3 describes the building of an altar, so that the sacrificial cult can recommence, and a foundation for the rebuilding of the temple. With this information the author wishes to emphasize that the sacrificial cult had also ceased to be practiced in Jerusalem during the exile, and that we can thank the returning families for reinstating true YHWH religion in Judah.

In Ezra 4 we read about the first clashes with the people who lived in the land. The people who hailed from Judah and Israel before the return of the first contingency of Jews from Babylon were hostile to the returnees. They tried in all kinds of ways to put up obstacles to rebuilding the temple and the walls of Jerusalem. Some scholars, especially in earlier times, interpreted this conflict as referring to an opposition between "Jews" and "Samaritans." But this is probably oversimplified. In Ezra 5 we read about how the prophets Haggai and Zechariah both urge the rebuilding of the temple and encourage the Jews to carry on with their reconstruction work. (Both of these prophets have books named after them in the Book of the Twelve Prophets.) Ezra 6 recounts how the Persian authorities helped to set things right for the Jews so that they could recommence their efforts and complete the building of the temple. After this, the Jews celebrated Passover in Jerusalem.

The second section of the book, Ezra 7–10, begins with the story of the scribe (*sopher*) Ezra, who, during the reign of the Persian Artaxerxes, left Babylon and traveled to Jerusalem. We know of several Persian rulers with this name. It remains highly uncertain which one is meant here. Ezra brought with him, in his following, a number of priests, Levites, and temple servants. Ezra 7 also contains the so-called decree of Artaxerxes. Here the Persian ruler provided, in the form of a written document, a message that Ezra had full royal support for his future work in Judah. Further, all the officers of the king would assist Ezra and put things in order for him. In Ezra 8 we find a list of those families who returned from Babylon to Jerusalem together with Ezra, and an account of the journey itself.

Ezra 9 contains the characteristic commandment against mixed marriages, that is, marriages of Jews with non-Jews. The prohibition is followed up in Ezra 10, the last chapter of the book, which describes how the people were forced by Ezra to follow the will of YHWH and to divorce their foreign wives. The last half of chapter 10 contains a list of persons from known families who had married non-Jewish women. It is made clear in many different ways that it was important for Ezra to avoid foreign influence of any kind, and it is against this background that the prohibition to marry foreign women must be understood. The tone of the book of Ezra is thus different from the tone in other parts of the Hebrew Bible. Against the background of Ezra 9–10 it becomes clear that we are now on the way out of "Old Testament times" and on the way into Judaism. With the prohibition against foreign women, Ezra made an important contribution to the particularism and ethnocentrism that was later to become one of the distinct characteristics of exclusivist forms of Judaism.

THE BOOK OF NEHEMIAH

The book of Nehemiah can roughly be divided into two main parts. The first section, 1:1–7:72, contains an overview of the work of Nehemiah. The second main part, 8:1–13:31, recounts the story of Ezra reading the law to the people.

In chapter 1, we learn how Nehemiah receives a message about the miserable state of affairs in Jerusalem, and how he turns to YHWH with a prayer for help. Chapter 2 recounts, in the first person, how Nehemiah, the cupbearer of the Persian king Artaxerxes (the cupbearer was a high-ranking official in the royal bureaucracy, no mere butler), is given permission by the king to travel to Jerusalem to rebuild the city walls. The bulk of chapter 3 consists of a list of the workers who participated in the reconstruction of Jerusalem's walls and city gates. We may also read about the non-Jewish opponents who ridicule the Jews' attempts to rebuild the walls and try to prevent them from doing the work. In Nehemiah 4, the account of the opposition between the Jewish construction workers and the ill-disposed peoples of the area continues. Nehemiah 5, however, gives the impression that the difficulties of the returned Jews are not only due to other nations. Here, tensions among the Jews themselves are revealed. In chapter 6 we meet Nehemiah's opponents again, and read about their attempt to stop the building activities. When all of their hostile efforts fail, the work on the walls can finally be completed. Chapter 7 relates the finishing of the city gates, how the returnees moved into Jerusalem, and how they settled in the rest of the towns of Judah. On the basis of genealogies documenting which families returned first, Nehemiah can decide who is to settle in Jerusalem. We notice that those who could not find documents to prove their family relationship are barred from the priestly office as unworthy.

With chapter 8 we reach the second part of the book of Nehemiah. The chapter recounts how Ezra the priest gathers the people and reads the law of Moses to them.

HISTORICAL AND LITERARY PROBLEMS IN THE BOOKS OF EZRA AND NEHEMIAH

Even a quick reading through of the books of Ezra and Nehemiah shows us that they, despite a number of datings, do not give any clear chronological exposition of the events that are related. Neither can the account in any way be said to give a complete portrayal of the history of the Jews in the period it deals with. Rather, attention seems to be concentrated on certain main concerns: the temple and the city walls, the priesthood, the Levites, the proclamation of the law, and the prohibition of marriage to foreign women.

The references that we do find to known political figures in the contemporary periods do not make it simpler to date the books of Ezra and Nehemiah. Several passages in the books refer to the Persian ruler Artaxerxes. However, we know three kings with this name who ruled Persia in this period: Artaxerxes I (464–423 BCE), Artaxerxes II (404–358 BCE), and Artaxerxes III (358–337 BCE). Even though many scholars have chosen to identify the Persian king with Artaxerxes I, this identification remains uncertain.

Another Persian ruler who is mentioned in the biblical sources is Darius. But here again there are several possibilities. Darius I ruled 521–485 BCE, and Darius II, 423–404 BCE. When the conditions are like this, it is obviously not always simple to understand the relative chronology of the texts. A lot of hard work has gone into trying to solve these problems. The only certain thing that seems to have come out of it all is that, due to the nature of the sources, we have to be very careful with our assumptions.

The books of Ezra and Nehemiah contain several "documents" that claim to be historically authentic. A closer investigation of these documents shows, however, that we soon run into problems also on this issue. At the center of the book of Ezra stands the so-called edict of Cyrus, in which the Persian ruler Cyrus, after having conquered Babylon in 539, gives the Jews permission to return to their homeland from Babylon. But this "document" is found in two different versions: one Hebrew version in Ezra 1:1–4 (and partly also in 2 Chr. 36:22–23), and one Aramaic version in Ezra 6:3–5 (see also 5:13–15). If we compare these two documents, we soon see that even though the two documents are most likely one and the same, they are not identical in their wording.

In the Hebrew version, we can read about how the Persian ruler Cyrus has been given power by YHWH to rule over "all the lands of the earth," and that YHWH has commanded him to rebuild the temple of Jerusalem. Further, Cyrus wishes to give one of the Jews who is in Babylon the task of traveling to Jerusalem to rebuild the temple, and he commands all the Jews who are dispersed in the different countries to support the building financially.

In the Aramaic version in Ezra 6:3–5, the wording differs. Also in this text Cyrus gives the order that the temple in Jerusalem must be rebuilt. He even details the measurements of the building, and informs about what materials will be used for the reconstruction. But in this version it is said clearly that the expenses are to be covered by the Persian ruler's treasury. It is emphasized further that the silver and gold that belong to the temple of Jerusalem, and that Nebuchadnezzar took away to Babylon, shall be brought back to Jerusalem.

Both documents are dated to the first year of Cyrus's rule, that is, 538 BCE. As we are dealing with quotations from purportedly existing documents, it is self-evident that they are not the same document. It follows that both documents cannot be authentic. But even if we were to suppose that one of them is authentic, we still run into major problems. The whole authenticity debate has been characterized by a historicist approach to ancient documents, and today we do not believe anymore that is possible to make definite conclusions in areas like these. Also, the argument could be turned the other way around. Forgeries, too, are important for historical reconstructions. If it is a good forgery, the texts certainly can contain a lot of historical information.

Other important biblical sources for knowledge about Judaism in the Persian period are the prophetic books of Haggai and Zechariah. According to the colophons in the books that bear their name, these prophets were active around twenty years after Cyrus had taken over power from the Babylonian Empire. But from the books of Haggai and Zechariah it is not clear that these prophets' contemporaries knew about any edict of Cyrus. When both of these prophets zealously encourage the rebuilding of the temple, they do not point to groups of returned Jews, to any kind of royal edict, or to the existence of any plans for the rebuilding of the temple whatsoever. On the contrary, the preaching of these prophets assumes that the people do not want to rebuild the temple.

There are problems connected also to the individuals in the books of Ezra and Nehemiah. The primary problem concerns the relationship between the main characters, Ezra and Nehemiah. Secondarily, the relationship between the two persons Zerubbabel and Sheshbazzar is not simple to work out.

If we take the time to read the books of Ezra and Nehemiah carefully, the problems quickly pile up. In spite of what we read in the book of Nehemiah about how Nehemiah was responsible for the rebuilding of the city walls, Ezra 9:9 gives the impression that Jerusalem already has a wall when Ezra arrives in the city. For this and similar reasons many scholars believe that Nehemiah must have come to Jerusalem before Ezra. Perhaps it is also because of this that the list of names in Nehemiah 12:2 puts Nehemiah before Ezra. Further, some have remarked that the description we find in Ezra 10:1 gives the impression that Jerusalem was fairly densely populated by Jews in the time of Ezra. From Nehemiah 7:4 it is clear that in his time the city was sparsely populated.

But this rational way of discussing historical problems presupposes that the books of Ezra and Nehemiah contain historically correct information, and that we can use our modern, Western logic in interpreting these texts. This is something we cannot do without qualification. Scholars oriented more to tradition history have claimed that the two persons Ezra and Nehemiah have been connected only at a late stage in the development of the traditions. In this way the impression was created that they were active at the same time. When we today find the book of Ezra before the book of Nehemiah, this could be because the editor attempted to emphasize Ezra. Such a conscious emphasis on the person of Ezra does not seem improbable when we see the way the book of Ezra portrays him as a hero. Because Ezra was associated with the priesthood it is likely that influential priests wished to emphasize him. Perhaps they felt it was a defeat that Nehemiah, who was not a priest, was to get all of the honor and glory for having rebuilt the walls of Jerusalem and the temple. They avoided this discredit by placing Ezra chronologically before Nehemiah. If this is so, it is possible that the Chroniclers themselves were behind this reworking of the traditions. They wished in all ways to highlight the temple with the priesthood and the Levites, and to call attention to the influence of religion on the development in Judah. Many scholars today support this type of explanation.

This reshuffling of Ezra and Nehemiah compared to the order we are used to does not solve all the problems. However, such an explanation has some advantages. In any case this careful chronological reevaluation is perhaps preferable to more radical attempts to reject Ezra as a historical person. Scholars who have chosen such a radical solution consider Ezra a fictional ideal character created by the Chroniclers to market their particular theological interests. But it is precisely the lack of coherence in the book of Ezra that speaks against such a radical solution to the problem. Among other things, we notice a gap of around sixty years between Ezra 6 and 7. A presentation that was purely imaginative would hardly give such a haphazard impression as the one that we find here. It is probably closer to the mark to assume that we are dealing with a work that was heavily edited. That the edict of Cyrus is written in Aramaic can, however, strengthen the theory that at least parts of the work are purely literary. Perhaps the authors wished to give the work an increased trustworthiness by constructing "authentic" documents in the language of diplomacy of that day, namely Aramaic. If this was the case, however, we should remember that there is no such thing as "pure fiction." A falsified document could at the same time yield important historical information about Persian imperial policy, perhaps confirming or even supplementing what we know from other sources.

We run into further complications if we look more closely at the two other main characters of the story in Ezra and Nehemiah, Zerubbabel and Sheshbazzar. Here too the problem is associated with the unclear nature of the sources and with issues of chronology. In Ezra 1 we read that a certain Sheshbazzar led the first contingency of returned Jews from Babylon to Jerusalem. According to Ezra 1:8, Sheshbazzar was of royal descent. From Ezra 5:16 we learn further that Sheshbazzar was the first governor of the province of Judah and that he laid the foundations for the new temple. That is the extent of the information we get from the sources about Sheshbazzar. If one of the explanations about the name Sheshbazzar is correct, there is also an alternative form, Shenazzar. A person by this name is mentioned in 1 Chronicles 3:18 as someone who was the grandson of King Jehoiachin, who was led into captivity to Babylon by Nebuchadnezzar.

Even if very little is told about Sheshbazzar, it is more than enough to create problems, because the same things that are told about Sheshbazzar are also told about another person, Zerubbabel. Both were of royal descent and were governor of Judah (Ezra 5:14 and Hag. 1:1). Both figures appear in association with the return from Babylon during the reign of Cyrus (Ezra 1:11 and 2:2). It is said about both that they started to rebuild the temple (Sheshbazzar in Ezra 5:16, Zerubbabel in Ezra 3:2, 8; 5:2; Haggai 1; Zech. 4:9). In Ezra 1:11 Sheshbazzar is mentioned as the leader of the Jews who had returned from Jerusalem following the edict of Cyrus, and who brought with them the silver and gold vessels that had been taken from the temple. It may confuse us, therefore, to discover that in Ezra 2:2 (see also Neh. 7:7) Zerubbabel is the one who is mentioned first among the families who left Babylon. About Sheshbazzar we find no information whatever.

If we compare the different information that we have at our disposal regarding the two figures Sheshbazzar and Zerubbabel, we understand why some scholars have claimed that behind these two names hides one and the same person. Later Jewish tradition has also wavered in its views on whether we are dealing with two different people or one person. We can see this from the apocryphal book of 1 Esdras (6:18), which recounts that the silver and gold vessels of Jerusalem were delivered to "Zerubbabel and Sheshbazzar the governor." Some manuscripts have deleted "and" between the two names, and have thus understood it to refer to one individual, not to two different persons.

It is nevertheless most likely that the story concerns two different figures. A common argument among those who have claimed that we are dealing with two different names for the same person has been that Sheshbazzar must have been the person's Babylonian name, while Zerubbabel was his Jewish name. However, neo-Babylonian inscriptions show that Zerubbabel is a common Babylonian name. Further, the way in which this name is composed departs from what is ordinary for Hebrew names. And it is less likely that a Jew would have had two different Babylonian names, instead of one Jewish and one Babylonian. In addition, the books of Haggai and Zechariah indicate that Zerubbabel was active during the reign of Darius, but not a single word is mentioned about him as also having been active during the reign of Cyrus. Perhaps the most acceptable explanation for all of this is that the "author" of Ezra 2 has transmitted the tradition wrongly, and has referred to a list that originally belongs to the context of events that were to have taken place during the reign of Darius, not during the reign of Cyrus.

According to Ezra 6, Darius had a positive attitude toward the reconstruction of the temple in Jerusalem. Perhaps the other events related in Ezra 2 also fit better the conditions under Darius than under Cyrus. If these speculations are correct, then what the text says happened to Zerubbabel is a chronological mistake. It is possible that this mistake has been made purposely. Perhaps the Chroniclers wished to highlight Zerubbabel in order to take some of the glory away from his predecessor Sheshbazzar and his pioneering endeavor. So it has turned out that Zerubbabel, not Sheshbazzar, stands as the shining name in later Jewish tradition. If this explanation is correct, this is an example of the Chroniclers' free use of sources and of their desire to emphasize individuals whom they considered to be more important than others.

THE TIME OF THE EXILE (586–539 BCE)

The exile and the return from exile play an extremely important role in Judaism. In the time following the exilic period, the negative aspect of this fateful event grew out of proportion until it finally became an iconic disaster. We should be aware, however, that this traditional view of exilic Judah is not historically reliable. The biblical sources are complex and do not lend themselves easily to historical reconstructions. A reading of the texts of the Hebrew Bible does not make clear in how many rounds and in what scope the population of Judah was deported. The image that the Chroniclers draw of the situation in the land some two hundred years before their own time is the most negative in the whole Bible: Judah lay desolate and empty. Even though this popular view was somewhat modified, it has been strong in the consciousness of succeeding periods, all the way until the present. God's judgment and punishment were all-encompassing.

Not a few scholars have let themselves be influenced by the Chronicler's negative view. Therefore, they have claimed that Judah in the exilic period was completely devastated, with regard to population as well as politically, culturally, and religiously. Important biblical works such as the Deuteronomistic History, Deutero-Isaiah (Isaiah 40–55), and Ezekiel must therefore have been composed in Babylon, scholars have claimed. But the concept of a total deportation represents an artificial and mechanistic way of understanding how ancient societies functioned. It is not feasible that all of the population in 586 BCE would have been brought into exile, and that they, almost fifty years later, came back as one group. Rather, we have to accept that the large majority of the population stayed in the homeland. Archaeological excavations and surveys have gradually also made clearer that there were uninterrupted settlements in Jerusalem and the Judean towns after the catastrophe in 586 BCE.

If we examine the duration of the "exile," it lasted from 586 to 539 BCE, that is, forty-eight years. The seventy-year period that is mentioned in the Bible (Jer. 25:11–12; 29:10; Zech. 1:12; 2 Chr. 36:21; Dan. 9:2) must not be understood literally. It is difficult for those of us who have grown up in a Western culture to get used to the idea that numbers and figures in the Hebrew Bible are often not exact. In the case of the exile, the number seventy is used symbolically of a period of great significance, not as a literal figure to designate a number of years. When it comes to the total number of people who were deported, it is hard for us to know the exact figure. The Old Testament itself gives a number of different figures. What remains clear is that a total deportation of the whole population did not take place. Besides the royal household and some of the leading families, the Babylonians probably deported a number of skilled workers and others who could be of use to them. However, this would imply that the number of Judeans in Babylonia could have been substantial. In fact, most of them never returned, and the Diaspora in Babylonia over time developed into a major Jewish center.

From a historical point of view, therefore, the exile was never the momentous event that it became in the historical and theological reflections of subsequent generations. Nor has there been a complete return from the exile of the scope and significance that the Chronicler wishes to imply.

Moreover, we should realize that the study of the history of Diaspora Judaism in Babylonia has its own set of problems. There were Jewish colonies in

Babylon long before the so-called Babylonian exile. These settlements owed their existence to a number of transfers and migrations, voluntary and involuntary, over a long period of time.

The Jewish Diaspora in Babylon also continued to be a center of power long after the Jews allegedly had moved back to Judah. Over time, some of these exilic Jews gained a position of wealth and social stature that would not have been possible in the province of Judah. Very much later, early in the twentieth century, the Jews in Baghdad and elsewhere made up one of the largest ethnic minorities in Iraq.

There can be little doubt, however, that a return of some kind occurred in Persian times, and probably over a long period. It is this return that is reflected in the books of Ezra and Nehemiah. It may be that Nehemiah's book was the earlier of the two, and that he represented the Persian government. It also seems clear that the returnees belonged to the landowning, higher tier of society. Apparently, there were many priests and Levites among those who returned. There is little reason to doubt that there must have been tensions between those who had remained in the land and those who returned from Babylon. This too is documented in the books of Ezra and Nehemiah.

What further seems possible is that the returnees played an important role in the reconstruction of Judah, both financially and culturally. It follows from the books of Ezra and Nehemiah that priests and Levites played an important role among the returnees. The Chroniclers, who may have belonged among the returning families, portray it as if the segments of the population who lived in Judah more or less consisted of an "impure" mixed group also known as "Samaritans." This somewhat imprecise term came to be used about the mixed population in the northern kingdom after the fall of Samaria in 721 BCE. (The negative ring that the term "Samaritans" carried among Judeans is well known also from the New Testament.) Those who returned, on the other hand, were "pure." The Chroniclers' exposition in the books of Ezra and Nehemiah attempts to give the impression that the returnees came in the nick of time and reinstated the pure YHWH religion that had been forgotten. This profile of the returning families was important for the Chroniclers. But with this the exile passes from being a historical event to becoming a piece of ideological rhetoric.

The portrayal given by the books of Ezra and Nehemiah legitimizes the significance of certain families as founders and reformers of the YHWH religion, and as the defenders and keepers of true Judaism. By being responsible for the reconstruction of the temple in Jerusalem and the city walls, these families secured for themselves a position for all posterity. This is seen clearly from the importance attached to genealogies in these books. Again we are dealing with ideological documents rather than with "historical" ones.

The books of Ezra and Nehemiah do, however, reflect something of what happened in history. We can reasonably assume that the returned families played a role like the one demonstrated here. At the same time, the work takes on significance as a document of legitimization for the type of religious and social structure that was dominant in Judah around 350 BCE. In this way, these sources reflect the contemporary, nascent Judaism, and the increasing importance of the priesthood.

THE BOOKS OF CHRONICLES

For practical reasons we are, in the present context, dealing with three different works, Ezra, Nehemiah, and 1 and 2 Chronicles, as one work. We refer, moreover, to both the authors/editors of Ezra and of Nehemiah and of 1 and 2 Chronicles, and of the combined historiographical work that runs from the beginning of Ezra to the end of 2 Chronicles, as stemming from the same scribal and theological circles.

The present form of the work, consisting of four separate "books" in English translations, is late. In order to tie the two main parts together (the books of Chronicles on the one hand and the books of Ezra and Nehemiah on the other) an editor of the work has let the closing words of 2 Chronicles (the edict of Cyrus) repeat the beginning of the book of Ezra. It is possible that the final composition of the work is to be attributed to a single author. However, it is more probable that in late postexilic times a distinct school of thought desired to express its view of the history of the Israelite people. In all of these cases, we simply refer to the authors/editors of these works as "the Chroniclers," or collectively as "the Chronicler."

For various reasons, this represents a much too simplified way of approaching these texts. However, it does give us the possibility of considering the books of Ezra, Nehemiah, and 1 and 2 Chronicles as one large history. In this way the books of Chronicles make up a parallel work to that of the Priestly and the Deuteronomistic histories. The work of the Chronicler is the most broadly conceived of all the Old Testament works of history, and tells the story of ancient Israel all the way from Adam down to the Persian king Cyrus II, around the mid-sixth century BCE.

In the Hebrew Bible the books of Chronicles are called *Divre hayyamim,* "words of the days," or "annals." It is this title that is reflected in English "Chronicles." The Septuagint uses the term *Paraleipomena,* "things that have been omitted," "things that have been passed over," for the books of Chronicles. From this term it is clear that the Greek translators saw the work as a kind of addition, a supplement, to the rest of the histories in the Hebrew Bible. This has often been the way it has been viewed, even in more recent times. But this view does not adequately appreciate the Chronicler. The Chronicler's History is a separate, independent work. It is a parallel to the other biblical histories, not a supplement.

The Chronicler's History departs markedly from both the Priestly History and the Deuteronomistic History. This applies not only to the Chronistic style and language but also to the overall ideology that dominates this work, its "view of history."

The Books of Chronicles: On Sources and Dating

The Chroniclers present us with an alternative portrayal of the history and religion of ancient Israel. For that reason the question of the sources they may have had at their disposal becomes important. Scholars assume that the work was written between 400 and 200 BCE, but we have very little to go on. Our knowledge of Jewish history and literary history in the period 400–200 BCE is limited. Tentatively, we date the work to around 350 BCE.

What is clear is that the Chroniclers must have known the Deuteronomistic History (Joshua, Judges, Samuel, and Kings), or at least versions of this work. Not only is the Chronistic account construed according to the same mold; there are also verbatim quotes from the Deuteronomistic History. That the Chroniclers' view of punishment and reward is completely in line with the Deuteronomists' view is not a point we should accord much weight, however. We are, on this issue, dealing with an instance of a common Near Eastern theology of retribution, well known also outside ancient Israel. When disaster struck, whether it was a defeat in battle or crop failure, it was interpreted as punishment from the gods. If one humbled oneself and turned to the gods with a prayer of forgiveness, the disaster might come to an end.

It is interesting to note that the Chroniclers themselves list a number of different sources that they seem to have had access to. Among these, we find "the Books of the Kings of Israel and Judah" (e.g., 2 Chr. 27:7), "the Book of the Kings of Judah and Israel" (e.g., 16:11), "the Book of the Kings of Israel" (20:34), "the Annals of the Kings of Israel" (33:18), and "the Commentary on the Book of the Kings" (24:27). As people in the ancient world were not as careful with source citations as we are today, it is possible that these references are to one and the same work. It could perhaps be different terms for the books of Kings in the form that we know them today in the Deuteronomistic History. That all of these references should be to the same work, however, is unlikely. It is more probable that some of them are works that have been lost to posterity.

Other works that are referred to by the Chroniclers and that we do not have any specific knowledge of are "the records of the seer Samuel, the records of the prophet Nathan, and the records of the seer Gad" (e.g., 1 Chr. 29:29), "the prophecy of Ahijah the Shilonite and the vision of the seer Iddo concerning Jeroboam son of Nebat" (2 Chr. 9:29), "the records of the prophet Shemaiah and of the seer Iddo" (12:15), and "the story of the prophet Iddo" (13:22). Again, it could be that behind all of these references are works that are known by other names today, and that actually exist in the canonical Hebrew Bible. For example, it is likely that the canonical book of Samuel is to be found behind the title "the records of the seer Samuel." However, we also have to assume that some of the references are to literary works that have been lost to us. Such references to lost works are important in that they remind us that the Old Testament in its present form contains only a selection of ancient Israelite traditions. It is also significant that the Chroniclers utilize works that we know today, for example, the books of Kings. In this way we are able to get valuable insights into the Chroniclers as historians.

The Books of Chronicles: Theology

Just like the authors of the Priestly and Deuteronomistic histories, the Chroniclers would hardly qualify as "historians" in our sense of the word. Their task was not to reconstruct the past but to interpret it. The Chroniclers wished to impart their understanding not of how it was but of how they wanted it to have been. Like all "history writing" in antiquity, their accounts are not based on an interest in reconstructing the past for the present, but on a desire to bring a message to the present. Like the other "historians" of the Hebrew Bible, the Chroniclers too are highly tendentious and exhibit a fair amount of freedom in handling their sources. The material is pressed and tailored; and, in order to make a point, the writer does not stop at suppressing the sources, or even sometimes completely rewriting them. The books of Chronicles, therefore, give us also valuable information about how the biblical writers worked.

Whether we are dealing with the Deuteronomistic, the Priestly, or the Chronistic work of history, the primary and overall aim of all of these histories is the opposite of that of the modern historian. Instead of a critical weighing of sources to reconstruct the past, the biblical writers try to use the sources to give an account of the course of events that fits with their own politically and theologically tinted view of how things should be. In itself, there is nothing unusual about this.

The Chronicler wanted to portray history in the way that it would be understood by contemporary society. As historical background for the work, we thus have to imagine the conditions in Jerusalem around 350 BCE. The

Chronicler's view of history comes across very clearly in the description of King David and the Davidic monarchy. The story of David and his son Solomon is allotted much more space than that of any other king. If we look at the content of the books of Chronicles, we find that this long narrative treats the history of Israel from creation until the Persian period. However, a total of 40 percent of the text is reserved for the story of David and Solomon. Also, the David of the Chronicler is a purely ideal character; none of his negative characteristics that we know from the Deuteronomistic History are included in the Chronicler's account. Thus the story about David and Bathsheba and her husband Uriah, which we find in 2 Samuel, is not recounted. Neither is the story of the opposition between David and his son Absalom. What is essential to the Chronicler is the emphasis on David and the significance of the Davidic monarchy for Israel.

In the Chronicler's contemporary society there did not seem to be much hope for the Judeans. Politically and economically, as well as culturally and religiously, the Jews were oppressed. The Chronicler struggles to hold up the past as an admonition, as encouragement, and as an ideal; only David and his descendants represent the true kings and only Jerusalem can be the center of worship for the one true God, YHWH. The whole exposition is colored by this concern. Also the many genealogies in the first nine chapters of 1 Chronicles bear the mark of having been composed against this background. The tribe of Judah, the tribe of the hero king, comes first. This tribe is also described in great detail. The tribes of the northern kingdom, however, were made as anonymous as possible. Some of them are allotted only a few verses.

In his eagerness to show that David and his descendants are the true kings, and that Jerusalem and Judah are the right places to worship YHWH, the Chronicler consciously demotes the northern kingdom and its history. Once again, the reason is partly to be sought in the Chronicler's own time, for example the opposition to the "Samaritans." This is the same attitude that we find reflected in the New Testament. As we have seen, however, the Chronicler is in happy agreement with the Deuteronomists on this issue. They also portray the kings of the northern kingdom, Israel, as the villains.

The Chronicler's portrayal of the kings is highly schematic and characterized by stereotypical phrases. The kings are categorized as "good" or "bad" according to whether or not they worshiped YHWH. Of the good kings it is ordinarily said that they destroyed the places of worship and divine statues in Israel. When the traditions include information that the kings had suffered defeat on the battleground, this is always set directly in association with apostasy from YHWH. We also notice how kings often start out as good. When the priest they are relying on for support dies, they can no longer stay the course. They fall from YHWH, and become "bad" kings. The big bad wolves are first of all the northern kings. Very often the downfall of a "good" king in Judah begins after he has committed the mistake of allying himself with the terrible king of the north.

The temple in Jerusalem and the worship there, with the priesthood and their various tasks, are crucial to the Chroniclers. Religion is important and is seen as a national gathering point in the times of crisis in which the nation found itself. Also in relation to the temple, however, the Chroniclers feel free to use their sources liberally. Even though the sources tell us that Solomon built the temple in Jerusalem, the Chroniclers give David the honor for this. However, it would not be possible, even for the Chroniclers, to claim that David himself built the temple. This would be too much of a departure from the tradition. Instead, the Chroniclers portray the event as if it was David who had the idea to build the temple, and that it was he who collected the material for the temple and who, before his death, was able to hand over the complete plans for how to build it. Instead of being the one who actually had the temple built, Solomon, in the Chronistic version, is reduced to being the obedient tool of his famous father.

As mentioned above, Jerusalem and Judah were at quite a low point politically, economically, and culturally in the period that the Chroniclers were active. Around 350 BCE many Jews lived outside Judah, which was a province under Persian dominion. The national, political, social, and religious feelings of inferiority must have been great in this period. It is therefore worth noticing that the Chroniclers, despite their strong emphasis on the Davidic monarchy, do not call for the reestablishment of the monarchy. The significance of David and the Davidic monarchy lies first of all in the symbolic meaning that the David traditions had for the temple and for temple worship. It is not David or the secular kings who are the true kings in the eyes of the Chroniclers. The only true king is YHWH.

In the politically oppressed Judah of the time of the Chroniclers, it is the priests who have power in daily life. It is YHWH who stands at the center of the Chroniclers' portrayal of ancient Israelite history. Therefore, they can allow themselves to contend against the texts and to rewrite them. Yet another example of such a rewriting of the sources can be found in the account of David's census. In 2 Samuel 24 there is a story about how YHWH provoked David into counting the people. For the Chroniclers it is offensive that YHWH has acted in this way against an unassailable, ideal king. For that reason they simply change the tradition and substitute Satan for YHWH.

As a result of their particular view of religion and its importance it is no wonder that one of the points where the Chroniclers differ markedly from other sources is in their view of the priesthood and its significance. The Chroniclers are not alone in stressing the importance of the priests, though. Many of the ideas about the priests and their role that we find in the Priestly History are closely related to what we find in the Chroniclers. However, the Priestly view in this case is also a late development that is hardly representative of the "classical" understanding of the priests and the cult in early Israel.

An essential difference between the "old" and the "new" views of the priests is clearly expressed when it comes to the role of the high priests. In earlier times, the Israelite high priests occupied themselves above all with the temple and cultic activities. In Persian times (sixth to fourth centuries BCE), the high priest begins gradually to apply his influence also to issues of civil law. In the past, this area had been the domain of the kings.

In the theological history of the Chroniclers we meet a type of theocracy. And as the "history writers" of this theocracy, the Chroniclers can change the old traditions. An illustration of this in relation to the role of the high priest can be found in 2 Chronicles 26:16–21, the story of how the high priest chased King Uzziah out of the temple because Uzziah wanted to burn incense inside the building. As a cultic act, the burning of incense was, according to the tradition, a prerogative of the priests. But it is questionable that the high priest in the time of Uzziah had the power to throw the king out of the temple. The priesthood of the Chroniclers' time, however, did have this authority.

Another characteristic of the Chroniclers is that they attribute much more power to the Levites than other sources in the Hebrew Bible. Some have claimed that the Chroniclers must have belonged to the Levites, but we cannot know for sure. It is just as likely that the Chroniclers, in their eagerness to attribute more power to the priesthood, wanted to improve the conditions of the Levites as well. At least it is clear that the Chroniclers wanted to adjust the status of the Levites to a higher level compared to the priests, the "sons of Aaron." According to the Priestly work, it was only this last group that constituted the true class of priests, and who had the privilege of performing priestly duties. The Levites in the Priestly work are considered to be a type of lower servants associated with the temple service. But in the books of Chronicles we find several descriptions of Levites performing ritual functions that, according to the Priestly writer, were reserved as a duty of the priestly class. This information is found in Josephus, *Jewish Antiquities* xx 9:6.

Much of what we find in Chronicles reflects conditions of the authors' time. For instance, the elevation of the status of the Levites, so that Levites are given priestly tasks, had probably not yet occurred in the time of the Chroniclers. This perspective emphasized by the Chroniclers should perhaps be seen as propaganda writing, agitating for the position of the Levites rather than a reflection of the contemporary view of their function and status. Again, some scholars have seen this as an indication of Levitical interests behind the work of the Chroniclers. In later Judaism at least some of the improvements that the Chroniclers indirectly suggested were implemented. In the first century BCE, for example, it was decided that the Levitical temple singers were to wear garments of linen of the same type as ordinary priests. This information is found in Josephus, *Jewish Antiquities* xx 9:6.

5

The Prophets

Isaiah, Jeremiah, Ezekiel, Hosea, Joel, Amos,
Obadiah, Micah, Nahum, Habakkuk, Zephaniah,
Haggai, Zechariah, Malachi, Daniel

In the Hebrew Bible the Nevi'im, "Prophets," appears as the second part in the canonical order, immediately following the Torah, "Law." The Nevi'im consists of Joshua, Judges, Samuel, Kings, Isaiah, Jeremiah, Ezekiel, and the Book of the Twelve: Hosea, Joel, Amos, Obadiah, Jonah, Micah, Nahum, Habakkuk, Zephaniah, Haggai, Zechariah, and Malachi.

In the Hebrew text the Nevi'im is divided in two parts. The first part consists of "the Former Prophets," Joshua, Judges, Samuel, and Kings. The second contains "the Latter Prophets," Isaiah, Jeremiah, Ezekiel, and the Book of the Twelve. The division into two in the Jewish canon took place in the Middle Ages.

The location of the Latter Prophets after the poetic books follows the Greek translation, the Septuagint. The different orders of biblical books in translations of Hebrew and Greek versions of the Old Testament show that the order of the canonical books had not been settled when the translation of the Septuagint took place (in the third century BCE).

The Old Testament prophets are significant in Western tradition. In both Judaism and Christianity we find clear testimony to the importance Amos, Micah, Jeremiah, Isaiah, and Ezekiel have for Western cultural and religious history. The scientific study of ancient Israelite prophecy is not very old, however, barely a hundred years. Before the so-called historical-critical work on the Bible began, in Christian tradition the prophets were almost exclusively seen as the forerunners of Christ or as preachers of the coming of Christ. Their message was read messianically or christologically. Often, the interpretations stood quite far from the historical context in which the prophetic message originated.

SOME HIGHLIGHTS FROM THE HISTORY
OF RESEARCH

The greatest name in Old Testament research in the nineteenth century is undoubtedly Julius Wellhausen (1844–1918). Both in Christian tradition, with its doctrine of scriptural inspiration, and in Orthodox Jewish tradition, the classical theological question of the relationship between "the Law and the Prophets" had remained unproblematic and was not an issue of debate; the Law was given to Moses on Mount Sinai, and the Prophets enter the stage only later. Through his studies of the Pentateuch, Wellhausen was able to demonstrate that the Law (Torah) belonged among the latest parts of the Old Testament. This claim caused an uproar in his day, and the church was quick to name Wellhausen a heretic.

Wellhausen did not write much about the prophets. However, he did see them as the creators of Israel's religion. In their time the prophets fought against the paganism of the popular cult and advocated the worship solely of YHWH. Wellhausen was not original in his view of the prophets. He built in large measure on his teacher Heinrich Ewald.

Ewald (1803–1875) published several works about the prophets. He was interested in the prophets as a phenomenon not just in ancient Israel but also in other cultures. He viewed the biblical prophets as idealists, the bearers of a religious truth. All humans have within them the kernel that allows them to understand true religion, but this kernel is sleeping, he claimed. It was the task of the prophets to awaken this sleeping kernel in their audience. With this understanding of the prophets, Ewald turned against the individualistic, romantic understanding of the prophets that we find, for example, in Johann Gottfried Herder (1744–1803) and Johann Gottfried Eichhorn (1752–1827). It is typical for most nineteenth-century work on the prophets that it fluctuated between romanticism and idealism.

However, the real pioneer of prophetic research was Wellhausen's friend Bernhard Duhm (1847–1928). Duhm, too, had studied with Ewald in Göttingen, and received, as did Wellhausen, decisive impressions from his teacher. His first work on the theology of the prophets was published in 1875. What is new with Duhm (in contrast to predecessors like the romanticist Herder and the idealist and historian Ewald) is that he, with the prophetic books as his point of departure, wanted to describe the development of ancient Israelite religion. Duhm's agenda was identical to that of Wellhausen in relation to the history of ancient Israel. One of Duhm's interests had to do with the relationship between the law and the prophets; could the prophetic period have developed subsequent to a period dominated by Mosaic law? To this, Duhm answered a definitive no.

Karl Heinrich Graf (1815–1869) had started this scholarly revolution by claiming that the books of Moses in reality came from late postexilic times. Duhm and Wellhausen had supported Graf's thesis, and gradually it would attract more and more followers. The religion that had existed in ancient Israel before the prophets was, according to Duhm, no Mosaic legal religion, but a popular natural religion. Duhm shared this view with Wellhausen. What set the prophets apart from the old times was their new religious insight, which positioned them to break away from the old.

For Duhm the early prophets (those mentioned in the "historical" works) are clearly distinct from the so-called writing prophets. Duhm pointed to a development that he maintained had occurred within prophetic religion. While the early prophets remained stuck in the popular natural religion, something completely new arose with the prophet Amos: the connection to nature was replaced by an ethical grounding. The power that drove the religious prophetic movement forward was an ethical idea. On this point Duhm revealed more clearly than anywhere else that he (like Ewald and Wellhausen) was strongly influenced by German idealism. He wanted to separate himself from any sort of theological framework and to begin his work without presuppositions. Yet he was not able to carry out such a project—no one can.

The most famous and undoubtedly most influential of Duhm's contributions to prophetic research is his commentary on Isaiah (1892). Here the idealist, speculative tendency that we find in many of his earlier works withdraws more to the background. With his commentary on Isaiah, Duhm delivered a significant contribution to prophetic research. First, he attempted to reconstruct an original text, based on his reasoning that the prophets had originally been good writers. In those places where the text in some way did not make sense or in any other way was "destroyed," Duhm "corrected" the text to get back to the "original." Duhm's approach became very popular in prophetic studies. Today this is one of the methods that have come under attack, and not many believe that we can regard the prophets as "authors" in this way.

Metrics, the study of the structure of verses, played just as important a role as textual criticism when Duhm reconstructed his "original text." He emphasized that these texts are poetic, and underlined the aesthetic and artistic aspects of the texts of Isaiah. We can say that Duhm "rediscovered" the poetic dimension in the prophets. According to Duhm, however, the point of all exegesis is to reach the message that the prophets really had said and meant. He claimed to be able to do this by discerning and delving into the individual writer's personality and individuality. We therefore often call such an interpretation of the prophets "neo-romanticist," because it is close, in many ways, to Herder and romanticism.

One influence of Duhm that we can trace all the way up to our own day is his literary-critical identification of the four so-called Servant Songs in the book of Isaiah: Isaiah 42:1–4; 49:1–6; 50:4–9; and 52:13–53:12. These texts do not, according to Duhm, belong with Isaiah 40–55, but are later additions.

Duhm was also the first to separate Isaiah 56–66 from the rest of the book, and attribute these chapters to a "Third Isaiah" (Trito-Isaiah), who was active in late postexilic times. Even though Duhm's criteria for sorting out parts of the book of Isaiah as "inauthentic" cannot be accepted today, his work nevertheless paved the way for the view that there is a long and complicated process behind the origin of the prophetic books.

Duhm's commentary on Jeremiah (1901) was equally epoch-making. He determined that large parts of the book of Jeremiah were secondary. These additions to the words of the prophet Jeremiah included not least the many prose speeches, which in language, phraseology, and theology are strongly reminiscent of Deuteronomy. With this analysis Duhm initiated the process that was to become one of the main themes of discussion in the later Jeremiah debate.

As mentioned above, Duhm's understanding of the development of ancient Israelite religion is typical of his time. The moral idealism of the nineteenth century haunts every corner of his work. Characteristically, Duhm operated with a theory of three different stages of development in Israel's religion. This development is well described in his mature work on "Israel's Prophets" (1916). From being "demonist," the religion of ancient Israel developed to become a "dynamistic" folk religion. The highest stage in the development was prophetic religion. The great, and new, aspect of the prophetic movement was that it wrenched the religion free of the "demonist" and the "dynamistic" folk religion. The prophets appear almost as "protestant" theologians who invent an ethically superior religion. But with this emphasis on the ethical there occurred a downplaying of religion. Prophetic religion could almost be reduced to the formula: Fear God and love your neighbor! At the same time, Duhm emphasized that the prophets were not thinkers or theologians in the ordinary sense of the word, but received their messages through emotional, ecstatic experiences. This is a clear development in Duhm's view from his earlier thoughts.

Duhm's ethical and idealist views of the Old Testament prophets had a great influence on the following generations of prophetic scholars. With his idealist point of departure, Duhm could, in spite of his historical orientation and his criticism of "timeless truths," let the ethical values that the prophet-theologians represent expand beyond both Judaism and Christianity, and become expressions of universal ethical ideals.

What must remain one of the greatest contributions of Duhm is that, in line with Graf and Wellhausen's views on the relationship between the law and the prophets, he was able to regard the biblical prophets as separate from the books of Moses and study them independently. The texts themselves and their content could thus come to the fore. With this Duhm also laid the foundation for all subsequent prophetic research.

In the period immediately following Duhm, particularly his interest in the prophets' "ecstatic experiences" came to dominate research. Through the reading of prophetic texts it became clear that the prophets could not be considered as "normal" in the eyes of nineteenth- and twentieth-century scholars. The focus on the prophets as individuals also contributed to focusing attention on their somewhat peculiar behavior.

Gradually, the forthcoming new science of psychology was drawn more and more into the discussion. An important name in Old Testament research here is Gustav Hölscher (1877–1955), who published his major book on the prophets in 1914. Hölscher was strongly influenced by the work of the psychologist Wilhelm Wundt (1832–1920). A main concern of Hölscher was to understand the call narratives and vision accounts of the prophetic books as expressions of ecstatic experiences, and that these can be understood with the aid of psychology. Hölscher used the term "apathetic ecstasy." His understanding was that individual consciousness retreats to the background during the "ecstatic experiences" and is replaced by "hallucinations" and "illusions." After discussing parallel phenomena in the Near East, Hölscher attempted to explore the whole of the prophetic literature through a combination of history of religions and psychological methods. The Israelites had inherited the simple ecstatic prophecy from the ancient Canaanites, Hölscher maintained. Gradually this developed more in the direction of a higher form of prophecy, permeated by a new, moral spirituality.

Even though other scholars also participated in the debate, particularly the two Norwegians Sigmund Mowinckel (1884–1965) and Ivar Seierstad (1901–1987), it was the Swede Johannes Lindblom (1882–1974) who was to set the tone of subsequent discussions about prophetic ecstasy. Lindblom worked on ancient Israelite prophecy throughout his long life, and wrote a number of books and articles about the subject. Lindblom's views are most accessible in his now classic work, *Prophecy in Ancient Israel* (1962). Hölscher and earlier scholars had maintained that the experiences of the prophets were "hallucinatory." Lindblom claimed that he could give an acceptable explanation for the Old Testament prophets' ecstatic experiences based on studies in psychology of religion and extensive studies in religious ecstasy. Lindblom distinguished between "absorption ecstasy," where the personality disappears totally into something else, and "concentration ecstasy," where deep concentration removes the prophet from ordinary consciousness and severs contact with the outside world. According to Lindblom, only this last type of ecstasy can be associated with the biblical prophets.

Today we are more careful when it comes to discussing prophetic ecstasy. Information about the phenomenon is now based more on what we can find described in the texts. It is clear that "ecstasy" formed an important part of prophetic activity. However, we no longer believe that it is possible to discern the inner psychological experiences of the prophets on the basis of the texts. Perhaps we should see this approach to texts as a final remnant of a romanticist understanding of the prophets, with its concentration on the personality and the individual.

Important new impulses in Old Testament prophetic research were to come particularly from the well-known German scholar Hermann Gunkel (1862–1932). Gunkel is best known for his work on the Old Testament as literature, and as the founder of the form-critical method. Although he worked primarily with Genesis and Psalms, and did not write much about prophecy, what he did publish was to have a great influence. A coincidence brought Gunkel into prophetic studies. His student Hans Schmidt had finished writing his commentary on the prophets (published 1915). When World War I broke out, Schmidt had to go to war. In 1914 he sent a letter to Gunkel, asking him to write the introduction to the commentary. As a result, Gunkel was forced to think through his ideas about prophecy in ancient Israel.

The roughly sixty pages of introduction to Schmidt's book came to have a much bigger influence on the subsequent development of prophetic research than the modest number of pages would indicate. In his earlier studies on prophecy, Gunkel had shown that he understood "ecstasy" to be the core experience of all prophetic activity. Nevertheless, he claimed that the content of the prophetic words was most important. He saw the prophets' task as political. The prophets were key players in their contemporary societies, and their message was dependent on their contemporary history. With this claim, Gunkel stood quite far from Hölscher's so-called apathetic ecstasy. The prophets were in every way conscious individuals. The prophets' inner religious experience, their inner piety, was, however, also important to Gunkel. He clearly inherited this understanding from the romanticist movement.

Gunkel's most significant contribution to research on Old Testament prophecy is found in his application of genre studies to prophetic texts. Hölscher maintained that the ancient Israelite prophetic movement had started out as a very simple form of oral oracle delivery. Much later, in postexilic times, it had developed to become a purely written authorial activity. "The ecstatic becomes a writer, the prophet becomes a poet," as he put it. Gunkel held similar views. The prophets were originally not writers but speakers. The original prophetic words had always been very brief. For this reason it became important to Gunkel to isolate individual "units" of the text. Gradually, there occurred a development whereby the "units" became longer and longer. Finally, they came to consist of larger prophetic compositions of "about a chapter in length."

Another development that occurred, according to Gunkel, was the movement from poetry to prose. "Enthusiasm speaks according to its nature in poetic form, the rational thought in prose." Only later were the prophetic words collected. Through the redactor's work new elements entered into the text that did not originally belong to the prophet's own words. Here Gunkel found the book of Ezekiel to be an exception. Ezekiel was, according to Gunkel, the first prophet who really wrote a book.

It is Gunkel's great achievement to have demonstrated the degree to which the Old Testament texts are literature and how this literature is governed by set conventions of set literary types or genres (German *Gattungen*). To us today a free imagination is considered an important attribute of a great writer. In the ancient Near East it was knowledge of the conventional literature and the ability to combine and use well-known genres and poetic devices that characterized artistic quality.

Gunkel next turned to the prophetic texts with the same interest with which he previously had approached other biblical texts. His overall approach was literary-critical and literary-historical. The questions he wanted to ask were: What type of popular genres did the prophets use, what did they look like originally, and how did they eventually develop?

According to Gunkel, the different genres and compositional techniques used in prophetic words or texts are extensive. They include promises, threats, descriptions of sin, admonitions, priestly laws, historical reviews, rhetorical disputations, songs of different kinds, religious poems, imitations of profane poems, songs of lament, songs of joy, short lyric pieces, liturgies, parables, allegories, and so on. The task of the exegete, according to Gunkel, is to clarify the various genres, that is, to conduct a study of literary history, and to explain how this literature has come into existence. The exegete must attempt to explain how the prophetic words have developed from brief promises and threats about the future to more elaborate and advanced poetry, historiography, sermons, and legal teaching. Prophetic poetry represented the epitome of ancient Israelite literature, according to Gunkel.

The strength of Gunkel's approach is clear: he wanted to force the exegete back to the text, away from the speculative focus on personality and psychological individualism. His significance for subsequent prophetic research was profound. Genre research, the attempt to designate the different literary genres of the prophetic books, became the main task of prophetic research in the period from Gunkel up until our own day.

In Germany in the 1950s and 1960s the tradition-historical study of prophetic literature continued with much detail and ever-increasing diligence. As it gradually became clear to scholars that the prophets were dependent on traditions from their own contemporary society, interest focused on what seemed to be new and what could be old in their message. The earlier somewhat simplified understanding of the relationship between the law and the prophets had disappeared in the wake of tradition history. No one believed any longer (and neither had Wellhausen) that the message of the prophets had been created in a vacuum. After a while it became clear that the law also had a history that went far back into preexilic times. Even if the Mosaic law had been written down only in late, postexilic times, this did not mean that it could not have had a long oral and written prehistory.

A central name in modern prophetic research is Gerhard von Rad (1901–1971). The second volume of his influential *Old Testament Theology* (published in German in 1960) has the subtitle *The Theology of Israel's Prophetic Traditions*. To von Rad, the study of the prophets represented a direct continuation of his extensive tradition-historical studies of the development of the pentateuchal traditions. Von Rad's primary interest was in the tradition process itself. He saw the transmission of tradition as a living process that was partially oral, and that each generation received anew, worked over and accommodated, and made into its own. In the different layers of the tradition it was possible to find the views on religion, society, and self-understanding that each generation found important.

Wellhausen had switched the order of the prophets and the law. For Wellhausen and his followers it was the prophets who played the most important part in the religious development of ancient Israel. Von Rad, however, insisted on seeing the whole issue in light of the development of the traditions of election in the Pentateuch. The prophets built on these very same ancient traditions. Therefore the "law," the torah, must be the oldest. The characteristic of prophecy is that it interprets the faith and history of ancient Israel in light of the law, in a critical period of the history of Israel.

The prophets give the law a new and radical meaning. At the same time, they represent a renewal of the ancient "kerygmatic salvation history" but with the opposite result. Salvation history is no longer the story of God who has chosen a people, but the story of God who judges his people. The national decline that the Israelite people experienced from the eighth to the sixth century BCE forms part of YHWH's salvation history. History becomes the necessary punishment for rebellion, apostasy, and disobedience. But the prophets see beyond their time. They also see that YHWH once again will forgive his people, that he will "reelect" his people in the future. In this way, the prophets project salvation history into the future. They always presuppose the promises of the law. The future reelection will happen just as the past election once happened.

By associating the literary composition of the Pentateuch with the theological concept of salvation history, von Rad made a brilliant theological contribution to the hermeneutical problem of the Old Testament. However, this scheme requires the prophets to be relegated to a spectator's seat, with a direct view of the grand salvation-historical drama as a macrostructure of the whole Old Testament. No matter how attractive this angle may seem, it relies on external theological prejudices, and may transform biblical prophecy into something it is not.

Von Rad's student and successor in Heidelberg, Hans Walter Wolff (1911–1993), has also provided a number of important contributions to the tradition-historical study of the prophets. Wolff has, in particular, tried to show how the tradition-historical approach casts light on the social and cultural background of the prophets. In an article on "Hosea's spiritual background" (1956), Wolff developed the thesis that Hosea's background was to be found in cultic circles in northern Israel. Here Levites kept alive several of the ancient YHWH cult's salvation-historical institutions, as well as legal traditions. These prophetic Levitical circles must be seen as the predecessors of the prophets, according to Wolff.

This thesis came to have some influence through Wolff's commentary on Hosea from 1965 (Eng. trans. 1974). Here he joins those scholars who claim that cultic traditions play a major role for the understanding of the prophets. But when he gets to the prophet Amos, Wolff is no longer satisfied to place the prophet into a cultic situation. A number of scholars had claimed that Amos could be understood only in such a cultic context. For example, the Norwegian scholar Arvid S. Kapelrud (1912–1994), in *Central Ideas in Amos* (1956), had tried to show that Amos was a cult prophet. Wolff was not satisfied with the attempt to understand Amos in light of the cultic traditions of ancient Israel, and his studies of Amos led him to the view that Amos had his "spiritual background" in the tribal wisdom of ancient Israel. Later he made similar claims about the prophet Micah. Inspired by Wolff, other scholars have tried to show that the prophet Isaiah also had his background in ancient Israelite wisdom traditions.

Seen in hindsight, none of these explanations seem very convincing, and they confirm that we cannot easily use form-critical and tradition-historical observations to reconstruct the "original" environment of the prophets. At the same time, therefore, these scholars have also unintentionally exposed the many uncertainties of this method. We have to be very careful before we claim that the prevalence of a certain vocabulary or phraseology tells us anything about whether a prophet belonged to a particular historical setting.

The same caution should be applied when it comes to possibilities of getting access to "original" and "genuine" prophetic utterances. The idea of prophetic religion in ancient Israel was discovered in the nineteenth century. Gradually, scholars have become aware that the prophetic books, just like the other biblical books, have gone through a long and complicated process of development. With the help of the various methods that were used (literary criticism, tradition history, form criticism, redaction criticism), it came to be the foremost task of biblical scholars to attempt to distinguish between the original words of the prophets and what had been added later in the tradition process. Since then, a lot of scholarly energy has gone into trying to reconstruct the prophets' ipsissima verba, what the prophets "really said."

Since this short survey of the history of Hebrew Bible prophecy scholarship has focused on certain illustrative highlights, it is naturally quite uneven. In reality, twentieth-century prophecy scholars used not only historical-critical methods but applied a rich variety of approaches. Modern researchers have dissected and reworked the prophetic corpus of the Hebrew Bible again and again in efforts to gain new insights. Methods that have been used are theological, philological, historical, archaeological, folkloristic, sociological, anthropological, linguistic, and literary. Especially after the mid-1960s, approaches influenced by structuralism and narratology (the Bible as literature) became quite popular. Toward the end of the century, a growing number of scholars worked with approaches to the final form of the texts, slowly replacing, or supplementing, traditional historical-critical methods.

PRESENT-DAY PROPHETIC RESEARCH

Today, one hundred years or so after critical scholarship of the Bible seriously got under way, there is still no real consensus about how to view the prophetic movement in ancient Israel. Several of the questions that were posed at the beginning of the twentieth century still seem relevant. Who were the Old Testament prophets? What function did they have in ancient Israelite society? What role have they played in the development of ancient Israelite religion? Such questions imply that prophetic research is still heavily dominated by historical interests.

In the most recent period, however, we have been witnessing an increasing dissatisfaction with the results of much traditional historical-critical research. Following a radicalization of the question of the prophets' ipsissima verba, an increasing number of scholars now claim that the problem is about to become obsolete because the biblical prophetic texts, in their present shape, do not go back to preexilic named prophets at all. Instead these books are postexilic compositions of a completely different character. What we are witnessing is a radical, but necessary, reorientation within the study of biblical prophecy.

We have observed above that the biblical traditions show a strong tendency to attribute as many as possible of the books of the Bible to named authors. At the same time it is unthinkable that the texts, in their present shape, can go back to these postulated authors. It is enough to mention some of the better-known examples. Modern biblical research has shown us that the books of Moses cannot go back to Moses, that the psalms of David cannot go back to King David, and that Proverbs cannot go back to King Solomon. This raises the interesting question, why should this be any different with the prophets? What is it that makes the superscriptions of the prophetic books more reliable than the superscriptions of other biblical books? Work on the book of Isaiah, for example, has long since shown that this book consists of not one but two or three different prophetic books. I shall here mention only a small selection of recent publications that address this type of question within prophetic studies.

A leading commentator on Isaiah, Otto Kaiser, claims that the core of Proto- or First Isaiah, Isaiah 1–39, consisted of a handful of prophetic utterances. These prophetic words come from the beginning of the fifth century BCE, and had as their purpose to interpret the collapse of the kingdom of Judah. In the beginning of the book of Isaiah we read, "The vision of Isaiah son of Amoz, which he saw concerning Judah and Jerusalem in the days of Uzziah, Jotham, Ahaz, and Hezekiah, kings of Judah." According to Kaiser, this "Isaiah of Jerusalem," who would have been active around the mid-eighth century BCE, disappears into legend.

With the so-called Deutero- or Second Isaiah, Isaiah 40–55, the overall consensus places it in the sixth century BCE. But also here we witness the same type of tendencies as the one Kaiser represents. For example, Jean M. Vincent claimed in 1977 (*Studien zur literarischen Eigenart und zur geistigen Heimat von Jesaja, Kap. 40–55*) that there was no such prophet Deutero-Isaiah, but that Isaiah 40–55, which for the most part comes from cult prophecy at the Jerusalem temple, is a result of the work of several authors and editors. The various traditions were transmitted through several generations before they were collected into one text in postexilic times.

A similar view has been upheld by the Englishman John H. Eaton in *Festal Drama in Deutero-Isaiah* (1979). And in one of the latest substantial commentaries Robert Carroll (1941–2000) claims that the book of Jeremiah has little to do with the preexilic prophet Jeremiah (1986). What we find in the biblical book of Jeremiah is an anthology created by the Deuteronomistic redactors in exilic and postexilic times. The result is a prophetic book in the form that the redactors' contemporaries thought a prophetic book should have.

In Denmark the Aarhus scholar Knud Jeppesen published a thesis on the book of Micah, "Tears Are Not Wounds" (1987). The debate about the "authenticity" of Micah has at times been heated. The most radical scholars have wanted to make substantial cuts in the book, and have seen up to two-thirds of it as late additions. The remaining third is then supposed to have gone back to a prophet Micah, who, according to the book's superscription, lived at about the same time as "Isaiah of Jerusalem." Jeppesen's thesis, in brief, is that the book of Micah in its present form can be read as a comprehensive unified composition that was composed in the exilic period. The authors, or editors, of the book of Micah have combined ancient Micah traditions with their own message. The purpose of the composition is the desire to convince the audience about the causes of the destruction of Jerusalem and the deportation into exile, and why they now have good reason for new hope.

In this view, the purpose of the work is the same as that of Deutero-Isaiah (Isaiah 40–55). Jeppesen points to the possibility that the exilic redactors of the book of Micah may be identical with the redactors of the book of Isaiah. According to Jeppesen, the rise of ancient Israelite prophetic traditions must be sought in legends of the same type as those in the Deuteronomistic History. In the course of time, interest shifted from the stories about the prophets to the words they had spoken. Gradually the historical framework of the prophetic words disappeared. With this, the foundation was laid for the use and reuse of the prophets' words by each new generation. Parts of the traditions were transmitted orally, and parts in writing. From this traditional material it is not possible to reconstruct any ipsissima verba.

The apparent contradiction between what the prophetic texts themselves claim to be and what modern biblical researchers believe they are has come even more into focus with the most recent developments within what has been called "inner-biblical exegesis." This term sums up an increasing attentiveness among biblical scholars that textual interpretation is not something that is limited to the postbiblical period. Textual understanding and textual interpretation not only represent a "post-textual" phenomenon, but also play an important role in the reworking of biblical textual traditions and in the development of the biblical texts.

More than ever before, today scholars are aware that there has been a tendency to draw an artificial distinction between the fixed text and later reworking of this tradition. Editing and reworking do not begin after the text, but do themselves constitute elements in the growth of the text. Thus prophetic books need to be evaluated through a dual aspect that considers the text/ tradition both as what is being transmitted and as the interpretation that the transmitters by necessity work into the text as they appropriate it and pass it on. The interpretation of the "scholar-scribes" is worked into the text to such a degree that it can no longer be distinguished from the "original" (even the terminology "original" can no longer be upheld, and becomes absurd in this context). The interpretation itself becomes part of the text. Among researchers who have worked with the prophetic traditions along these lines are Martti Nissinen and Ehud Ben Zvi.

The above examples can be seen as quite representative of some of the latest developments within prophetic research. It is not a novelty that scholarship questions the nature of the historicity of Old Testament prophets, of course. One problem in particular has been that the Deuteronomistic History (Deuteronomy, Joshua, Judges, Samuel, and Kings), which tells the story of the Israelite people from the settlement of the land to the time of the exile, with a few exceptions does not mention the writing prophets. Because of this, scholars already at the beginning of the twentieth century claimed that the prophetic books of the Old Testament were late postexilic pseudonymous compositions.

PROPHECY AS A PHENOMENON

We see how, in the wake of recent research, a number of new fundamental and central questions immediately arise. Did the prophets not exist at all? Have all of the biblical prophetic texts in reality been written at a much later date, and under totally different circumstances, from what the texts themselves tell us? Are Amos, Micah, Hosea, Jeremiah, Isaiah, Ezekiel, and the other prophetic texts only a set of pseudepigraphical literary creations from late postexilic times that lay claim to a number of legendary figures in order to increase their trustworthiness? What about the whole ancient Israelite prophetic movement? Is it simply a fiction?

All of the above questions reveal that we need to start thinking about prophets and prophecy in new and different ways. As with all biblical research that has been conducted under the label "historical-critical," prophetic research has been characterized by an ultrapositivistic empiricism, where discussions about so-called historical truths have dominated the scene. But historical research the way it is (or should be) done in the academy today has changed greatly since the breakthrough of historical consciousness in intellectual history in nineteenth-century Germany.

An increased awareness has led to other ways of understanding what we really mean, or can mean, when we say that something is "true" in history, for example, in the work of Hans-Georg Gadamer and Paul Ricoeur. For example, prophetic texts can be true in the same way that a historical novel is "true," as a representative presentation of historical possibilities. Future prophetic research, therefore, must to a greater degree concentrate on the phenomenon of prophecy, and to a lesser degree on hypothetical reconstructions of individual historical prophets. This does not imply that we should leave the history problem. Rather, we should adjust our history project to a more realistic one.

A clear tendency in recent research is to give more and more of the biblical material a late date. "Late" is in itself an imprecise term. Even though a few researchers seem to think that the traditions were created in the postexilic period, most scholars agree that the material received its final form and was fixed in writing at a late date. The essential question has always been, which traditions existed prior to the final editing? What did these traditions look like? I think that if we can learn anything from the history of research of the Old Testament it must be that we cannot really answer these questions. At the same time, the biblical material is so diverse and so complex that the possibility for it to have come about in any other way than through a reworking of previously existing traditions is not likely. This means that the foundation for many of the traditions must come from earlier times.

Today we could attempt in various ways to reach back to ancient Israelite prophecy as a historical phenomenon. Among them, comparisons between the texts of the Hebrew Bible and prophecy in extrabiblical sources should be a high priority. From a long range of Near Eastern texts (e.g., the Mari texts, Neo-Assyrian royal inscriptions, and West Semitic inscriptions) we know that certain persons stood in a privileged relationship with the deities and communicated their message. There is a long series of very clear parallels between extrabiblical prophecy and what we can read in the Hebrew Bible about the activity of the prophets. The phenomenon described in the Old Testament, what we, grossly oversimplifying, call ancient Israelite prophecy, can therefore not be written off as a purely literary phenomenon. Judged against the background of the existing Hebrew Bible traditions, as well as the extrabiblical material, it is obvious that prophets must have existed in ancient Israel.

Equally relevant for "prophecy as a phenomenon" is the ways prophets and prophecy are described in the historiographical and other parts of the Hebrew Bible. Again, we are witnessing a change in attitude among scholars working with prophecy. Formerly, it was believed that the kind of prophecy that is described in, for instance, the Deuteronomistic History represents an earlier and more primitive form of prophecy. The "real" prophets were the great "prophets of doom," Isaiah, Jeremiah, Ezekiel, and the Twelve "Minor" Prophets. Today, many see considerable similarities between the kinds of prophecy described in these two groups of texts.

A major prophetic figure in the Deuteronomistic History is Samuel. First Samuel 3 tells the story of how YHWH revealed himself to Samuel in Shiloh, and how all the people understood that "Samuel was a trustworthy prophet of the LORD (YHWH)." In the story of Samuel we can also read about how the prophet appeared as a kind of psychic who could be used for seemingly everyday tasks such as to say where the lost she-donkeys had gone (1 Samuel 9). In the same chapter, we can read about how the prophets received wages for their work, which are also mentioned in 1 Kings 14.

According to 1 Samuel 28 there were several ways of coming into contact with YHWH. It could happen through dreams, by Urim, or through prophets. Prophetic activity is indicated in Hebrew by the noun *nabi'* (or *navi'*, plural *nevi'im*), "prophet," and the verb *nibba'*, "to prophesy." Also used are the verbs *chazah* and *ra'ah*, "to view" or "to see" (prophetically), with the nouns derived from them: *chozeh* and *ro'eh*, "seer." "Man of God," *'ish ha'elohim*, is another term that appears.

One characteristic of prophecy is the state of ecstasy that the prophets could attain. The word *nibba'* can mean to prophesy, but is sometimes used in the sense of "being in [or: to be put into] prophetic frenzy." Trancelike, ecstatic states are well known from many cultures, not just in antiquity. The term "ecstasy" is an imprecise term that is used of a number of different states ranging from being fully conscious to being completely cut off from the self, time, and space. We do not have enough information in the Hebrew Bible to be able to say much about prophetic ecstasy. That it refers to a complete loss of consciousness is, however, not likely. We also have to count the possibility that the phenomenon could have varied according to different contexts and times.

It is clear from the Deuteronomistic History that the prophets played a major role in their societies. In 1 Kings it is a priest and a prophet who perform the task of anointing Solomon as king. In 2 Kings 9 a prophet anoints King Jehu. The prophets also perform the role as advisors to the kings in many different contexts.

Many miracle stories are associated with the activity of the prophets in the Deuteronomistic History. In 2 Kings 4 several wonder stories are told about the prophet Elisha. Among other things, in one of two feeding miracles twenty loaves of rye bread are enough to feed the whole people during a famine.

In times of disaster, particularly during times of national crisis, the prophets became important figures. In 1 Kings 14 we read about how King Jeroboam's wife disguises herself and seeks out the prophet Ahijah from Shiloh, in order to find out what will happen to her sick son. In reality, this story contains more than a tragic family event. Since the death of a king's son might have dynastic implications, this narrative too concerns an issue of national importance.

Dramatic and heavily tendentious is the story in 1 Kings 18 about the contest on Mount Carmel between the 450 prophets of Baal and 400 prophets of Asherah on the one side, and the lone prophet of YHWH, Elijah, on the other. But the issue at stake is typical: there is a crisis in the country, there is drought and famine. We read again and again in the Bible that drought in ancient Israel means famine and death. In times such as these, the people turned to YHWH through their prophets to ask for help. At the same time, the story of the prophets on Mount Carmel vividly illustrates the contest that was going on in polytheistic Israel. Which of the gods was stronger? Was it YHWH or Baal?

Both the issues of the intercessory prayer in times of crisis and the contest with the "foreign" deities stand in the center of ancient Israelite prophecy. This holds true for the Deuteronomistic History as well as the so-called writing prophets. Phenomenologically, we cannot see any difference between the two groups of prophets. When rain did not fall and the drought came, the Deuteronomists saw this as punishment from YHWH (see Deut. 28:23–24). A similar view is expressed by the writing prophets, as in 1 Kings 18 (see Amos 4:7–8; Joel 1; Jer. 3:3; 14:1–7). Also the "divine contest" is important in the writing prophets. Through their accusations, followed by the exhortation of the audience to leave "foreign gods" and follow YHWH as their only God, the prophets stand close to the Deuteronomists on this issue. In texts such as Isaiah 2:6; 27:9; Jeremiah 7:31; 11:13; Ezekiel 6:6; 8:14; Hosea 8:4–6, 14; Micah 1:7; Zephaniah 1:4–5; and Zechariah 10:2 we find examples of this type of polemic against other gods.

The texts give us a fairly clear impression of the type of religion that the prophets fought against in their contemporary society. Ancient Israel was a clearly polytheistic landscape where YHWH was being worshiped as one of several gods. From these texts it is also clear that in the eyes of the prophets the Israelites did not consist of a group of faithful YHWH worshipers, but that they worshiped several gods. As such, the prophets of YHWH acted almost as missionaries who propagandized the YHWH cult. At stake here is exactly what we find in the story about the divine contest on Mount Carmel in 1 Kings 18. The reward that the prophets held up to their audience, should they choose to follow YHWH, was clear. Salvation in ancient Israel was of this life, completely devoid of eschatological concepts of the other side. If the people followed YHWH, and obeyed him as their God, they would be saved from war, drought, famine, disease, and exile. It is in this context that we must understand the prophetic words of judgment against the Israelite people. The last issue, "exile," reflects the historical fact that throughout the first millennium BCE the Assyrian and Babylonian empires used deportations as a means of controlling their empires.

One issue of ancient Israelite prophecy that easily lends itself to misunderstanding is the oracle of judgment against the prophet's own people. This has to do, not least, with the nature of prophetic language, with a frequent use of rhetorical and poetic expressions. Next, it also has to do with a lack of ability to set the prophetic words of judgment against the people into a larger context. When we pay the necessary attention to the fact that we are dealing with a piece of Near Eastern rhetoric in a highly poetic form, it will become clear that the "words of judgment" cannot be understood as absolute and final, but as conditional and educational. They serve a function of threat and warning more than any real judgment. There is therefore no reason to wonder, as many have done, why we find in the prophetic texts a mixture of harsh words of judgment and words of salvation side by side. If people turn to YHWH, things will go well. If they do not, things will go badly. This is the logic of the Old Testament prophetic words of judgment.

Wars in the ancient Near East were all so-called holy wars, for the gods stood behind a nation and guided the military actions. The deities even joined in actively on the battlefield. It was also this way in ancient Israel. Therefore it is not so strange that the prophets also played a significant role in many different situations of war. In Judges 6 YHWH sends a prophet to assist the Israelites just when they are about to lose to the Midianites. The account in 1 Samuel 15 is also illustrative. Here the prophet Samuel claims authority over Saul by pointing out that he was the one who was sent by YHWH to anoint Saul king, and then he intervenes in the battle against the desert people, the Amalekites. And 1 Samuel 7 describes Samuel as intercessor and intermediary between YHWH and the people prior to a battle against the Philistines. Another illustration is found in Judges 20, where the priest Phinehas, the grandson of Aaron, consults YHWH before the battle (Judg. 20:28). Phinehas received the following answer from YHWH to the question of whether they should go out to war against the Benjaminites: "Go up, for tomorrow I will give them into your hand."

Even though we cannot consider these accounts "historical," they still give a good illustration of the phenomenon of holy war, and the significance of the role of the prophets in warfare in ancient Israel. Like so many narratives of the Hebrew Bible, they therefore give away historical information at least indirectly. The step from intercessor to advisor was not very far, and this gave the prophets a powerful position in society. In the war account in 1 Kings 20 about the Aramean king Ben-hadad and King Ahab of the northern kingdom of Israel, a prophet appears as an advisor in military affairs. We notice the role of the gods in this story. After the Israelites had won an overwhelming victory, the men of the Aramean king explain the defeat to him. They lost because the Israelite gods are mountain gods. If the battle had taken place on the plains, the Arameans would have won. The victory over the enemy was simultaneously a show of the gods' power.

The role that prophets played in warfare is also seen in the story about the seer Balaam in Numbers 22–24. Balaam was a well-known seer who was summoned to curse the Israelites so that Balak, the Moabite king, would defeat their army. In the account of Balaam we see how the role of the prophet appears as both divinatory (he sees the future) and performative. In this lies the key to understanding a central part of the prophetic literature, the oracles of judgment against other nations. The performative component in many ways constitutes the lost element in the understanding of ancient Israelite prophecy.

That prophets played such an important role in situations of war has left clear traces also in the writing prophets. The powerful poetic language is, in part, strongly colored by the concept of holy war. The oracles of judgment against other nations stand in a category of their own in the writing prophets. Nevertheless, these oracles have almost always been viewed as less important in recent biblical research. Earlier scholars, like Hermann Gunkel, emphasized the words against the nations, and even spoke of them as the foundational prophetic form. More recent scholars, like Claus Westermann, have disregarded them almost completely. But we cannot neglect the fact that oracles of judgment against other nations make up large parts of all the prophetic books (see, for example, Isaiah 13–23; Jeremiah 46–51; Ezekiel 25–32; 35; 38–39; Amos 1:1–2:3). In fact, two prophetic books in the Book of the Twelve, Obadiah and Nahum, consist almost entirely of oracles of judgment against other nations. The historical context for the oracles of judgment against other nations was holy war, possibly including the practice of cursing the enemy on the battlefield. The extent to which this phenomenon eventually became poetic remains an unanswered question. We have to consider that what we have now in the various large collections of prophetic texts is a type of rhetorical national and theological literature severed from any concrete situation of war.

We find further interesting information about prophecy as a phenomenon in, for example, the book of Jeremiah. From the account of Jeremiah's calling in the beginning of the book we see that he was called to be a prophet to the nations, not to Judah. In Jeremiah 28:8 Jeremiah speaks about the prophetic role to his adversary, the prophet Hananiah, saying, "The prophets who preceded you and me from ancient times prophesied war, famine, and pestilence against many countries and great kingdoms."

In Jeremiah 21 we read about the role of the prophet as intercessor. Here the last king of Judah, Zedekiah, sends two of his priests to Jeremiah with the following petition, "Please inquire of the Lord (YHWH) on our behalf, for King Nebuchadrezzar of Babylon is making war against us; perhaps the Lord will perform a wonderful deed for us, as he has often done, and will make him withdraw from us." In this text the prophet's role in times of crisis is quite clear. As the intermediary between YHWH and the people, here represented by the king, the prophet is asked to consult YHWH in order to find out the attitude of the Deity. The prophet has the function of intermediary or intercessor. The answer that the king's delegation receives is clearly not what they had hoped for. Instead of giving them hope, Jeremiah imparts that YHWH will not help them, but that they are facing disaster. Only if they give themselves over to the Babylonian king will they survive.

Another text of interest in relation to prophecy as a phenomenon is Jeremiah 14. Here the situation is different, but also in this case there is a situation of crisis, a critical period of drought. The drought and its consequences are described in verses 1–6. Later, Jeremiah steps into the situation (vv. 11–16).

> The LORD said to me: Do not pray for the welfare of this people. Although they fast, I do not hear their cry, and although they offer burnt offering and grain offering, I do not accept them; but by the sword, by famine, and by pestilence I consume them.
> Then I said: "Ah, Lord GOD! Here are the prophets saying to them, 'You shall not see the sword, nor shall you have famine, but I will give you true peace in this place.'" And the LORD said to me: The prophets are prophesying lies in my name; I did not send them, nor did I command them or speak to them. They are prophesying to you a lying vision, worthless divination, and the deceit of their own minds. Therefore thus says the LORD concerning the prophets who prophesy in my name though I did not send them, and who say, "Sword and famine shall not come on this land": By sword and famine those prophets shall be consumed. And the people to whom they prophesy shall be thrown out into the streets of Jerusalem, victims of famine and sword. There shall be no one to bury them—themselves, their wives, their sons, and their daughters. For I will pour out their wickedness upon them.

In this text we are given a good impression of both the prophet's role as intercessor and the opposition between Jeremiah and the prophets that he calls false prophets, those who are not sent by YHWH.

The intercessory function is illustrated further in the beginning of Jeremiah 15, with the following interesting utterance, "The LORD (YHWH) said to me: Though Moses and Samuel stood before me, yet my heart would not turn toward this people." As we can see, here Moses and Samuel are counted among the greatest prophets and therefore also as the greatest intercessors or intermediaries. So great is the people's failure, according to Jeremiah, that even these great men of God would not be able to change the fate of the people.

In yet another text, Jeremiah 35:15, we read, "I have sent to you all my servants the prophets, sending them persistently, saying 'Turn now everyone of you from your evil way, and amend your doings, and do not go after other gods to serve them, and then you shall live in the land that I gave to you and your ancestors.' But you did not incline your ear or obey me." As we see here, it is not only the worship of the Israelites that the prophets are concerned with, but also their conduct in life (for other examples see Isa. 1:23; 59:3–7; Jer. 9:2–6; Ezek. 9:9; Hos. 10:4; Amos 2:6–8; Mic. 2:1–2; Hab. 1:3–4; Zeph. 3:1–4).

The style and content of the quote from Jeremiah sounds unmistakably Deuteronomistic. The common view among scholars is, again, that we here are dealing with a Deuteronomistic reworking of the book of Jeremiah, and thus not a genuine prophetic oracle. It is, however, a more likely model that the Deuteronomistic tradition itself builds on ancient prophetic material. A common denominator for the prophets whose books have been handed down to us is that they are very negative in their attitude to their contemporary society. They chastise and criticize their society and utter strong oracles of judgment against their own people. The disapproval by the prophets is religious, but also of a moral and political character.

In their criticism the prophets point to the past. The present is seen as a decline compared to an earlier golden age. In Isaiah 1:23 the leaders of Israel are criticized, "Your princes are rebels and companions of thieves, everyone loves a bribe and runs after gifts, they do not defend the orphan, and the widow's cause does not come before them." Against this, the prophets posited better "earlier times." In Isaiah 1:26 we read, "And I will restore your judges as at the first, and your counselors as at the beginning. Afterward you shall be called the city of righteousness, the faithful city."

Similar ideas are expressed in Jeremiah 2:2: "Go and proclaim in the hearing of Jerusalem, thus says the LORD: I remember the devotion of your youth, your love as a bride, how you followed me in the wilderness, in a land not sown." After this, there follows a long recapitulation of the salvation history of Israel. The portrayal, which talks about the exodus from Egypt, the settlement of the land, and the apostasy that began as soon as Israel took possession of the promised land, is strongly reminiscent of the Deuteronomists.

Also in Ezekiel we find similar ideas. Chapter 16 portrays, in highly poetic language, a newborn infant girl who grows up to be a beautiful woman. This image portrays the relationship between YHWH and the people from the time of the election. In Ezekiel 16:43 we read, "Because you have not remembered the days of your youth, but have enraged me with all these things; therefore, I have returned your deeds upon your head, says the Lord GOD." The issue at stake in Ezekiel 16 is completely in line with the salvation-historical view of the Deuteronomists, but the style and language differ somewhat.

Also in the Book of the Twelve Prophets we find the concept of the good times of the past. In Hosea 9:10 we read, "Like grapes in the wilderness,

I found Israel. Like the first fruit on the fig tree, in its first season, I saw your ancestors. But they came to Baal-peor, and consecrated themselves to a thing of shame, and became detestable like the thing they loved." The episode alluded to is found in Numbers 25. And in Amos 3:1–2, "Hear this word that the LORD has spoken against you, O people of Israel, against the whole family that I brought up out of the land of Egypt: You only have I known of all the families of the earth; therefore I will punish you for all your iniquities."

It is an important point for several of the prophets that the apostasy began very early, already in the desert period. This is clear in the text from Hosea cited above. Amos 5:25 mentions the worship of "foreign" gods also in the desert. And in Jeremiah 7:25–26 we read, "From the day that your ancestors came out of the land of Egypt until this day, I have persistently sent all my servants the prophets to them, day after day; yet they did not listen to me, or pay attention, but they stiffened their necks. They did worse than their ancestors did" (see also Jer. 2:5–6 and 11:7–8). Something similar can be found in Hosea 6:5: "Therefore I have hewn them by the prophets, I have killed them by the words of my mouth, and my judgment goes forth as the light."

As with several other biblical authors, the prophets conceive of an earlier ideal time and a people who have "left YHWH." This ideal period is a purely theological concept, and has nothing to do with any historical reality.

There is no reason to think that the prophets have invented the traditions that they use. Just like the other biblical authors, they stand as transmitters and reusers of traditions that come from earlier generations and that they find relevant in the present. It is probably futile to inquire further about the origin and development of these traditions. As the transmitted tradition has probably changed greatly through the centuries, this type of attempt too often ends in pure speculation. In the prophets we possibly find the concepts of election, ideal past, and apostasy in their earliest accessible form. We have reason to assume that the prophets were the predecessors of the Deuteronomists. With this being the case, we understand that the prophets of ancient Israel played a very important role in the development of Old Testament religion.

THE PROPHETS AND THE "CLASSICAL" RELIGION OF ANCIENT ISRAEL

A major part of the prophets' message consists of criticism leveled at the religious and moral conduct of the people, and especially of the leadership. The Deuteronomists describe the history of Israel and Judah from the point of view that the people "originally" followed YHWH but later left him. The prophets claim that this happened already in the time of the desert wanderings. The Deuteronomists, Priestly writers, and Chroniclers all understand the history of Israel from the perspective of election, covenant, and apostasy.

There is reason to assume that it is thanks to the prophetic establishment and its custodianship that these traditions were kept for posterity. The reworking and transmission of these fundamental theological concepts made it possible for subsequent generations of learned scribes to receive and to make use of them. Now, the prophets did not invent election, covenant, and apostasy. There were most likely traditions that they built on, but we do not have access to them. In the prophetic literature, traditions about election are used consciously in order to put a certain perspective on prophetic activity. We know that the religion of ancient Israel did not distinguish itself in any large measure from its neighboring cultures in the ancient Near East. What distinguished Israel from its surroundings was the power that lay in the prophetic movement, which later was adapted by the Deuteronomistic, Priestly, and Chronistic circles.

What we associate with the "classical" YHWH religion, as we know it from the Hebrew Bible, clearly did not exist in ancient Israel, but constitutes a postexilic phenomenon. The most important single cause of the synthesis that we find in the historiographical works of the Old Testament was presumably conditions surrounding the fall of Jerusalem. With the demise of Judah as a political entity, and the deportation of the royal family and some of the leading circles to Babylon, there arose a need for an ideological trial, characterized by national and theological reflection on the catastrophe that had struck the people.

This means that the prophets played a significant role in the development that led to what became "classical" YHWH religion. From the biblical sources, it appears that some prophets fought for the religion of YHWH early on as the only acceptable religion. In the same way, the prophets of Baal fought for their religion. When the religion of YHWH finally ended up victorious in the late postexilic period, the traditions of the competing prophets were lost for posterity. The bitter fight that "our" prophets fought in their many political but also religiously polemical and prophet-critical utterances is crowned with victory. As regards "the other," the so-called prophets of Baal and the false prophets, there are only a few notes and episodes scattered here and there. One such example would be the Hananiah story in Jeremiah 28.

That the "classical" prophets were saved for posterity, and not all of those who now are forgotten (those who, according to Ezek. 13:9, "shall not be enrolled in the register of the house of Israel"), can be explained by the fact that they were proven right after the fact. The prophets who prophesied "peace, peace" (Jer. 6:14; Ezek. 13:10; Mic. 3:5), became the losers. That this was not the case in the prophets' own time can be seen from the biographical parts of Jeremiah and Amos. Here we learn that the "classical" prophets were not considered "classical" in their own time, but represented the opposition, and only one alternative among many.

THE BOOK OF ISAIAH

The book of Isaiah does not consist of one unified work, but contains collections of various prophetic utterances. It is customary to divide the book into three main parts. In chapters 1–39 we find the first Isaiah (Proto-Isaiah), in chapters 40–55 the second Isaiah (Deutero-Isaiah), and in chapters 56–66 the third Isaiah (Trito-Isaiah). Whether it is correct to talk about a "third Isaiah" is somewhat controversial; some scholars think that we must look at all of Isaiah 40–66 as a collection of its own.

Scholars have divided the book of Isaiah in this way for several reasons. Common to all of them is that they take the background that is reflected in the various collections as their point of departure. A reading of the first part of the book, Isaiah 1–39, will draw up an image of a historical background where the most important events are the Syro-Ephraimite wars and the military threat of the Assyrians against Jerusalem. Both of these reflect conditions from the last half of the eighth century BCE. The content of Isaiah 1–39 consists of a mixture of oracles of judgment against Judah (with the prophet's own condemnation of the people for their transgressions), oracles against the neighboring nations, and a few oracles of blessing/promise to the people. The so-called messianic prophecies occupy a category of their own, especially Isaiah 7:14–17; 9:2–7; and 11:1–5.

The Hebrew word *mashiach*, "messiah, anointed one," can be used about any person who is anointed, but is used primarily about the kings of the Davidic dynasty (see Pss. 18:50; 89:20; 132:10, 17). According to 2 Samuel 7:8–16, the Davidic king is YHWH's specially chosen ruler. In the Hebrew Bible, the word *mashiach* ("messiah") is also sometimes associated with a prophetic expectation that YHWH will raise up an ideal king from the Davidic dynasty who will sit on the royal throne of Israel. But it is important to note that the prophetic books do not use the term "messiah" about this future king (see in addition to Isa. 7:14–17; 9:2–7; and 11:1–5 also Jer. 33:15 and Ezek. 37:23–24). In Daniel 9:25 the reconstruction of Jerusalem is associated with the arrival of the anointed one (a prince). The word "messiah" does not appear in the Hebrew Bible as a term for a future figure of salvation. This usage appears only in late times, perhaps as late as the first century CE. Even though the Christian usage has its background in the Old Testament, it is important to be aware that this represents a radical new reading of ancient Israelite concepts.

Isaiah 40–55 is usually referred to as "Second Isaiah" or "Deutero-Isaiah." A quick reading of Isaiah 40–55 reveals that we are dealing with a completely different historical background from what we find in Isaiah 1–39. Now it is no longer the Assyrians but the Babylonians who are on the stage. With Deutero-Isaiah we no longer find any threats of punishment and destruction. The judgment is already a fact. In 586 BCE the Babylonian king Nebuchadnezzar had conquered Jerusalem; taken control of the city walls, the royal palace, and the temple; and exiled some of the leaders of the people to Babylon. Therefore the tone of Isaiah 40–55 is quite different from that of Proto-Isaiah. It is not judgment but comfort that dominates. Already the opening words in Isaiah 40:1 strike the chord, "Comfort, O comfort my people, says your God." Now Judah is to be rebuilt as a nation, and the people are to return to their land. YHWH's sentence of judgment is over.

A particular problem in Deutero-Isaiah concerns the "Servant Songs," Isaiah 42:1–4; 49:1–6; 50:4–9; and 52:12–53:12. This group of texts is often referred to as "the songs of the suffering servant of the LORD (YHWH)." Ever since Bernhard Duhm distinguished the texts as separate from the Deutero-Isaian corpus, the discussion has continued. Do the texts originally belong within Isaiah 40–55, or are they later additions? Should they be understood collectively, as referring to Israel, or individually, as referring to a concrete historical person or a future figure? The literature on the so-called Servant Songs has in time grown to a disproportionately large corpus.

However, some scholars have claimed that these texts are not as mysterious as has been claimed. Rather, the group of texts fits in well with the message of Isaiah 40–55, and can probably best be understood as figurative references to the Judean people, who, after having gone through great suffering, now face a new future. This understanding is also in line with how Jewish tradition has understood the texts. One exception is Isaiah 53, which some early Jewish traditions understood as a text about the Israelite people, and others interpreted messianically, as relating to a future eschatological savior figure. Early Christianity, on the other hand, interpreted Isaiah 53 christologically, as a prophetic utterance about the suffering of Christ. However, in the original Hebrew text, Isaiah 53 too may be read in the same way as all the other Servant Songs, as a narrative about the people of God.

The last part of the book of Isaiah, chapters 56–66, is often called "Third Isaiah" (Trito-Isaiah). We are now no longer in the period just before the fall of Babylon, but in the Second Temple period, in the time of Ezra and Nehemiah. We are standing in the transitional period between Old Testament times and early Judaism, and it is characteristic that among oracles of salvation from YHWH to his people we also find emphasis on the Sabbath and the Law.

Some of the most recent research on Isaiah appears to put less emphasis on the division into three different prophetic books. It still seems to hold that the book of Isaiah does not consist of a collection of prophetic utterances that go back to one single prophet who lived in the eighth century BCE, but that it is a collection of various prophetic speeches edited in the Persian period. Recently, some scholars have begun to show interest in the redactional unity of the book and to look closer at the theology of the redactors. They have claimed that many similarities in the book of Isaiah can be found across the division into three separate collections.

THE BOOK OF JEREMIAH

The superscription of the book of Jeremiah, found in 1:1–3, attributes all fifty-two chapters of the book to the prophet Jeremiah, who was active in the dramatic last decades before the fall of Jerusalem in 586 BCE. There are several theories about what the relation might be between the material that exists today in the book of Jeremiah and the prophet Jeremiah. They range on a scale from a total denial of the possibility of finding any traces of the historical prophet Jeremiah to the acceptance of the bulk of the book as historically genuine.

A reading of the book of Jeremiah gives an impression of a long and complicated process of composition. This is clear not least from the seemingly arbitrary arrangement of the material in the book. Despite the historical framework, much of the material is not presented as a coherent narrative but appears helter-skelter. This makes it difficult to find the thread of the book. Further, there are many duplicate texts (e.g., 6:12–15 = 8:10–12; 7:1–15 = 26:1–6; 23:5–6 = 33:15–16).

Moreover, the text of the Septuagint (LXX) is one-eighth shorter than the Masoretic Text (MT). For example, the MT Jeremiah 33:14–26 and 39:4–13 are missing from LXX. Also the order of the material is different in LXX. While the oracles against other nations in MT are placed last in the book (chaps. 46–51), they appear after 25:13 in LXX. Even the internal order of the oracles against the nations is different in LXX and MT. While there used to be several different explanations for this, the discovery of fragments of the text of Jeremiah among the Dead Sea Scrolls has shown that there must have existed two different Hebrew versions of the book of Jeremiah prior to the standardization of MT. While the fragments 4QJer[a] correspond to MT, 4QJer[b] corresponds to LXX.

The material in the book of Jeremiah appears, then, as a fairly unedited collection of prophetic utterances. The content includes both prose and poetry. The poetry consists mostly of various oracles of judgment and oracles of salvation against Judah and Jerusalem. We find these mainly in Jeremiah 1–25. Another collection of poetry, Jeremiah 46–51, contains oracles of judgment against other nations. In a category by itself stand the so-called laments of Jeremiah (11:18–12:3; 15:10–21; 17:14–18; 18:18–23; 20:7–18). Such individual songs of lament are not found in any other prophetic book.

The prose in the book of Jeremiah is of various types. Examples of prose can be found in 7:1–15; 11:1–23; 13:1–11; 16:1–13; 17:19–27; 18:1–12; 21:1–10; 22:1–5; 25:1–14; 34:8–22; 35:1–19. Because of the many points of similarity between some of the prose texts and the style and language of the Deuteronomists, many scholars have seen these prose pieces in the book of Jeremiah as Deuteronomistic reworkings. But this is not necessary. In a category of their own stand the many biographical accounts—for example, those in Jeremiah 26–29 and 36; these are also unusual in a prophetic book, though they do occur in some (e.g., Isaiah 37–39).

The theology of the book of Jeremiah is characterized by concepts about the covenant that YHWH has entered into with his people. Jeremiah constantly points to YHWH's acts with his people in history. At the same time, history is a witness to a people that has fallen away from their God. Jeremiah uses imagery from the relationship between man and woman. Israel has been unfaithful and has followed other gods, like Baal and Asherah. With the breach of the covenant follows violation of justice. The people, especially their leaders (kings, priests, and prophets), have transgressed against the law of YHWH. Against this background Jeremiah admonishes the people to repent. The prophetic activity of Jeremiah took place during the last years of the kingdom of Judah. The prophet plays a major role during the dramatic occurrences around the fall of Jerusalem in 586 BCE; he interprets the fall of Jerusalem as punishment from YHWH for the sins of the people.

The book of Jeremiah is one of the most important sources for the history not only of Judah but for the entire ancient Near East in the period of the neo-Babylonian rise to power. However, due to the nature of the texts, it has to be used with great caution for historical reconstructions.

THE BOOK OF EZEKIEL

According to the superscription in 1:3, the book of Ezekiel is attributed to the priest Ezekiel, son of Buzi, who was active in the sixth century BCE. According to 1:1, Ezekiel was among those exiled to Babylon, where he received the call to be a prophet. The book gives a clear impression of being thoroughly edited and follows a consistent pattern. We do not know who this redactor was.

The tone of the book of Ezekiel differs in many ways from what some may associate with prophecy. With respect to style and content, the book of Ezekiel makes us think of priests rather than prophets. The whole book shows signs of the priestly way of understanding religion. For example, the role of purity (clean and unclean) and holiness is similar in Ezekiel and in the Priestly History. Trito-Isaiah (Isaiah 56–66), Haggai, and Malachi contain similar traits.

However, we should not look upon Old Testament prophecy too narrowly. Although Ezekiel differs in some ways from other prophetic books, it also has a number of traits in common with them. We find a visionary call narrative, accusations, and words of doom and words of salvation to Judah and their leaders, as well as words against foreign nations. In the same way as Hosea and Jeremiah, Ezekiel describes the apostasy of Israel with imagery from the marriage between man and woman.

At the center of the book's concept of religion stands the holiness of the temple, particularly the vision of the temple, Ezekiel 40–48, with the holiness of YHWH as the focus. The Temple Mount has here become the mountain of the world, and Jerusalem the center of the universe. We find ourselves no longer in history, but in an "eschatological" future vision. The future is that of the holy people with the temple at the center. A comprehensive set of rules will secure that the people and temple are kept holy and protected against all impurity.

Some regard Ezekiel as a transitional figure between the Hebrew Bible and early Judaism. The book then becomes important to our effort to bring greater clarity to this difficult period.

THE BOOK OF HOSEA

In the Hebrew Bible the book of Hosea appears as the first prophet of the Book of the Twelve, immediately following the book of Ezekiel. In the Septuagint, and in most modern translations, the book of Daniel is placed between Ezekiel and Hosea. According to the superscription of the book (Hos. 1:1), the contents go back to the prophet Hosea, son of Beeri, who was active in the northern kingdom in the eighth century BCE. Hosea is thus the only northern prophet whose word has been transmitted to posterity. In the superscription, Hosea is placed in about the same time period as the prophet Amos.

The text of Hosea is characterized by rich poetic language, with an extensive use of imagery. At the same time, a major problem with the book is that the Hebrew text in many places is corrupt (that is, damaged) and often difficult to understand.

The book can be divided into two main parts, Hosea 1–3 and Hosea 4–14. Chapters 1 and 3 refer to the prophet's marriage and family life. In many ways the text is unclear, but the description seems to recapture in imagery the breach of the covenant between YHWH and the people. If this is the case, the main issue in Hosea 1–3 is the breaking of the marriage covenant. In the same way that Hosea's wife has been unfaithful, the people have been unfaithful to YHWH.

The second part of the book, Hosea 4–14, is less coherent, and gives a motley impression. The section consists for the most part of oracles of judgment against Israel for having broken the covenant with YHWH, especially for having followed other gods. Hosea is very concerned with the mercy of YHWH and his love for his people. At the center of the prophetic message, we find the covenant between YHWH and his people. Because of this, the traditional theological concept of YHWH's interactions with his chosen people in history plays a major role in the book of Hosea, thus offering a striking similarity between Hosea and the Deuteronomists. Hosea shows a close relationship to the Deuteronomists also through the harsh and consistent attack on gods other than YHWH.

THE BOOK OF JOEL

The book of Joel is the second of the Twelve Prophets in the Hebrew Bible, but the fourth in the Septuagint. According to the superscription, the text goes back to "Joel son of Pethuel." Because the text does not operate with any chronology, the date of the book has been a major question. Some consider Joel the earliest prophetic book (ninth century BCE), and others among the latest (fourth century BCE). We do not have a basis on which to date the book of Joel with certainty.

Even though the meaning of the message found in the book of Joel is problematic, two issues stand out clearly. Joel 1:1–2:11 describes a plague of locusts. In an agricultural society like ancient Israel, the population was completely dependent on satisfactory crops. Drought and crop disease were tantamount to crop failure and famine. The huge swarms of locusts are notorious in the Middle East. When these come in great multitudes and consume everything that grows in the fields, catastrophe is inevitable.

However, there is not only one way to understand the locusts in Joel 1:1–2:11. Many scholars see a description of a contemporary plague of locusts. Because disasters were seen as punishment from the Deity, prophets were asked to seek YHWH for help in times of crisis. Through intercessory prayer, the prophet could perhaps move YHWH to turn his rage away from the people.

Because the book of Joel seems to follow a particular liturgical pattern (the communal lament), with the description of the plague in 1:1–2:11, the prayer of intercession in 2:12–18, and the oracle of salvation in 2:18–3:26, many scholars have seen Joel as the prototype of a cultic prophet. But it is also possible that we are dealing with a type of prophetic rhetoric describing a future situation. In that case 1:1–2:11 should be understood as an oracle of judgment; the prophet is speaking about a future plague that will strike the people if they do not turn to YHWH. A combination of the two ways of understanding the text of Joel is also possible.

Another major issue in the book of Joel is the concept of the "day of YHWH," which Joel weaves into his preaching. We find the "day of the LORD" several times in the prophets. The concept entailed an expectation that YHWH would intervene in history in a particular way on behalf of his people, on *yom yhwh*, literally "the day of YHWH." One expectation of "the day of YHWH" included victory over the enemy in war, and a prosperous future for Israel. But the prophets also turned this expectation into something negative, and let "the day of the LORD" count as YHWH's judgment on his own people.

In Amos 5:18–20 and Joel 1:15 we find examples of how the day of YHWH expressed judgment on Israel, while Joel 3:19 contains a future oracle of salvation for Israel. The rhetoric of the prophetic description of the "day of YHWH" can assume cosmic dimensions (e.g., Joel 3:4). In these detailed descriptions, we find the background for the subsequent eschatological and apocalyptic views of early Judaism. In the Old Testament itself we do not find these views; the prophets always had in mind an immediate future, described with poetic words and expressions. Other important "day of YHWH" texts are Isaiah 13:9–13; 24:1–6, 18–23; 34:1–4; Ezekiel 13:5; Obadiah 15; Zephaniah 1:1–18; Zechariah 14:1–21; and Malachi 4:5.

THE BOOK OF AMOS

The book of Amos is the third of the Twelve Prophets in the Hebrew order, but second in the Septuagint. According to the superscription of the book, the content goes back to "Amos, who was among the shepherds of Tekoa," and who was active around the mid-eighth century BCE. "Shepherd" can be a little misleading, and recent studies have shown even more clearly that "shepherd" here is used as a title for someone in a high position.

For the most part, the book of Amos consists of oracles of judgment against Samaria and Israel (the northern kingdom). Some of the oracles have the form of visions. In 7:1–9:4 we find five visions (7:1–3, 4–6, 7–9; 8:1–3; 9:1–4). Also the genre of "oracles against the nations" is represented in the book (1:3–2:3). We further find the notion of "the day of YHWH" in 5:18–20 (see further on this expression above, under Joel). In Amos 7:10–17 we find a biographical section. Many scholars have seen the closing oracle of salvation, 9:8–15, as a very late addition to the book, but this is not necessary. The tendency to want to distinguish certain parts of the book of Amos (and of other prophetic books) as "later additions" is primarily caused by the understanding that Amos preached only oracles of judgment, and that there was no room for a brighter future in his preaching. This way of reading the text may be based on a misunderstanding of the ancient Near Eastern rhetoric used in prophetic books, and militates against the prophetic role in general. Also the so-called doxologies (see 4:13; 5:8–9; 9:5–6) in the book have been contested. This is not necessary. It is not uncommon to find in the Hebrew Bible hymnic statements to underline certain points made in the text.

The main theme in Amos is the preaching of YHWH's judgment against the people because they have violated the divine rules by oppressing their fellow citizens. They have also worshiped other gods than YHWH. At the same time, there are also some more positive tones in the book. As with the other prophets in the Hebrew Bible, the oracles of judgment are conditional oracles. If Israel repents and follows YHWH and worships him as their God, YHWH will take care of his people and provide them with a prosperous future.

THE BOOK OF OBADIAH

The book of Obadiah is the fourth book in the Book of the Twelve in the Hebrew Bible, and the fifth in the Greek Bible. With its twenty-one verses, it is the shortest book in the Hebrew Bible. In the superscription, we are told succinctly that what we have before us is "the vision of Obadiah." That is all we are told. The dating of the book has varied from the ninth century BCE to late postexilic times. We do not, however, have any secure foundation to date it.

The book of Obadiah contains an oracle against Edom, the neighboring state of Israel, and is as such an example of the prophetic genre "oracle against other nations." Edom lay in an area that today is part of Jordan, southwest of the Dead Sea. According to tradition, Israel and Edom were related through their ancestors Esau and Jacob. Esau was the forefather of the Edomites, and Jacob of the Israelites. In spite of this there do not seem to have been good feelings in ancient Israel for their neighbors to the south, and there were continuous conflicts between the two peoples.

Despite its brevity, the book of Obadiah is a good representative of prophetic literature.

THE BOOK OF MICAH

According to the superscription in 1:1, the book of Micah goes back to a "Micah of Moresheth," who was active in the eighth century BCE. The book is number six of the Book of the Twelve according to the Hebrew canon, but third in the Septuagint.

The content consists of a mixture of oracles of judgment and oracles of salvation to Israel and Judah (Samaria and Jerusalem). The accusations in Micah concerning the greed and gluttony of the upper classes, as well as the wrongdoings of priests and prophets, remind us of not a few other prophetic books. The judgment of YHWH follows as a result of this, and because the people have not followed YHWH as their God.

The book of Micah seems well composed, though there is a general consensus that the content of the book comes from not one but different periods. The well-organized structure of the final form as we have it today is a product of the postexilic redactors. However, from the point of view of "prophecy as a phenomenon," much of what we find in the book of Micah fits well into the pattern of how we may understand the nature of prophecy in the ancient Near East in general. For this reason we also have to reckon with the possibility that we are dealing with older traditions that reflect historical prophecy in an earlier age. It is remarkable that even if these prophetic traditions have been reworked and reused by subsequent generations, they are still recognizable as typical prophetic genres.

THE BOOK OF NAHUM

According to the superscription in 1:1, the book of Nahum, the seventh in the Book of the Twelve (from here on, the order in both Hebrew and Greek versions is the same), contains "the vision of Nahum of Elkosh." The whole text is one long oracle of judgment against Nineveh, which the Neo-Assyrian king Sennacherib had made the capital of his empire in the transition period from the eighth to the seventh century BCE. The city fell to Babylonian and Median troops in 612 BCE. The issue in the book of Nahum is therefore identical to that which we find in Jonah. Despite its different genre, the book of Jonah, too, contains a word against Nineveh. A prophetic book that also contains just a single message against another nation is Obadiah, which is one short oracle against Edom.

With regard to content, the book of Nahum can probably be divided into two parts. In chapter 1 we find a hymn that describes the theophany of YHWH. The rest of the book consists of an oracle of judgment against Nineveh. The Hebrew poetry of the book is of a very high quality, and is strongly colored by concepts of holy war.

THE BOOK OF HABAKKUK

The book of Habakkuk is the eighth in the Book of the Twelve. According to the superscription in 1:1 (see also 3:1), the text contains "the oracle that the prophet Habakkuk saw." The dating of the book is highly problematic, but some scholars think that it goes back to a prophet who was contemporaneous with Jeremiah, early in the sixth century BCE.

The message of Habakkuk seems to take as its point of departure the Babylonian rise to power in the Near East. The Babylonians are regarded as an evil people, but their growth is seen as part of the salvation plan of YHWH all the same. Because of their evil deeds, however, the Babylonians must be punished. In Habakkuk we find examples of accusations and judgment both against Israel and against another nation. In a position by itself stands the psalm or hymn of Habakkuk (3:1–19). In its present context, this hymn is an answer to "a prayer," and thus functions as an oracle of salvation to Israel.

In spite of the seeming disparity of the material, the book seems well composed. Because of its liturgical structure some scholars have claimed that we have an example of a so-called cult prophet, that is, a professional prophet who had his activity in the temple.

Among the many interesting discoveries at Qumran is a commentary on Habakkuk 1–2, *Pesher Habakkuk* (1QpHab). In addition to being an important textual witness to the Masoretic Text of Habakkuk, the commentary shows how the Qumran community interpreted the Old Testament prophets. Habakkuk plays a role also in the New Testament, when Paul uses this prophet as the textual basis for the teaching about "justification by faith" (Rom. 1:17; Gal. 3:11).

THE BOOK OF ZEPHANIAH

The book of Zephaniah is the ninth book among the Twelve. According to its superscription, the content goes back to "Zephaniah son of Cushi son of

Gedaliah son of Amariah son of Hezekiah," who was active in the last part of the seventh century BCE.

The book of Zephaniah contains classic prophetic genres. The people in Judah are accused of many transgressions and are threatened with punishment from YHWH. A main theme in Zephaniah is the concept of "the day of YHWH" (Zeph. 1:14–18), which is well known from the prophetic literature (see under Joel, above, for more details). Following oracles of judgment against other nations, the book ends with an oracle of salvation to Judah.

THE BOOK OF HAGGAI

The book of Haggai comes as the tenth book of the Twelve Prophets. It is concerned with the efforts of Haggai to encourage the people to rebuild the temple in Jerusalem. Based on the information in the superscription, the prophet's activity has traditionally been dated to 520 BCE. A prophet Haggai is mentioned in Ezra 5:1 and 6:14 as contemporary with Zechariah. It is common to set the year 539 BCE as the end of the exile, when the people could start to return to Judah. This was the year that Cyrus conquered Babylon, and the Persians took over the Neo-Babylonian (Chaldean) Empire. In reality we are dealing more with processes than with exact years.

Because the return took place only in limited numbers, and the inhabitants who had lived in the land during the exile showed lack of will and ability, the rebuilding of the temple after the exile seemed slow. The main topic in Haggai is that the current crisis in food production and the famine are a punishment from YHWH for the bad state of the temple building. The book of Haggai is related to Priestly and Chronistic theology, but this does not have to mean, as some have indicated, that the book has been extensively edited.

THE BOOK OF ZECHARIAH

The book of Zechariah is the eleventh in the Book of the Twelve. Compared to the others, Zechariah gives a more incoherent and disparate impression. Scholars generally agree to divide the book into two main parts: Zechariah 1–8 and 9–14. According to the superscription, chapters 1–8 go back to a prophet Zechariah who was active at the same time as Haggai, around 520 BCE. In Ezra 5:1 and 6:14 these two prophets are described as contemporaries.

After the Achaemenian king Cyrus had conquered the Neo-Babylonian Empire, the consolidation of the Persian Empire, including the province of Judah, could begin. Together with Haggai, Zechariah took part in the reconstruction of the temple. The Second Temple was completed in 516 BCE, according to conventional chronology.

The second part of the book of Zechariah, chapters 9–14, is often called "Deutero-Zechariah" or Second Zechariah, and consists of a mixture of different prophetic oracles that are difficult to date. However, it is reasonable to assume that they are later than Zechariah 1–8. Parts of Deutero-Zechariah show similarities to the book of Malachi. Even though most scholars agree that Zechariah 1–8 consists of a separate collection of visions and prophetic words, some scholars have recently also started to show interest in the relation between the two parts and the redactional unity of the book of Zechariah.

THE BOOK OF MALACHI

The book of Malachi is the last of the Twelve Prophets, and in the Christian canon it is also the last book of the Old Testament (the Hebrew canon ends with Chronicles). Style and content betray a postexilic time. The name of the prophet in Hebrew, *mal'aki* (Mal. 1:1), means "my messenger," and was originally probably not a personal name. The name is perhaps taken from Malachi 3:1. The Greek translation, the Septuagint, understood Hebrew *mal'aki* as a term, not as a name.

The messenger formula itself is important in the book of Malachi, and is used to legitimize the prophetic role. The book contains six speeches in the form of a dialogue, in which the audience is criticized for not having related to God in the correct way. The content is characterized by concern with everyday life, such as the keeping of the sacrificial cult and preoccupation with the tithe. We find ourselves in the transition period between the Old Testament and early Judaism.

THE BOOK OF DANIEL

In the Jewish canon the book of Daniel is placed between the books of Esther and Ezra. In the Septuagint and in the Christian canon, it is placed between Ezekiel and Hosea. Most scholars agree on dating the book to around the mid-second century BCE. This makes Daniel the latest book in the Hebrew Bible. Daniel is differently placed in the Jewish and in the Christian canon because it is such a late text. In the tripartite canonical process of the Hebrew Bible, Torah was canonized in the Persian period and Nevi'im in the late or very late Persian period. For this reason, Daniel had to be placed in Ketuvim.

Daniel 2:4b–7:28 is written in Aramaic, the rest of the book in Hebrew. There is no good explanation for this bilingual feature.

Many have discussed the genre of the book. Is Daniel a prophetic book or not? It is hardly justified to call it a prophetic book in the ordinary sense of the word. It is not really typical of the Hebrew Bible at all. It is also one of the books that is most difficult to understand. The setting of the book of Daniel is Babylon during the exile. But even though the book contains geographical and chronological information, the content is purely literary and gives us no foundation for extracting historical information.

The book of Daniel can be divided into a haggadic part and an apocalyptic part. The first part (Daniel 1–6) contains a number of stories about Daniel that refer to him in the third person. The second part (Daniel 7–12) contains four visions in which Daniel himself speaks in the first person.

In early Jewish and early Christian times, the literary genre of apocalypse became common. The terms "apocalypse" and "apocalyptic" are not found in the Old Testament, but are taken from the book of Revelation in the New Testament (Greek *apokalypsis* means "revelation"). In the apocalypses the supernatural world is revealed and communicated through angel-like beings. There is a focus on concepts of end times and judgment, often accompanied by cosmic changes, and an extensive use of imagery.

Daniel 7–12 is the only example of an Old Testament apocalypse (although some call Isaiah 24–27 and Zechariah 9–14 examples of "early apocalyptic"). Well-known extrabiblical apocalypses are *1* and *2 Enoch*, *4 Ezra*, *2* and *3 Baruch*, and the book of *Jubilees*. The apocalypses usually have fictional authors. They are attributed to famous figures in the past rather than to contemporary authors. In Judaism the genre of apocalypse came to an end in the first century CE. In Christianity it continued for several hundred years.

Broadly speaking, we find two types of apocalypses. In the historical apocalypses, the end of days is expected to occur through catastrophes and upheaval (Daniel, Revelation). Even though this type of apocalypse reveals events that are supposed to take place in the end times, such apocalypses often take incidents in their own time as points of departure. This kind of apocalypse admonishes courage and faith in times of trial and persecution. A completely different apocalypse describes the visionary on a journey up into the heavenly spheres, where he receives insight into secrets. An angel often accompanies him on the journey. Examples of this type of apocalypse are the books of *1 Enoch* and the *Apocalypse of Abraham*.

6

The Poetic Literature
and Wisdom Literature

*Psalms, Song of Songs, Lamentations,
Job, Proverbs, Ecclesiastes*

Poetry plays a much bigger role in the literature of the Hebrew Bible than we might think. When we speak of biblical poetry, we usually have in mind Psalms, Song of Songs, and Lamentations. These books are collections of poetry. In addition, we count the wisdom books of Job, Proverbs, and Ecclesiastes as part of the poetry of the Bible. But it is important to be aware that the presence of poetry in the Hebrew Bible is not limited to these books. There are poetic texts in very many places. For example, in the prophetic literature much of the language is poetic.

A problem for many modern readers of the Bible is that they do not realize that biblical language makes extensive use of images. The main reason that many texts have not been adequately understood has been a lack of ability among readers to see the extent to which the authors make use of stereotypical language, poetic techniques, and imagery.

A separate problem concerns the question of what distinguishes poetic literature in the Bible from prose. In the early phase of biblical research, intense discussions went on in order to discover and reveal the metric system of the ancient Israelites. Much of what was written in this pioneering period on the topic is unfortunately not satisfactory in view of today's insights, and would also be regarded as too speculative. In more recent times, however, scholars like Robert Alter, Adele Berlin, and James Kugel, among others, have brought our knowledge of this intricate field much further along.

The poems and songs of the Hebrew Bible were not written in quantitative meters like ancient Greek poetry. Neither do we find any regular rhythm or regular rhyme as we are used to from (say) poetry in English. The characteristic quality of biblical poetry is the repeated use of one short sentence, usually composed of two short segments, where the last segment in some way relates to the first. The most common designation for this phenomenon is "parallelism." The term goes back to the eighteenth-century scholar Robert Lowth, who used the Latin term *parallelismus membrorum*. The extent, function, and significance of this parallelism have been the subject of much debate in biblical research.

Another issue of some concern in recent research is increasing awareness of problems in relation to scholarly attempts to distinguish between "poetry" and "prose" in Classical Hebrew literature. Both of these terms, "poetry" and "prose," are taken from very different literary traditions than the biblical. Lately, many have questioned how adequate these terms are for ancient Hebrew literature. For example, there is no indication at all that the ancient Hebrews themselves were aware of any such distinction. When attempting to distinguish between poetry and prose, scholars have traditionally understood poetic texts to follow specific rules of composition, to make extended use of imagery and parallelism, and to express their message in a more evocative, emotional, imaginative, and associative way than texts that were called prose.

Within biblical research there has been a tendency to characterize texts that are made up solely of parallelisms as poetry, and all other types of literature as prose. But we can find imagery and parallelisms in so-called prose literature too. It is therefore more usual today not to draw such a sharp distinction between poetry and prose. In the academy the same is the case with the study of nonbiblical literature.

THE PSALMS

Few Old Testament books can be said to have had as much an impact on Western cultural history as the biblical book of Psalms. In the Christian era, probably no other book has been as widely known. Church history, intellectual history, literature, and art history all attest to this. An indicator from the recent past is the many editions of the New Testament that have been printed together with the Old Testament Psalms.

According to the Bible's own information, the main bulk of the book of Psalms goes back to King David. The word "psalm" itself comes from the Greek translation of the Hebrew word *mizmor*, meaning "song," which occurs in the heading of several psalms (e.g., Psalms 3; 4; 5). A more archaic expression in English is the word "psalter," from Greek *psaltērion*, which refers to a stringed instrument. The Hebrew Bible's own name for the book of Psalms, *Tehillim*, means "praises." This term is probably more appropriate, and it is less likely to cause misunderstandings, than the term "psalms." Psalms is the only book in the Bible whose units are not chapters but discrete poems, organized into collections of individual psalms. There are five such collections: Psalms 1–41; 42–72; 73–89; 90–106; and 107–150. We also need to note that there are a number of discrepancies between the numbering of the psalms in the Septuagint (the Greek translation) and in the Hebrew Masoretic Text.

When we look more closely at this book, we find that it constitutes a motley collection of different types of poetry. The collection does not go back to David, but must be dated quite variously. Because of the great variety within the collection, the biblical psalms cannot be reduced to a common formula. The earlier understanding of these songs, or psalms, was naturally influenced by the traditional belief that they went back to King David. It was thus commonly assumed that the biblical psalms were pious, personal, occasional poetry. As scholars became aware of the complex character of the book of Psalms and began to doubt its Davidic origin, they began to regard the psalms as late compositions. At the beginning of the twentieth century, hardly any scholar claimed that the psalms were older than the Babylonian exile (that is, earlier than 586 BCE). Many regarded this pious poetry in the same way as the Christian congregation's hymnal, and assumed that the biblical psalms belonged to the postexilic community's worship. The psalms were for use by individuals at home or in the congregation's worship, perhaps performed by a choir.

After a while, however, scholars started to dismiss the possibility that the psalms were the poetry of individuals. Rather, they are anonymous works that have been transmitted through the centuries to be performed either by individuals or a congregation. Gradually, it also became clear that similar literature existed among Israel's neighbors in Babylonia, Egypt, and Ugarit. With the discovery of texts from the second millennium BCE showing striking similarities to the Old Testament psalms, the pendulum swung back in the other direction regarding the question of dating.

Specific psalms in the book—for example, Psalms 29 and 68—show striking similarities with ancient Ugaritic poetry. While prior to the discovery of the Ugaritic texts (1929) these psalms had been regarded as late, postexilic compositions, some scholars today believe that these are among the earliest texts in the Hebrew Bible. Other psalms, such as 1 and 119, represent a completely different era and intellectual background, and are regarded by many as belonging to the latest texts of the Hebrew Bible. However, we cannot be certain that these scholars are correct in their early or late dating. What we can be sure of is that the songs, or whatever we choose to call them, that we find in the book of Psalms stem from different environments and probably widely differing time periods.

As time passed, the psalms were collected into larger units that, in turn, were collected into one book, ending up with the 150 different "psalms" that we find today in our editions of the Bible. Most likely, the Old Testament book of Psalms represents only a small selection of the many psalms that were in circulation in ancient Israel at various points in time. It is of particular interest that a number of psalms were discovered at Qumran that are not found in the Hebrew Bible but that clearly represent exactly the same type of literature. This discovery of authentic noncanonical psalms must be characterized as very significant, not least from a canonical-theological point of view. At Qumran we find yet another testimony to the long and laborious development in that process of selection that lies behind the finally fixed, written version of the Old Testament.

We also find indications within the book of Psalms itself that the work we now have is made up of a collection of earlier, smaller collections. For example, Psalm 72 ends with the following verse: "The prayers of David son of Jesse are ended." This could indicate that this is the ending of a previous collection of psalms, and that the psalms following have been added to the collection at a later point in time. Also within the present collection we find specific subgroups that might indicate that smaller collections had existed prior to their collection into larger units. For example, Psalms 120–134 constitute a separate collection under the subtitle *shir hamma'alot*, "a song of ascents." Perhaps this group of psalms has been made up of pilgrimage songs that were in use during the ascent to Jerusalem. Other groups are the so-called Asaph psalms (50 and 73–83) and the Korahite psalms (42–49 and 84–88, except for 86, which is a "prayer of David"). There are also psalms that are attributed to other authors (e.g., Moses, 90; Solomon, 127). A particular indication that we are dealing with originally separate collections of psalms has been found with the so-called YHWH psalms and the so-called Elohim psalms. The point of departure for the assumption that there had been a separate collection of Elohim psalms was the frequent use of the divine name Elohim in Psalms 42–83. This analysis is parallel to what we find in the Pentateuch, where the use of different names for God led to the identification of two different sources.

Also in other ways the book of Psalms displays signs of having been established through a long period of transmission and editing. Particularly striking are the many doublets in the work. Thus Psalm 53 is identical to Psalm 14, Psalm 70 is identical to the last five verses of Psalm 40, Psalm 71:1–3 is identical to Psalm 31:2–4, and Psalm 108 is identical to Psalm 57:8–12 and Psalm 60:7–14. It is also noteworthy that psalms are found not only in the book of Psalms but also in a number of other texts in the Hebrew Bible. Isaiah 12 is a good example of a psalm of thanksgiving, and Lamentations 5 illustrates a typical communal lament. In Job 30 we find a characteristic example of a private lament. Second Samuel 22:2–51 is almost identical to Psalm 18, and in 1 Chronicles 16 we find quotations from Psalms 105; 96; and 106.

It is interesting that the Bible might contain references to other collections of poetry that have been lost to posterity. Numbers 21:14 refers to the "Book of the Wars of YHWH." This work might have been a chronicle, but some scholars have maintained that the quotation could indicate that this was a poetic work. The same regards the reference to the "Book of Jashar" in 2 Samuel 1:18. We do not have any clear proof, however, that these works were poetic.

The Psalms: Some Insights from the History of Research

Early biblical scholarship had claimed individual authorship and a postexilic date for the book of Psalms, understanding it primarily as the postexilic temple's community hymnal. The German scholar Hermann Gunkel (1862–1932) would change all of this. While reading the Psalms, Gunkel was struck by the fact that the same motifs, the same linguistic expressions, and even the same textual structure could be found in one psalm after the next. On the basis of these observations, he laid the foundation for all subsequent research on the Psalms.

Gunkel founded the method called form criticism within Psalms research. He wished to determine the individual psalms' literary characteristics, their genre (German *Gattung*). On the basis of the psalms' literary type, he attempted to distinguish the function that these psalms had in ancient Israel (German *Sitz im Leben*, "place in life, life setting"). It was important for Gunkel to emphasize that the psalms were not arbitrary poetry, but that they belonged in a context of worship—they were liturgical texts. Nevertheless, he did think that most of the psalms that we know of today, that is, the psalms that are collected in the book of Psalms, should primarily be regarded as poems by individuals who had sought to emulate the style of the ancient cultic psalms. The purpose of form criticism was not to study the literary genres in their final form, the way we now have them in the Hebrew Bible. Similar to other classical historical-critical methods like source criticism and tradition criticism, the purpose of form criticism was to reconstruct the original historical genres the way they existed in ancient Israel.

Gunkel's original classification of the various types of psalms has, roughly, been kept until today. Some new genres have been added, others have been revised or downplayed. Some scholars have probably also gone too far in their eagerness to discover hitherto unknown genres. However, on the whole, Gunkel's theories have dominated research on the psalms up until our own day.

In recent years, however, a change in intellectual climate has clearly taken place in biblical studies. The diachronic methods of historical-critical studies have been replaced more and more by a rich variety of synchronic approaches to the final form of the text. This change is probably necessary. Among the weaknesses of historical-critical approaches, particular mention should be made of a high degree of uncertainty when it comes to reconstructing "original" texts and their function in ancient Israel. Another major weakness is fragmentation. Historical-critical methods have mainly been occupied with the history of the text. This one-sided focus on how texts came into existence quite often led to a lack of interest in the texts themselves. Surely, from a hermeneutical point of view, what texts mean should always be the most important issue in the study of literature. Also, it is what texts mean today that is of interest to present-day readers, not what they meant in some obscure past. However, we should take care not to throw out the baby with the bathwater. If used with caution, historical-critical methods can still yield many valuable insights that are relevant also to "final-form" readers. Moreover, there can be a danger that some final-form readers forget the historical aspect. The texts are indeed texts from a distant past. If we do not take the historical implications seriously, final-form readings too may be unsound and inadequate, and fail to understand the texts.

In particular, Gunkel's view that the psalm types originally belonged in the ancient Israelite cult (temple worship) had caught the attention of biblical scholars. Here we must specifically mention the Norwegian scholar Sigmund Mowinckel (1884–1966). After Gunkel, Mowinckel is probably the most significant Psalms scholar of the twentieth century. As opposed to Gunkel, who thought that the psalms were pious copies of the original cultic poetry, Mowinckel claimed that the psalms were the actual cultic poetry itself. He attempted to place almost every psalm directly into a cultic context.

One of Mowinckel's most distinguished contributions to the study of ancient Israelite religion was his attempt to reconstruct a feast of YHWH's enthronement, which he claimed had been part of the great fall and New Year festival in ancient Israel. Many of the biblical psalms had had their original *Sitz im Leben* within this festival complex. According to Mowinckel, it was first of all the psalms that begin with the words *YHWH mlk*, "YHWH has become king," that belong here. On the basis of these so-called psalms of enthronement, Mowinckel began his wide-ranging work of reconstructing a feast of YHWH's enthronement. The festival celebration consisted of, among other things, a cultic drama in which fertility in fields and gardens, among cattle and flock, and among people in general was secured for the new year.

In spite of the significance of Mowinckel's work for Psalms research, his theories were not widely accepted, and he has hardly any followers today. He received the most support for his views in Scandinavia and Great Britain. In Gunkel's native country, Germany, research has taken a different course. Nonetheless, Mowinckel's influence, directly or indirectly, is clear.

The problems lie first of all in the sources themselves. The psalms, in the form that we have them today, most often appear to be short, independent compositions, severed from any historical or literary context. The content, as one would expect for poetic texts, is general, nonhistorical, timeless, and universal. It is not without reason that generation after generation has been able to identify with this religious poetry and feels that it speaks to them. The biblical psalms are suitable for most occasions. And this makes it all very complicated for the scholar of religion. There are plenty of indications in the psalms themselves that they might have had a connection to the cult. But due to strongly figurative language and a lack of any kind of context, the identification of a concrete and historical place in life may appear to be not only very difficult and hypothetical but perhaps even impossible.

It is therefore not so strange that today we have quite a few divergent theories about how the historical background of the psalms should be understood. Most likely, it is not possible to do as Mowinckel did and attempt to find a place in the ancient Israelite temple worship for all of the biblical psalms. Even though a liturgical context seems enticing for quite a number of the texts in the book of Psalms, it is also clear that many of them most likely had their *Sitz im Leben* in the sphere of private piety or even belonged in a noncultic context, particularly those whose language reveals that they are probably of a late date. Such a noncultic context would be likely also for the wisdom psalms.

Among important contributions to the discussion about the relationship between cult and biblical psalms are two representatives for the quite opposite view. Both Harry Torczyner (Naphtali H. Tur-Sinai) and Jürgen Becker claimed that, for example, the lament psalms that we find in the Hebrew Bible collection of psalms are purely pious poetry without any connection to the cult. The psalms are, according to this view, purely literary.

Many scholars still hold the view that Gunkel and Mowinckel were right when they saw a connection between the psalms and temple worship. When it comes to the question of what kind of connection, however, scholars have not reached any agreement. Again, we must keep in mind that we do not get much help from the Hebrew Bible itself in answering this question. The cultic framework that has been imagined is purely hypothetical or reconstructed.

Another illustration of how scholars have worked with problems concerning the relationship between text and history in Psalms is taken from discussions about how the genre of the individual psalm of lament may have originated. Scholarly theories to answer this question have been quite contested. Mowinckel thought that the individual who wished to put forth his lament over illness, misfortune, and so on before YHWH would seek out the temple to perform his prayer there. Many scholars have followed him in this. Hans Schmidt had a somewhat different view of the individual lament. He imagined that some of these psalms had their origin in a religious-legal (cult-juridical) procedure in the temple. A person who fell victim to false accusations could turn to YHWH with a prayer asking to be freed from his accusers (enemies). YHWH's ruling in the case was then uttered by the priests. In cases of acquittal, the lament would be succeeded by a new liturgy, the individual psalm of thanksgiving.

A similar view has been presented by Walter Beyerlin, who modified Schmidt's thesis, and claimed that the background for these psalms was an inquiry of the priests not by someone seeking acquittal, but by a person who asked for protection. Lienhard Delekat is even more consistent, and has understood these as well as other psalms as straightforward prayers performed in the temple in order to seek asylum. Yet other scholars think that the individual psalms of lament are not individual laments at all but psalms of thanksgiving. The logic behind this stance takes as its point of departure that someone in great distress—for example, an ill person—could not himself perform the lament in his present state. Only when his situation improved would it be possible to come to the temple to perform the lament and the thanksgiving. The lament thus makes up only the first part of the psalm of thanksgiving. In this understanding of the ritual, the individual who is giving thanks points to his previous state of distress, and subsequently performs the real task at hand, which is expressed in the psalm of thanksgiving. This view has been supported by, among others, Artur Weiser, Hartmut Gese, and Klaus Seybold.

In Scandinavia the royal interpretation of the individual lament has been particularly pronounced. In this view the speaking "I" of the psalm is understood as the king, speaking on behalf of his people. This view has been espoused by, among others, Aage Bentzen in Denmark and Ivan Engnell and Geo Widengren in Sweden. After the Norwegian Harris Birkeland had developed this idea further, Mowinckel also embraced the royal thesis. Other subscribers to this view have been J. Alberto Soggin in Italy and John H. Eaton in England.

Finally, we must mention the thesis of the German Erhard S. Gerstenberger, which distinguishes itself from all of the above. On the basis of Mesopotamian parallels, Gerstenberger attempts to reconstruct a type of healing ritual that would have taken place privately, in the individual's own family, independently of the official cult.

Many of these views are possible. But one cannot single out which thesis gives the "correct" answer to the question of the "real" *Sitz im Leben* of the individual lament. This has to do with issues already mentioned: difficulty in dating because of stereotypical phraseology, the use of universal poetic language, the fact that the psalms in their present context are completely separated from their "original" context, the timeless and universal content of the psalms, and so on. The individual psalm of lament does give us some information about ancient Israelite religion. Nevertheless, it remains difficult to reconstruct its rituals and cultic practice on the basis of the genre.

It may seem simpler to explain other genres, such as the communal lament. It seems clear that the communal lament belongs to a context of rituals that may have been performed in particular situations of crisis, accompanied by fasting and rituals of mourning. There may also be an apotropaic element in these psalms. But we know very little about the specific situation that they were performed in. Are the communal laments purely occasional rituals, performed, for example, in the vineyard during a drought? Or in times of war? Or have they also had a type of preventive function and been performed at specific intervals—for example, in the temple cult? Or have they, also with a preventive function, had their place in the annual festivals—for example, in the fall and New Year festival? Without doubt, the New Year feast represented a critical period in the annual cycle of an agricultural society. Often the question will be, again, where to lay the emphasis. A scholar like Claus Westermann sees the fundamental genres in the psalms more as praise and lament, performed as prayers to YHWH, and less as liturgies. Again, we must face the frustration that we do not have sufficient sources available, and we are, more or less, left to pure guesswork.

As we have seen, many will disagree with a cultic interpretation of the psalms. Also, it will not be possible, as some scholars have tried, to place all the psalms of the Hebrew Bible into specific literary genres. This can be a useful exercise, but should be done only tentatively. Exaggerated enthusiasm for classification may, in some cases, violate a sound interpretation of the texts. Instead of reading the psalms as they present themselves, one might pay too much attention to theories about how the texts have come into existence, and speculate about what they may have been used for in ancient Israel. We simply do not know what all of the various psalms have been used for. What we do know is that they all represent an important corpus of ancient Hebrew poetry, and that they express a deep and poignant faith, and that through all times they have been edifying. This must remain the most important concern in relation to the biblical psalms.

The Most Common Types of Psalms

It is not easy to determine the literary type of each individual psalm. Often we find what seem to be several different genres represented in one psalm. The most common psalm genre is the hymn, or psalm of praise and thanksgiving to YHWH, possibly performed in the temple or at festive occasions. Characteristic of the hymn is the call to glorify YHWH with joy and praise for his goodness and greatness. One type of hymn is the processional hymn—for example, Psalm 24:

> The earth is the Lord's and all that is in it,
> the world, and those who live in it;
> for he has founded it on the seas,
> and established it on the rivers.
>
> Who shall ascend the hill of the Lord?
> And who shall stand in his holy place?
> Those who have clean hands and pure hearts,
> who do not lift up their souls to what is false,
> and do not swear deceitfully.
> They will receive blessing from the Lord,
> and vindication from the God of their salvation.
> Such is the company of those who seek him,
> who seek the face of the God of Jacob. *Selah*
>
> Lift up your heads, O gates!
> and be lifted up, O ancient doors!
> that the King of glory may come in.
> Who is the King of glory?
> The Lord, strong and mighty,
> The Lord, mighty in battle.
> Lift up your heads, O gates!
> and be lifted up, O ancient doors!
> that the King of glory may come in.
> Who is the King of glory?
> The Lord of hosts,
> he is the King of glory. *Selah*

In Psalm 8, as in a number of other hymns, the motifs for praise are taken from nature:

> O Lord, our sovereign,
> how majestic is your name in all the earth!
> Your have set your glory above the heavens.
> Out of the mouth of babes and infants
> you have founded a bulwark because of your foes,
> to silence the enemy and the avenger.
>
> When I look at your heavens, the work of your fingers,
> the moon and the stars that you have established;
> what are human beings that you are mindful of them,
> mortals that you care for them?

Some psalms praise YHWH as king. It was the study of these psalms in particular that brought Mowinckel to the theory about a festival of YHWH's enthronement. Our example is taken from Psalm 97. In addition to the royal motif, we note the theophany motif, the destruction of those who practice idolatry, and the motif of doom.

> The LORD is king! Let the earth rejoice;
> let the many coastlands be glad!
> Clouds and thick darkness are all around him;
> righteousness and justice are the foundation of his throne.
> Fire goes before him,
> And consumes his adversaries on every side.
> His lightnings light up the world;
> the earth sees and trembles.
> The mountains melt like wax before the LORD,
> before the LORD of all the earth.
>
> The heavens proclaim his righteousness;
> and all the peoples behold his glory.
> All worshipers of images are put to shame,
> those who make their boasts in worthless idols;
> all gods bow down before him.
> Zion hears and is glad,
> and the towns of Judah rejoice,
> because of your judgments, O God.

Zion has a major symbolic function in the Hebrew Bible. Zion is not only a poetic name for Jerusalem, the city of David, and the temple. It is also an image of YHWH's support and help to his people. This usage has passed on to the New Testament, where Zion is used as a term for the community of the faithful (Heb. 12:22). In a group by itself stand the so-called Zion hymns. These psalms praise God's dwelling in Jerusalem. Our example is from Psalm 46.

> God is our refuge and strength,
> A very present help in trouble.
> Therefore we will not fear, though the earth should change,
> though the mountains shake in the heart of the sea;
> though its waters roar and foam,
> though the mountains tremble with its tumult. *Selah*
>
> There is a river whose streams make glad the city of God,
> the holy habitation of the Most High.
> God is in the midst of the city; it shall not be moved;
> God will help it when the morning dawns.
> The nations are in an uproar, the kingdoms totter;
> He utters his voice, the earth melts.
> The LORD of hosts is with us;
> The God of Jacob is our refuge. *Selah*

In Psalm 23 we find a most beautiful poem. The imagery is taken from pastoral life. The shepherd motif was much loved in the ancient Middle East. This image played a major role in religious poetry as an expression of the relationship between God and the people of Israel, and between God and humans. We can, for lack of anything better, characterize it as a psalm of trust.

> The LORD is my shepherd, I shall not want.
> He makes me lie down in green pastures;
> he leads me beside still waters;
> he restores my soul.
> He leads me in right paths for his name's sake.
>
> Even though I walk through the darkest valley,
> I fear no evil;
> for you are with me;
> your rod and your staff—
> they comfort me.
>
> You prepare a table before me in the presence of my enemies;
> you anoint my head with oil;
> my cup overflows.
> Surely goodness and mercy shall follow me
> all the days of my life,
> and I shall dwell in the house of the LORD
> my whole life long.

A very common type of psalm is the individual psalm of lament. A well-known example is Psalm 22. The passion narrative in the New Testament quotes this psalm several times.

> My God, my God, why have you forsaken me?
> Why are you so far from helping me, from the words of my groaning?
> O my God, I cry by day, but you do not answer;
> and by night, but find no rest.
>
> Yet you are holy;
> enthroned on the praises of Israel.
> In you our ancestors trusted;
> they trusted, and you delivered them.
> To you they cried, and were saved;
> in you they trusted, and were not put to shame.
>
> But I am a worm, and not human;
> scorned by others, and despised by the people.
> All who see me mock at me;
> they make mouths at me, they shake their heads;
> "Commit your cause to the LORD; let him deliver—
> Let him rescue the one in whom he delights!"

Yet it was you who took me from the womb;
you kept me safe on my mother's breast.
On you I was cast from my birth,
and since my mother bore me you have been my God.
Do not be far from me,
for trouble is near
and there is no one to help.

Many bulls encircle me,
strong bulls of Bashan surround me;
they open wide their mouths at me,
like a ravening and roaring lion.

I am poured out like water,
and all my bones are out of joint;
my heart is like wax;
it is melted within my breast;
my mouth is dried up like a potsherd,
and my tongue sticks to my jaws;
you lay me in the dust of death.

For dogs are all around me;
a company of evildoers encircles me.
My hands and feet have shriveled;
I can count all my bones.
They stare and gloat over me;
they divide my clothes among themselves,
and for my clothing they cast lots.

But you, O Lord, do not be far away!
O my help, come quickly to my aid!
Deliver my soul from the sword,
my life from the power of the dog!
Save me from the mouth of the lion!

From the horns of the wild oxen you have rescued me.

This psalm of lament is typical of the laments of the Hebrew Bible. We notice the extensive use of imagery. Some have attempted to interpret this text literally, in the direction of it describing, for example, serious illness with fever, delirium, and death. If we look more closely at the verses, however, we find that they are too all-encompassing for that. We encounter a number of images, and we must take care so as to read the texts on their own premises. If we do not show respect for the nature of the literature that we read, we risk violating the poetry and misunderstanding the texts. All of the images in Psalm 22 express deep spiritual distress and despair.

Another common denominator of the individual psalms of lament is the
remarkable change in mood that we find in them. While the first part is a
lament, the second part often breaks into a hymn. It is this change, among
other things, that has led scholars to think that these texts might have been
cultic texts performed in the temple. The second part of the lament, the
hymn, would then have been the praying subject's answer to the temple personnel. A response might have included reassurances that YHWH had heard
the prayer of the person in need, as well as promises of salvation from distress
and sickness. After the extended description of the lament in Psalm 22, we
thus read on:

> I will tell of your name to my brothers and sisters;
> in the midst of the congregation I will praise you:
> You who fear the Lord, praise him!
> All you offspring of Jacob, glorify him;
> stand in awe of him, all you offspring of Israel!
> For he did not despise or abhor the affliction of the afflicted;
> he did not hide his face from me, but heard when I cried to him.
>
> From you comes my praise in the great congregation;
> my vows I will pay before those who fear him.
> The poor shall eat and be satisfied;
> those who seek him shall praise the Lord.
> May your hearts live forever!
>
> All the ends of the earth shall remember
> and turn to the Lord;
> and all the families of the nations
> shall worship before him.
> For dominion belongs to the Lord,
> and he rules over the nations.

Related to Psalm 22 is Psalm 51. In this psalm, however, the component
of penitence is so overarching that it would be more correct to call this psalm
a psalm of penitence. Spiritual need, anxiety, guilt, and a strong need to do
penance are not, as some people may think, a "Christian invention." All over
the ancient Near East we know of how people have struggled with existential
problems of this kind and have expressed them in religious poetry. According
to tradition, Psalm 51 was composed by David after the prophet Nathan had
rebuked him for his adulterous behavior with the beautiful Bathsheba.

> Have mercy on me, O God,
> according to your steadfast love;
> according to your abundant mercy
> blot out my transgressions.

Wash me thoroughly from my iniquity,
and cleanse me from my sin.

For I know my transgressions,
and my sin is ever before me.
Against you, you alone, have I sinned,
and done what is evil in your sight,
so that you are justified in your sentence
and blameless when you pass judgment.
Indeed; I was born guilty,
a sinner when my mother conceived me.

You desire truth in the inward being;
therefore teach me wisdom in my secret heart.
Purge me with hyssop, and I shall be clean;
wash me, and I shall be whiter than snow.

A particular group of psalms is the wisdom psalms. These pious poems are saturated by the thought world of wisdom. Psalm 1 is an example of a wisdom psalm. Already the opening words, "Happy are those . . . ," refer to the fundamental teaching of wisdom that the righteous will prosper and the wicked will suffer.

Happy are those
who do not follow the advice of the wicked,
or take the path that sinners tread,
or sit in the seat of scoffers;
but their delight is in the law of the LORD,
and on his law they meditate day and night.
They are like trees
planted by streams of water,
which yield their fruit in its season,
and their leaves do not wither.
In all that they do, they prosper.

The wicked are not so,
but are like chaff that the wind drives away.
Therefore the wicked will not stand in the judgment,
nor sinners in the congregation of the righteous;
For the LORD watches over the way of the righteous,
but the way of the wicked will perish.

Naturally, a number of psalms in ancient Israel were dedicated to the king (the messiah or "the anointed one") and his world; these are called the royal psalms. Psalm 2 is a royal psalm for the Davidic dynasty. Some have suggested that this psalm might have been used in connection with enthronement ceremonies.

Why do the nations conspire,
and the peoples plot in vain?
The kings of the earth set themselves,
and the rulers take counsel together,
against the Lord and his anointed, saying,
"Let us burst their bonds asunder,
and cast their cords from us."

He who sits in the heavens laughs;
the Lord has them in derision.
Then he will speak to them in his wrath,
and terrify them in his fury, saying,
"I have set my king on Zion, my holy hill."

I will tell of the decree of the Lord:
He said to me, "You are my son;
today I have begotten you.
Ask of me, and I will make the nations your heritage,
and the ends of the earth your possession.
You shall break them with a rod of iron,
and dash them in pieces like a potter's vessel."

Psalm 72 is another example of a royal psalm. Here we find a different tone from Psalm 2. The warlike attitude that characterized Psalm 2 is replaced by a prayer for the king and his government. When we read this royal psalm from ancient Israel, we understand easily how in later times of political deterioration it could receive new content. Instead of being a psalm about the earthly king, it came to signify the eschatological savior king, the Messiah.

Give the king your justice, O God,
and your righteousness to a king's son.
May he judge your people with righteousness,
and your poor with justice.
May the mountains yield prosperity for the people,
and the hills, in righteousness.
May he defend the cause of the poor of the people,
give deliverance to the needy
and crush the oppressor.

May he live while the sun endures,
and as long as the moon, throughout all generations.
May he be like the rain that falls on the mown grass,
like showers that water the earth.
In his days may righteousness flourish
and peace abound, until the moon is no more.

May he have dominion from sea to sea,
and from the River to the ends of the earth.

May his foes bow down before him,
and his enemies lick the dust.
May the kings of Tarshish and of the isles
render him tribute,
may the kings of Sheba and Seba bring gifts.
May all kings fall down before him,
all nations give him service.

For he delivers the needy when they call,
the poor and those who have no helper.
He has pity on the weak and the needy,
and saves the lives of the needy.
From the oppression and violence he redeems their life;
and precious is their blood in his sight.

Long may he live!
May the gold of Sheba be given to him.
May prayer be made for him continually,
and blessing invoked for him all day long.
May there be abundance of grain in the land;
may it wave on the tops of the mountains;
may its fruit be like Lebanon;
and may people blossom in the cities
like the grass of the field.
May his name endure forever,
his fame continue as long as the sun.
May all nations be blessed in him;
may they pronounce him happy.

The moving poem Psalm 90 is often called a communal lament. The psalm opens with the motif of transitoriness, which is well known also from other biblical texts.

Lord, you have been our dwelling place
in all generations.
Before the mountains were brought forth,
or ever you had formed the earth and the world,
from everlasting to everlasting you are God.

You turn us back to dust,
And say, "Turn back, you mortals."
For a thousand years in your sight
are like yesterday when it is past,
or like a watch in the night.

You sweep them away; they are like a dream,
like grass that is renewed in the morning;

in the morning it flourishes and is renewed;
in the evening it fades and withers.

For we are consumed by your anger;
by your wrath we are overwhelmed.
You have set our iniquities before you,
our secret sins in the light of your countenance.

For all our days pass away under your wrath;
our years come to an end like a sigh.
the days of our life are seventy years,
or perhaps eighty, if we are strong;
even then their span is only toil and trouble;
they are soon gone, and we fly away.

Who considers the power of your anger?
Your wrath is as great as the fear that is due you.
So teach us to count our days
that we may gain a wise heart.

Turn, O LORD! How long?
Have compassion on your servants!
Satisfy us in the morning with your steadfast love,
so that we may rejoice and be glad all our days.
Make us glad as many days as you have afflicted us,
and as many years as we have seen evil.
Let your work be manifest to your servants,
and your glorious power to their children.
Let the favor of the Lord our God be upon us,
and prosper for us the work of our hands—
O prosper the work of our hands!

In addition to the various types of psalms referred to above, the psalm literature includes a number of other, less common genres. For example, the vehement curses found in some psalms stand in stark contrast to the lovely and beautiful poems cited above, and remind us that we find ourselves in a world that in many ways stands far from our own (see, for example, 31:17–18; 40:14–15; 59:10–13; 69:22–28).

It has been commonplace in biblical scholarship to tie the various literary genres to particular life situations in ancient Israel. The communal lament was performed by the people in times when war, famine, and other catastrophes threatened them; the individual lament was performed by persons with problems of various types; the individual psalm of thanksgiving accompanied the sacrifice of thanksgiving; and so on.

When we reconstruct historical situations in ancient Israel we have to re-create the processes that went before the final form of the text as we have it in our English Bible translations. This is always done on the basis of the Hebrew text. However, we should realize that the possible connections of these different literary types with concrete historical situations in ancient Israel are highly speculative.

Also, historical-critical methods are not, by far, the most used approaches to the study of the Hebrew Bible today. In recent years various literary and theological exegetical methods that relate to reading "the final form" of the text have become more and more commonplace, and rightly so. The meaning of biblical texts as we have them in their final form can often be more important than assumed former meanings in reconstructed texts.

At the same time, many of the insights from so-called historical-critical research are very useful. For instance, these methods are vital when it comes to realizing the historical problems that are involved in the reading and understanding of the texts of the Hebrew Bible. When such methods are applied, however, they should always be adjusted according to the theoretical and methodological mentalities of today.

One great advantage of the present-day intellectual climate is that the methods we use for the study of ancient texts are manifold and diverse. No one method is adequate. The choice of a particular approach in the study of the Hebrew Bible depends very much upon what it is that we want to do with the text.

THE SONG OF SONGS

In Biblical Hebrew the title is *Shir hashshirim*, "Song of Songs" or "Greatest Song." In Roman Catholic versions of the Bible, it is called "Canticles," from the Latin translation, *Canticum Canticorum*. In the Septuagint the book is called *Asma*, "Song." Many scholars have assumed that Song of Songs consists of several individual pieces that only later were collected into a unified composition. Nonetheless, the best way to read this text, too, is to read it as a unity.

During the course of the transmission process, authorship was attributed to King Solomon (hence it is often called "Song of Solomon"). This detail has probably played a significant role during the debates over whether this text should be included in the canon. Song of Songs has been one of the most problematic biblical texts throughout history because of the negative view of sexuality that has often characterized Judaism and Christianity.

Song of Songs is a collection of love poetry with strong erotic elements. Because the content of Song of Songs has caused offense throughout time (except for in its original environment), various ways of reinterpreting the poems have been sought. The simplest way was to read the texts as something entirely different from what they were. Up until the breakthrough of historical-critical research, the allegorical interpretation of Song of Songs was the main method. Within some orthodox Christian and Jewish traditions we still find examples of allegorical interpretations of these texts.

We read the beautiful opening words of Song of Songs 1:2–4:

> Let him kiss me with the kisses of his mouth!
> For your love is better than wine,
> your anointing oils are fragrant,
> your name is perfume poured out;
> therefore the maidens love you.
> Draw me after you, let us make haste.
> The king has brought me into his chambers.
> We will exult and rejoice in you,
> we will extol your love more than wine;
> rightly do they love you.

In Christian tradition, from the church fathers until our own time, there is a widespread use of allegorical interpretation, in which the woman in the poem is understood to represent the Christian congregation, and the man to represent Christ. Thus the texts can be interpreted as the bride, the Israelite congregation, longing for her heavenly groom, the Messiah. The praise of eroticism that we find in these poems was unacceptable to the interpreters of Scripture, whose idea of the human body and sexuality was influenced by a development that would have been foreign to the ancient Israelite understanding.

Some Jewish exegesis demonstrates similar approaches to the text. As one example, we may read the description of the woman in 7:3, "Your two breasts are like two fawns, twins of a gazelle." Jewish interpreters claimed that this was pure imagery, and that the one breast stood for Moses and the other for Aaron. Another example is found in 1:13: "My beloved is to me a bag of myrrh that lies between my breasts." Jewish tradition (for example, Rashi and Ibn Ezra) might interpret this as, "The tabernacle of YHWH's presence above the ark, enthroned between the cherubs."

I should add that both the Christian and Jewish examples of figurative exegesis that are mentioned here are not among the most bizarre interpretations. Rather, they are fairly representative.

After historical-critical biblical research began to make serious headway, two theories in particular became prominent in trying to explain what Song of Songs was really about. During one time period it was common to assume that Song of Songs was the dramatic performance of a cultic ritual, and that the beloved was a dying and rising deity. The classical prototypes of this ritual were Baal and Anat in Ugaritic religion and Tammuz and Ishtar in Mesopotamian religion. This ritual supposedly belonged to the great autumn and New Year festival. YHWH, the God of vegetation, died and then rose again, in imitation of nature, and as a part of a fertility ritual for the fields and pastures, where the vegetation dies and reemerges. Part of this ritual was the celebration of the holy marriage of the god and goddess, often referred to by the Greek term *hieros gamos*. We know today that there is very little basis for assuming that such a ritual existed in ancient Israel, for thinking that such a ritual would have been part of an autumn and New Year festival, or that any of these assumptions have anything to do with Song of Songs.

Another (possibly more plausible) theory has claimed that this text has to do with a wedding drama. According to this assumption, Song of Songs was divided into different acts with various actors and a choir. Some scholars imagined that King Solomon himself had played the main part; others claimed that this was a rural, popular performance.

Yet again it became clear that the basis for this type of speculation was weak. For one, both ways of understanding Song of Songs presuppose that it was originally one unified composition. But this is not at all certain, and the theory that we are left with today is that this is simply love poetry of various types that has been composed as a unified whole at a late stage. Of course there might be parts of an old wedding ritual in Song of Songs, but not everything found in it can in any plausible way be explained by such a theory.

The dating of these poems remains pure guesswork, and many scholars have given up trying to assign a date. As in all love poetry, we find in Song of Songs different motifs such as flirtation, the fear of losing the beloved, longing for love, and the description of the meeting with the loved one. Such common motifs are all but impossible to date.

LAMENTATIONS

The book of Lamentations, a lament over the fall of Jerusalem in 586 BCE, also belongs to the poetic literature of the Hebrew Bible. In the Septuagint the collection is called *Thrēnoi*, "laments." In the Hebrew Bible, the work is called *'Ekah*, "how," after the opening words of the lament:

> How lonely sits the city,
> that once was full of people!
> How like a widow she has become,
> she that was great among the nations!
> She that was a princess among the provinces
> has become a vassal.

> She weeps bitterly in the night,
> with tears on her cheeks;
> among all her lovers
> she has no one to comfort her;
> All her friends have dealt treacherously with her,
> they have become her enemies.

In the Septuagint and in the Vulgate, Lamentations is placed after Jeremiah, because it was earlier believed that Jeremiah was the author of Lamentations. In our modern Bible translations we have taken over this placement of the book. The mistaken idea that Jeremiah wrote Lamentations could partly be based on an erroneous reading of 2 Chronicles 35:25, where we read in the account of the death of the pious king Josiah, "Jeremiah also uttered a lament for Josiah, and all the singing men and singing women have spoken of Josiah in their laments to this day. They made these a custom in Israel; they are recorded in the Laments (*qinot*)."

In the Hebrew Bible the book of Lamentations is the third of the so-called Megilloth. *Megillah* means "scroll," and "the Five Megilloth" is the title given to the five scriptural scrolls, each of which is read on a particular annual feast in the Jewish world. Lamentations was read on 9 Av, the holiday that was celebrated in memory of the destruction of Jerusalem and the temple in 586 BCE. This is a late, postbiblical feast that entered the Jewish calendar only after the Roman general Titus (Roman emperor 79–81 CE) had conquered Jerusalem, destroyed the temple, and carried off the temple treasures to Rome in 70 CE. In the same way, Song of Songs was read during Passover, the book of Ruth at Pentecost, Ecclesiastes during Sukkot, and the book of Esther during Purim (14–15 Adar).

One might have thought that dating Lamentations is simpler than dating any other work in the Old Testament. Since the work consists of a lament over the fall of Jerusalem, it should date to the sixth century BCE. But the work is not unified. The literary genre of "city lament" is well known from the poetry in the Hebrew Bible and from the ancient Near East in general. It is likely that a substantial lament literature (now mostly lost) developed after the fall of Jerusalem in 586 BCE. This particular form of lament may have flourished during a long period of time, and it could be that we find parts of this transmitted tradition in the biblical Lamentations.

The genre "city lament" is not straightforward; indeed, we find various forms of lament in Lamentations. Most prominent among the laments is the funerary lament. We find one of the most beautiful poems in the whole Hebrew Bible in 2 Samuel 1:17–27, where David sings a funerary lament for Saul and Jonathan. In Lamentations the funerary lament is used in a transferred meaning, in that Jerusalem is personified, and the lament is uttered for the "dead" city as if for someone dear who has died. Such a figurative use of the funerary lament is well known from the Hebrew Bible. In Amos 5:1–2 the prophet uses the funerary lament in an oracle of judgment against Israel, in which he compares Israel with a deceased young woman:

> Hear this word that I take up over you in lamentation, O house of Israel:
> Fallen, no more to rise,
> is maiden Israel;
> forsaken on her land,
> with no one to raise her up.

In Lamentations the use of the funerary lament is most clear in 1:1–2, quoted above, in 2:10–11, and in 3:48–50. Since Jerusalem is personified as a woman in Lamentations, it is not surprising that we also find the individual lament richly represented: 1:12–16, 18–22; 2:20–22. In 1:20–22 the personified Jerusalem begs:

> See, O LORD, how distressed I am;
> my stomach churns,
> my heart is wrung within me,
> because I have been very rebellious.
> In the street the sword bereaves;
> in the house it is like death.
>
> They heard how I was groaning,
> with no one to comfort me.
> All my enemies heard of my trouble;
> they are glad that you have done it.
> Bring on the day you have announced,
> and let them be as I am.
>
> Let all their evil doing come before you;
> and deal with them
> as you have dealt with me
> because of all my transgressions;
> for my groans are many
> and my heart is faint.

We also find the communal lament represented in Lamentations. All of chapter 5 consists of one long communal lament, as we know it from the biblical communal laments. Lamentations 5:1–7 is characteristic:

> Remember us, O LORD, what has befallen us;
> look, and see our disgrace!
> Our inheritance has been turned over to strangers,
> our homes to aliens.

We have become orphans, fatherless;
our mothers are like widows.
We must pay for the water we drink;
the wood we get must be bought.
With a yoke on our necks we are hard driven;
we are weary, we are given no rest.

We have made a pact with Egypt and Assyria,
to get enough bread.
Our ancestors sinned; they are no more,
and we bear their iniquities.

We note with interest the theology in this lament. Here, as with the Deuteronomists, the Chroniclers, and the wisdom literature, it is clear that the cause of the catastrophe is the Israelite people's sins. The punishment is not meaningless; it comes from YHWH. It is he who is behind everything and in charge of the course of history.

With poetic texts it is often difficult to see what concrete historical events are being referred to. Poetry is by nature full of imagery, associations, and allusions. In Lamentations the description of the famine in the land after the catastrophe, or during the siege, is, however, unmistakable. We may begin to understand how horrifying the tragedy has been from texts like 4:9–10:

Happier were those pierced by the sword
than those pierced by hunger,
whose life drains away, deprived
of the produce of the field.

The hands of compassionate women
have boiled their own children;
they became their food
in the destruction of my people.

According to its genre, Lamentations is a lament of the destruction of the city of Jerusalem. Within a larger Near Eastern context, we see that Lamentations constitutes a small part of a large and widespread literary genre. From ancient Sumer we know of laments of the destruction of the temple from as far back as 2300 BCE. The oldest, more comprehensive city laments of this type are five Sumerian laments (transmitted in the Old Babylonian language). The laments in question concern Ur/Sumer, and the cities of Ur, Nippur, Uruk, and Eridu. We thus find the city lament attested as a literary genre in Mesopotamia through more than two thousand years, down to the cessation of the Akkadian civilizations.

Very roughly, the Akkadian city laments from the first millennium may be structured in the following way:

1. Praise of the deity responsible for the destruction.
2. Description of the destruction.
3. Lament of the destruction: "How long . . ."
4. Prayer to the god of destruction that his or her anger may no longer rule.
5. Prayer that the deity may see what he or she has caused.
6. Prayer to other gods (or goddesses) for intercession.
7. Further description of the ruins.

If we read Lamentations in the Hebrew Bible closely in light of this outline, we find similarities as well as differences. The similarities are, however, sufficient to see that we are within a common cultural sphere. A direct influence from the Akkadian material to biblical Lamentations is not likely to be proven. Again, we are dealing with different expressions of the same phenomenon in different but related cultures. As so often is the case, however, it is clear that the ultimate influence comes from the big sister (culturally speaking), ancient Sumer. The similarities are too dominant to be explained in any other way.

Lamentations is a powerful testimony for posterity to the traumatic effect that the destruction of Jerusalem, its temple and its walls, and the exilic situation in general had on Jewish self-understanding. At the same time, however, the work, which was probably created in Judah, and perhaps in Jerusalem, after the destruction, is a vigorous sign that life in Judah continued on even after the catastrophe had struck.

WISDOM LITERATURE: SOME GENERAL REMARKS

The wisdom literature makes up a highly interesting and important area of the Hebrew Bible. Many have attempted to define more closely what is meant by "wisdom" in the Old Testament, but no one seems to have succeeded in a way that is satisfactory to all. We count three of the Bible's books as "wisdom literature," Job, Proverbs, and Ecclesiastes. From the so-called apocryphal literature we may add the Wisdom of Solomon and the Wisdom of Jesus Son of Sirach (Ben Sira or Ecclesiasticus).

In the wisdom texts we encounter a different type of literature from what we find, for example, in the historical works or in the prophetic books of the Hebrew Bible. It is not possible, however, to separate Job, Proverbs, and Ecclesiastes completely from the rest of the biblical writings and isolate them. Furthermore, we find many examples of "wisdom literature" spread throughout the Old Testament, for instance in prophetic texts, as well as in the so-called wisdom psalms.

Even though it might be difficult to define the wisdom phenomenon in the Hebrew Bible, we can still say quite a lot about this type of literature. First, the name "wisdom" derives from the Biblical Hebrew word *chokmah*, which means "wise," "sensible," "insightful." Perhaps the most characteristic feature of a large majority of Old Testament literature is the continuous reminder of YHWH's acts of salvation for his chosen people. One of the traits of wisdom literature is that it does not reflect salvation history, and does not refer to it as a framework for understanding the relationship between God and the world. Humanity in general stands at the center, not the holy, chosen people. Even though wisdom literature cannot be placed within the framework of biblical salvation history, it is nonetheless fundamentally religious.

In the historiographical and prophetic literature, the acts of YHWH with his people throughout history can in many ways be seen as a kind of *creatio continua*, as a continuation of creation in history. In wisdom literature this is not the case. Here YHWH has created the world with its laws of nature, and it is up to the wise one to attempt to discover what constitutes this world order and to adjust accordingly. Wisdom is concerned with humans first, and secondarily with God. Wisdom literature inquires: What is the world like? What is the good life? How can one attain a good life? Ancient Israelite wisdom concerns knowledge and experience. The outlook is scientific, not mythic. The world created by God is beneficial and good. If wise persons can realize the natural laws and understand them, they will also be able to participate in the many worldly goods.

The world of wisdom portrays the struggle between good and evil, between two groups of humans, the righteous and the wicked, the wise and the fool. As a result, wisdom literature is characterized by a strong didactic element; one can and should learn to understand wisdom. Wisdom is nurtured in the relationship between humans, and is passed on from the sage to his pupils, from father to son, from the older to the younger generation. In wisdom, faith in YHWH is expressed primarily through behavior; the wise person knows that YHWH will reward correct behavior. For that reason, virtue plays a significant role in wisdom literature. Examples of desirable qualities are respect for YHWH's order, diligence, patience, moderation, endurance, humility, respect for the elderly, a son's respect for his father. To walk in the ways of virtue brings life; the opposite leads to destruction. That virtue is rewarded and vice is punished is, in short, the central message of wisdom's worldview.

The idea of divine retribution thus plays a prominent role in wisdom. There is, however, no real uniformity in the understanding of retribution in the Hebrew Bible. Just as with the Deuteronomists and the Chroniclers, the book of Proverbs contains the view that if one does good, one will be rewarded with good, but if one chooses evil, things will go badly. Human experience will often lead to this system being put to the test. In Ecclesiastes and Job, therefore, as a contrast to this straightforward view, we find a far more pessimistic tone. In Ecclesiastes in particular, pure skepticism is expressed. The author of Ecclesiastes does not doubt the existence of God, but he doubts that God is at all interested in getting involved in the welfare of human beings here on earth.

Wisdom Personified

A particular phenomenon in wisdom literature is the personification of wisdom as a woman. We encounter this motif in the book of Proverbs. Various explanations have been given, with some understanding it as a type of hypostasis of wisdom, and others seeing a hidden goddess behind "Lady Wisdom" in Proverbs. Since personification is a widespread poetic device in the Hebrew Bible, however, most scholars regard the occurrence in Proverbs as a typical example of personification.

"Lady Wisdom" plays an important role in Proverbs, in particular in the creation account in Proverbs 8, which states that she was present when God created the world. The text in Proverbs 8, however, also has to be read in its context, Proverbs 7–9. Here one will see how well the descriptions of "Lady Wisdom" and "Lady Folly" fit the common wisdom pattern of the struggle between good and evil, the wise and the fool.

THE BOOK OF JOB

The book of Job is not only a representative example of wisdom literature, but also one of the gems of world literature. The book takes its name from the main character in the story. The English form of the name is taken from Greek *Iōb*, which renders Hebrew *'iyyob*. Scholars have offered many explanations for the meaning of the name Job, though they have not reached a consensus.

Job has several prototypes in the Near East. For example, the "Sumerian Job" (also known as "A Man and His God"; at least early second millennium BCE) is about a man who has lost everything, like the biblical Job. A striking difference between the Sumerian Job and the biblical one is that the Sumerian sufferer knows about and admits his guilt all along, whereas Job is not aware that he has committed any sin. Job sees himself as an innocent sufferer, more like the "Babylonian Job" (a work also called "I Will Praise the Lord of Wisdom"; late second millennium BCE).

The author of the book of Job was a great poet, and mastered to perfection the ancient Hebrew poetic techniques of the craft, which he used to a great extent. When it comes to the question of dating and authorship, again, Job scholars have not reached any agreement. We simply do not have enough clues in the text to be able to make any conclusive statements about these issues. Sometime between the sixth and the third century BCE is perhaps the closest we can get to a date.

Also, the book of Job gives a somewhat disjointed impression, bringing us to suspect an extended process of editing and transmission behind the present shape of the text. Again, this is absolutely no hindrance to a successful final-form reading of the text. On the contrary! It is in the form that we now have it that the book of Job has captured such great interest among so many throughout the centuries.

It is not easy to decide the main genre of the book of Job. The book contains various genres. The most appropriate characteristic of the book of Job as a whole might be "drama."

The book of Job can be divided into five parts: prose prologue (Job 1–2), dialogue (Job 3–31), the Elihu speeches (Job 32–37), YHWH's revelation and speeches (38:1–42:6), and prose epilogue (42:7–17).

The story of Job belongs to the classics of Western culture. A man by the name of Job is well known for his fear of God, piety, righteousness, and great fortune. One day a council is held in heaven. God asks Satan, who has wandered around on earth, if he has noticed the righteous and God-fearing Job. Satan then asks the question of whether Job's piety and righteousness are without ulterior motives. If he should suddenly lose his whole fortune, would not Job renounce YHWH? YHWH takes on the challenge, and gives Satan power over all of Job's property, but he must spare Job himself. Satan then takes away everything that Job owns—even his children are killed. But Job's reaction is not what Satan had expected. Robbed of everything he has in life, Job exclaims:

> Naked I came from my mother's womb,
> and naked shall I return there,
> The Lord gave, and the Lord has taken away;
> blessed be the name of the Lord.
>
> Job 1:21

As for the contents of the book of Job, it consists of a number of different literary genres. With the exception of the prologue and epilogue, the book is poetry. About half of the poetry consists of "hymnic praise" and "individual songs of lament." Both of these literary genres are well known from the Old Testament Psalms. In Job we find hymnic material spread throughout the whole book—for example, in Job's speeches in 9:4–12; 12:13–25; and 26:5–14. Sometimes the material is very similar to what we may find in biblical psalms. Particularly striking is the similarity between parts of the book of

Job and Psalm 104. Examples of the genre of lament may be found in Job's speeches in 3:3–26; 6:2–7:21; 9:25–10:22; 16:6–17:9; and 29:1–31:37.

Not surprisingly, we also find genres from wisdom literature represented in several places in the book of Job. This type of literature is found most extensively in the last part of Eliphaz's second speech, 15:17–35, which for the most part consists of proverblike expressions. However, it would be wrong to reduce wisdom in the book of Job to proverbial statements. When we look closer, we find that wisdom in one form or another permeates the whole book. The main topic of the drama concerns whether Job has sinned unknowingly. His friends are convinced that he has. Since God is just, and wisdom is great, all Job has to do is to follow God's plan. If he admits his sin, he will again be richly rewarded. All of this has, at bottom, to do with wisdom or a wisdom mentality. In addition, one will find throughout the various poetic compositions imagery that is well known from wisdom. Particularly important are references to retribution, creation, and the natural world.

A genre that is developed further in the book of Job than elsewhere in the Hebrew Bible is the dialogue. There are several examples of dialogues in the Old Testament. Well known is the story of Abraham arguing with God about the destruction of Sodom in Genesis 18:22–32. In the book of Job, even though the dialogue as a literary tradition is developed to its most refined, the genre forms an integrated part of the wider wisdom drama.

The reason that the book of Job has had such wide appeal, not least in modern times, is not only its wonderful poetic form. Equally relevant is that it deals with a problem that is timeless, the questions of guilt and sin, of innocent suffering, and of the meaning of life.

Some scholars have characterized Job and Ecclesiastes in particular as examples of the world of wisdom being struck by a crisis. This is too simplistic. We must not think so mechanically about ancient societies that we do not allow them the right to also cast doubt on parts of their own tradition. Doubt and existential need are not modern inventions!

THE BOOK OF PROVERBS

The majority of the ancient Israelite proverbs that have been passed down to posterity are found collected in the biblical book called Proverbs. In Hebrew the book of Proverbs is called *Mishle shelomoh*, "the proverbs of Solomon," after the opening words. In the Septuagint it is called *Paroimiai*, "proverbs." The name "proverbs" is also reflected in the Latin translation, the Vulgate, *Liber Proverbiorum*. Most of Proverbs consists of short sayings and proverbs stated in poetic form.

Many see Proverbs as the embodiment of wisdom literature. As in most cultures where traditions are passed on from generation to generation, also in oral form, proverbs probably played a significant role in ancient Israelite culture. In the various cultures surrounding ancient Israel we find a considerable element of proverbial literature. Large collections of proverbs are particularly well known from ancient Sumer, but proverbs were widespread in Egypt, in Assyria, and in Babylonia. Most proverbs of the Bible are found in edited collections. Relatively few proverbs have been transmitted in context from ancient Israel. Examples of these are Genesis 10:9; 1 Samuel 24:13; 2 Samuel 20:18; 1 Kings 20:11; Jeremiah 31:29; and Ezekiel 18:2.

In the opening words of Proverbs, we find a full title, not unlike modern books, and an author, with a lengthy "subtitle," giving didactic instructions for use:

> The proverbs of Solomon son of David, king of Israel:
> For learning about wisdom and instruction,
> for understanding words of insight,
> for gaining instruction in wise dealing,
> righteousness, justice, and equity;
> to teach shrewdness to the simple,
> knowledge and prudence to the young—
> Let the wise also hear and gain in learning,
> and the discerning acquire skill,
> to understand a proverb and a figure,
> the words of the wise and their riddles.
>
> The fear of the LORD is the beginning of knowledge;
> fools despise wisdom and instruction.
> Proverbs 1:1–7

However, this motley collection of quite disparate proverbs does not have much to do with King Solomon. Because this king in the biblical tradition was famous for his great wisdom, most proverbs were naturally ascribed to him in the same way that the book of Psalms was attributed to King David. We read about Solomon in 1 Kings 4:29–34:

> God gave Solomon very great wisdom, discernment, and breadth of understanding as vast as the sand on the seashore, so that Solomon's wisdom surpassed the wisdom of all the people of the east, and all the wisdom of Egypt. He was wiser than anyone else, wiser than Ethan the Ezrahite, and Heman, Calcol, and Darda, children of Mahol; his fame spread throughout all the surrounding nations. He composed three thousand proverbs, and his songs numbered a thousand and five. He would speak of trees, from the cedar that is in the Lebanon to the hyssop that grows in the wall; he would speak of animals, and

birds, and reptiles, and fish. People came from all the nations to hear the wisdom of Solomon; they came from all the kings of the earth who had heard of his wisdom.

Proverbs are typical examples of tradition literature that does not go back to any real author but has been shaped over a very long period of time. We do not know precisely what time period this anonymous literature might come from. There is no reason to doubt, however, that this type of literature might be old, and may go back some time before the exilic period (end of the sixth century BCE). We may assume this because we know of proverbs from the surrounding world of ancient Israel that go quite far back in time, and the great likeness between the ancient Israelite proverbs and proverbs from the surrounding cultures is striking.

In the case of some Egyptian proverbs the similarities are so remarkable that various scholars have thought that the biblical proverbs have been taken over directly from extrabiblical cultures. But this is not at all the only way to see this. The ancient Near Eastern cultures were closely related geographically and culturally. A certain influence from large cultures like Egypt or Mesopotamia on their smaller neighbors, Israel among them, should not surprise us. In this case, as in many others, it is more likely correct to assume that we are dealing with different expressions within a larger common culture, rather than with any systematic or mechanical direct takeover of the cultural material of the neighboring nations. When it comes to cultural expressions such as proverbs, we know how great similarities can be between closely related societies, even in our own time.

It is difficult to be very specific about the transmission process of the book of Proverbs and its composition history. In the shape that the book has been handed down to us, it can hardly be claimed that it is of a particularly popular nature. Building on style and vocabulary, many scholars have thought that the collection came into existence at the court, or possibly in schools, or in schools with a close connection to the court or the temple. Others have argued that Proverbs must go back to a time before the establishment of the monarchy, before 1000 BCE, and that it reflects early tribal conditions. In this case Proverbs might derive from the tribal chief's ethical rules for the members of the tribal society.

Yet others have pointed out that Proverbs must originally have been some type of "popular" proverbial literature, and that this in turn had been exposed to elitist environments that later had shaped and developed it. Based on content, this might be the best explanation. We would then be dealing with a type of "popular" literature that may have found its use in different social contexts: education, law, everyday speech, and so on. For everyday speech, one may refer to the introductory formulae, found in several places in Proverbs, of the type, "Hear, my child, your father's instruction, and do not reject your mother's teaching" (Prov. 1:8). This type of formula would indicate that proverbs have been used by parents in their child rearing. The problem, however, is that the stylized formula "And you, my child . . ." may have little to do with family relationships. It is, rather, the traditional, formulaic reference to a disciple, well known from wisdom literature.

Finally, some explanations take their point of departure from the fact that not nearly all of the Bible's proverbs are specifically instructional in character. Since there existed in ancient Israel an intellectual class (the scribes), one may count on the possibility that people who have belonged to this class have sought intellectual stimulus and entertainment from this type of literature.

Common to all of the explanations mentioned above is that they reveal a strong need for theorizing, classifying, and explaining. All the explanations might be plausible, but we probably need to admit that this literature simply will not fit easily into such simple models. We must be satisfied with the observation that we do have this type of literature from ancient Israel, and that it might have its origin in so-called popular wisdom. Proverbs may have been instructive, but they could also just as well represent wisdom based on experience, a type of philosophy that was expressed in rhyme, aphorisms, and paradoxes, and that may have been literarily reworked in different stages, until it finally grew to an extensive, written literature. The distinction that some scholars wish to make between "written, learned" and "oral, popular" proverbs, or "earlier" and "later" types of proverbs is problematic. It is a major obstacle that the tradition processes that took place before the final standardizations of the texts cannot be distinguished or traced with certainty. Available to us are only those proverbs now extant in the Hebrew Bible. We must also observe that the book of Proverbs has had a great influence on Western culture, where classical as well as biblical proverbs have played, and still do play, a major role.

Below follow some examples of biblical proverbs. Some will nod in recognition when they read the words, and be reminded that these ancient proverbs seem to be just as timely today as they were three thousand years ago. Human nature has not changed much!

We notice how also the proverbial literature is set in a religious context,

> The eyes of the Lord are in every place,
> keeping watch on the evil and the good.
> 15:3

> The Lord is far from the wicked,
> but he hears the prayer of the righteous.
> 15:29

When the ways of the people please the LORD,
he causes even their enemies to be at peace with them.
16:7

The fear of the LORD is a fountain of life,
so that one may avoid the snares of death.
14:27

A number of proverbs characterize human nature and try to teach judgment of character.

The words of a whisperer are like delicious morsels;
they go down into the inner parts of the body.
26:22

Whoever belittles another lacks sense,
but an intelligent person remains silent.
11:12

Pride goes before destruction,
and a haughty spirit before a fall.
16:18

Fools think their own way is right,
but the wise listen to advice.
12:15

Even in laughter the heart is sad,
and the end of joy is grief.
14:13

A good name is to be chosen rather than great riches,
and favor is better than silver or gold.
22:1

Let another praise you, and not your own mouth—
a stranger, and not your own lips.
27:2

The simple believe everything,
but the clever consider their steps.
14:15

The poor are disliked even by their neighbors,
but the rich have many friends.
14:20

Wealth brings many friends,
but the poor are left friendless.
19:4

Gray hair is a crown of glory;
it is gained in a righteous life.
16:31

If one gives answer before hearing,
it is folly and shame.
18:13

In the world of proverbs, laziness is a great sin, and work is a virtue, as the following examples illustrate:

The lazy person does not plow in season;
harvest comes, and there is nothing to be found.
20:4

For the drunkard and the glutton will come to poverty,
and drowsiness will clothe them with rags.
23:21

Go to the ant, you lazybones;
consider its ways, and be wise.
6:6

THE BOOK OF ECCLESIASTES

In Hebrew the book is called *Qohelet*, after the alleged author. *Qohelet* has traditionally been translated "preacher"; the word appears seven times in Ecclesiastes but nowhere else in the Bible. In the Septuagint the book is called *Ekklēsiastēs* (the Greek rendering of *Qohelet*), meaning "member of the assembly." The meaning of Hebrew *qohelet* is much debated; we really do not know what it means. In Ecclesiastes 1:12 Qohelet says about himself, "I, the Teacher (*Qohelet*), when king over Israel in Jerusalem . . ." We may also read about the author in 12:8–9: "Vanity of vanities, says the Teacher (*Qohelet*); all is vanity. Besides being wise, the Teacher (*Qohelet*) also taught the people knowledge, weighing and studying and arranging many proverbs."

Ecclesiastes gives us yet another example of a biblical text that has been ascribed to an author other than the "real author." The only son of David who, according to the biblical tradition, was a king in Jerusalem was Solomon. The ascription of a piece of wisdom literature to Solomon is not surprising.

The biblical traditions speak several times of the great wisdom of King Solomon. As we have seen, the book of Proverbs is also ascribed to King Solomon.

The theme and general tone of Ecclesiastes are struck in a characteristic way through the opening words of 1:1–9:

> The words of the Teacher (*Qohelet*), the son of David, king in Jerusalem.
> Vanity of vanities, says the Teacher (*Qohelet*),
> vanity of vanities! All is vanity.
> What do people gain from all the toil
> at which they toil under the sun?
> A generation goes, and a generation comes,
> but the earth remains forever.
> The sun rises and the sun goes down,
> and hurries to the place where it rises.
> The wind blows to the south,
> and goes around to the north;
> round and round goes the wind,
> and on its circuits the wind returns.
> All streams run to the sea,
> but the sea is not full;
> to the place where the streams flow,
> there they continue to flow.
> All things are wearisome;
> more than one can express;
> The eye is not satisfied with seeing,
> or the ear filled with hearing.
> What has been is what will be,
> and what has been done is what will be done;
> there is nothing new under the sun.

In many ways the author comes across as something of a philosopher, with a terminology that one does not often associate with Hebrew literature (1:12–13):

> I, the Teacher (*Qohelet*), when king over Israel in Jerusalem, applied my mind to seek and to search out by wisdom all that is done under heaven; it is an unhappy business that God has given to human beings to be busy with.

Some readers consider Ecclesiastes to be the strangest book in the Bible. The skepticism and the many pessimistic points of view that characterize the work have led many Bible readers to see it as not appropriate to the biblical context. This opinion is not new. The views of Ecclesiastes that we find in Hillel and Shammai are telling. These two learned rabbis lived in the time of Jesus, and played a central role in the development of the important Jewish concept of the Oral Torah. For Hillel, Qohelet (Ecclesiastes) was a holy book, whereas for the stricter Shammai it was not. The reason why the book in the end did find its place in the Writings (Ketuvim), the last part of the Hebrew Scriptures, is possibly because it was ascribed to King Solomon. Ecclesiastes was canonized toward the end of the first century CE.

Further, a more careful study of Ecclesiastes shows that it is not so far from the outlook that permeates this work to other wisdom books in the Old Testament. This applies first and foremost to Job, but comparison may also be made to the type of thoughts expressed in, for example, Psalm 73:3–12.

> For I was envious of the arrogant;
> I saw the prosperity of the wicked.
>
> For they have no pain,
> their bodies are sound and sleek.
> They are not in trouble as others are;
> they are not plagued like other people.
> Therefore pride is their necklace,
> violence covers them like a garment.
> Their eyes swell out with fatness;
> their hearts overflow with follies.
> They scoff and speak with malice;
> loftily they threaten oppression.
> They set their mouths against heaven,
> and their tongues range over the earth.
>
> Therefore the people turn and praise them,
> and find no fault in them.
> And they say, "How can God know?
> Is there knowledge in the Most High?"
> Such are the wicked;
> always at ease, they increase in riches.

Ecclesiastes is made up of reflections in the form of a monologue, based on personal experience and observations. The Teacher's experiences are very pessimistic. "Traditional" wisdom takes as its point of departure a world that is an ordered entity, where each individual must experience what is demanded of him or her, and where the individual will be punished or rewarded depending on whether he or she behaves according to God's order. In Ecclesiastes the existence of such a divinely ordered universe comes under doubt.

The experience of Ecclesiastes is that the "wicked" are rewarded. There is one principle in the world, namely that everything repeats itself, and there is nothing positive in this. Faith in divine retribution, so strong in traditional wisdom, does not belong to this order. With weary monotony and cynical weltschmerz, Ecclesiastes points out that nature works indeed like clockwork in accordance with laws that have been established once and for all.

Ecclesiastes is a very advanced text that contains scientific truths, acceptable even today. For example, 1:7 is regarded as one of the first attestations of one of the basic laws of limnology (the scientific study of inland freshwater): "All streams run to the sea, but the sea is not full; to the place where the streams flow, there they continue to flow."

In contrast to the laws of nature is the fate of humanity. Human life must submit to arbitrary coincidence. Happiness on earth and joy over life is therefore meaningless. When death arrives it is all over. Therefore pleasure becomes even more important. Eat and drink and love while you can! Soon comes old age and death, and it is all over. Again, we are dealing with a profound text containing several philosophical ideas (pessimism, hedonism, existentialism).

This philosophy was apparently too provocative for some of the ancient scribes. Toward the end of the work, an editor has added his own comments in order to adapt the text more to a traditional, orthodox view of the relationship between God, Torah, and the pious. The unknown commentator says about Qohelet that he was a wise man, and that wisdom is important. At the same time, he warns against this type of writing, and lets the book end in a hortatory speech that is contrary to the controversial content of the book. Only in this way could this work be accepted as part of the Jewish canon (12:12–14):

> Of anything beyond these, my child, beware. Of making many books there is no end, and much study is a weariness of the flesh.

> The end of the matter; all has been heard. Fear God, and keep his commandments; for that is the whole duty of everyone. For God will bring every deed into judgment, including every secret thing, whether good or evil.

Novellas

Jonah, Ruth, Esther

Three small literary works in various ways distinguish themselves from the rest of the Old Testament: the books of Jonah, Ruth, and Esther. All of these compositions must be regarded as being quite interesting examples of ancient Hebrew storytelling. For lack of a better term, we might characterize Jonah, Ruth, and Esther as Classical Hebrew "novellas."

THE BOOK OF JONAH

The book of Jonah is undoubtedly one of the least typical books of the Hebrew Bible. Even though it is placed as the fifth of the Book of the Twelve in the Hebrew Bible (sixth in the Septuagint), it distinguishes itself from the other prophetic books. While the prophetic books for the most part contain collections of various oracles of doom and salvation, the book of Jonah contains a story about a prophet. Although there are biographical notices also in the other prophetic books—for instance, in Amos, Hosea, Isaiah, and Jeremiah—the Jonah narrative reminds one more of the stories about prophets that we find in the Deuteronomistic History. Even if there are similarities to other prophetical stories in this literary work, the several supernatural traits found in the stories about the legendary Elijah the Tishbite may constitute a close parallel.

In the superscription the name of this prophet is given as Jonah ben Amittai. A prophet by this name is mentioned in 2 Kings 14:25, and is said to have been active during the reign of Jeroboam II, that is, in the eighth century BCE. Most researchers date the book of Jonah much later, to the sixth–fifth century BCE.

It is not easy to understand the book of Jonah. The genre is not clear. For example, some scholars have called it a parable, some a legend, and others have referred to it as a novella. This last term is probably the one that best characterizes the content of the book. We are dealing with a prophetic novella, the primary purpose of which was to entertain. The story is dynamic, has humor, and contains didactic elements with ironic undertones. With the account of the stay inside the belly of the fish we also have a fairytale motif.

Especially when reading the story in Hebrew, we discover that the Jonah narrative is full of humor. The account takes its point of departure from the prophet who resists. To resist a calling is not an unusual phenomenon in the Old Testament (see, for example, Judg. 6:15; 1 Sam. 9:21; Jer. 1:6). But in Jonah a big point is made of the issue, and the resistance has far-reaching consequences. One main point in the Jonah story has to do with the inscrutability and power of YHWH, and may recall in some ways the moral of the book of Job.

From the book of Jonah we can also learn about how the ancient Hebrew authors worked. Even though the book should be read as a unit, it may seem to modern readers to be composite. It is clear that the author (we might prefer the term "editor") makes use of a whole range of traditional motifs and compositions. Particularly illustrative of how the ancient authors worked is the prayer of Jonah in the belly of the fish (chap. 2). Here we find a psalm of thanksgiving, closely related to the psalms of thanksgiving that we find in the book of Psalms. It is less important to us today whether the prayer in Jonah 2 was entirely composed by the author or inserted partly or completely from other materials by an editor. Moreover, speculations over a possible closer relationship to similar psalms that we have access to in the present book of Psalms have not always been convincing. We have to respect the way the ancient Hebrew authors worked. In spite of its impression of being composite, the book of Jonah is a well-composed unit, and the author meant the story to be read as a whole.

THE BOOK OF RUTH

The story of the Moabite woman Ruth, who leaves her family and her homeland to follow her Hebrew mother-in-law, Naomi, to her hometown Bethlehem, belongs among the most beautiful of the biblical stories. The book of Ruth represents the art of Hebrew storytelling at its prime, with suspense, undertones of eroticism, and a happy ending, when the foreign widow is married to a "Judean of good family." The whole story is set into a context of a family genealogy, with the Moabite woman Ruth becoming the great-grandmother of King David.

The main theme in the book of Ruth is the faithfulness of the foreign woman. As childless and a widow, Ruth leaves her homeland, her family, and her religion to go with her mother-in-law to Judah. In Judah, Ruth continues to show her faithfulness by seeing to her mother-in-law's care by providing food for the home.

Again, this short, novella-like narrative bears witness to the diversity of the Hebrew Bible. For example, the story stands in contrast to the animosity toward foreigners and the prohibition against marriage with foreign women that we find in late texts such as the books of Ezra and Nehemiah. In addition to faithfulness, one of its main points is that the lineage of David is secured through the marriage of the foreign woman.

We also find many references to ancient Hebrew law in the book of Ruth. We may read about purchases and sales of property, and in the description of Boaz it becomes clear that not only is he a relative, but he is also a *go'el*, a "redeemer." A *go'el* is the person who, on behalf of the family, was responsible for buying back property that had been sold out of the family, and relatives who had been sold as slaves. Because two different "redeemers" appear in the book of Ruth, this brings some tension into the story before it all ends with marriage between Ruth and Boaz.

Another juridical institution that is touched on in the book is that of the levirate. A levirate marriage entailed that the brother of a man who died without leaving any descendants was obliged to marry the deceased brother's widow. The firstborn of their sons would take his deceased father's place and continue the lineage. From the book of Ruth (4:10) it seems that Boaz's role in relation to Ruth was similar to the levirate.

Because the view of marriage and foreign women stands in such a contrast to the books of Ezra and Nehemiah, many scholars have claimed that Ruth must be dated very early (900–700 BCE). We cannot, however, disregard the possibility that there may have been different points of view on mixed marriages also in later periods. Even though the content of the book in many ways gives an archaic impression, we have no hard evidence for dating the book of Ruth.

THE BOOK OF ESTHER

The book of Esther is special in more than a few ways. The setting is in the Persian Diaspora, and the homeland is not mentioned. The work is many-faceted and difficult to assign to a genre. The book of Esther is suspenseful and entertaining, but it is historically quite improbable. Perhaps it can best be characterized as a "secular novella." The composition has no religious undertones, and some biblical scholars have for that reason wondered why it has ended up in the Jewish canon. In Christian tradition the discussion of whether the book of Esther should be part of the canon continued into the fourth century CE.

None of the persons mentioned in the book of Esther is known from extra-biblical literature or can be identified in any other way. The names of the main characters, Esther and Mordecai, have etymological connections to the names of the Mesopotamian deities Ishtar and Marduk. Esther's Jewish name is Hadassah (Esth. 2:7). Some researchers believe that the royal name Aha-suerus might be a Jewish variant of the Persian name for Xerxes, who reigned 486–465 BCE. The name Marduka/Mordecai is also known from lists of Per-sian civil servants from the sixth century BCE. We do not know much more than this. Possibly, the story of Esther and Mordecai as we now know it was written in Judah as late as the fourth or third century BCE, and carries with it memories from a life in the Diaspora in Persia. The book of Esther is, in that case, one of the very latest books of the Bible.

There are some strong indications that the story about the Jewish girl Esther who became queen in the Persian kingdom has been shaped over a long time. Apparently, there existed several different versions before the text developed into the form that we know today. It is interesting in that connection to notice that the Greek translation, the Septuagint, has a much more extended text, with sixteen chapters instead of the ten that we find in the Hebrew Bible and in Protestant/Reformed Bible editions. In these traditions the extended Esther text is not canonical but is called "the Additions to Esther," and is counted among the apocryphal writings. Since the Vulgate adopted the Old Testa-ment books from the Septuagint, the Roman Catholic canon also includes "the Additions to Esther" and other apocrypha. However, Catholics call these texts not "apocryphal," but "deuterocanonical," to indicate their higher status among Catholics than among Protestant and Reformed churches.

The book of Esther contains the account of the first pogrom in history, and is characterized by strong national glorification and ethnic awareness, with an attitude of hostility toward non-Jews. It is typical that Christianity, in particular in its more anti-Jewish circles, has not cared much for the book of Esther. The infamous statements of Luther are illustrative; he wished that the books of Maccabees and Esther had never existed. However, it would be anachronistic not to regard such statements as expressions of the attitude of the time.

In Judaism the book of Esther has played a major role, with the evil Haman as the symbol of all the cruelty and the prejudices that have threatened Jew-ish existence throughout the centuries, and with the hope for a way out of the misery. It is possibly a misunderstanding that the theme of revenge is central to the book. The account that we find in Esther 9 can just as easily be understood as a theme of self-defense than as a theme of revenge. The book of Esther definitely deserves its place in the canon as an expression of the rich variety of the Old Testament, and as a constant reminder that the Bible cannot easily be reduced to one formula.

The book of Esther, together with Song of Songs, Ruth, Lamentations, and Ecclesiastes, make up the Five Megilloth, the festival scrolls. The book of Esther is the festival legend of the Feast of Purim. The connection to this Jewish feast is most likely secondary. Purim is celebrated as a festival of joy to remember that the greatest threat to Jewish existence in ancient times had a happy ending. In spite of the fact that the Jewish festive culture normally has a level-headed view of alcohol, the Talmud's prescriptions about Purim says that the participants in the feast must drink wine until they no longer are able to distinguish between "Cursed be Haman" and "Blessed be Mordecai." In the modern period Purim is a feast of joy with the exchange of presents, a festive dinner, and the reading of the book of Esther in the synagogue. Over the last few centuries European carnival celebrations have also influenced the celebration of Purim.

Glossary

Adar. Twelfth month in the Hebrew calendar, formed from Akkadian *adaru*, the twelfth month in the Mesopotamian lunar year. In the postexilic lunar Jewish calendar, with a year that began in the spring, it corresponds to our February/March. The Jewish feast of Purim is celebrated on 14 Adar.

Akkadian. A generic term for the Semitic dialects Assyrian and Babylonian. Akkadian is the oldest known Semitic language, going back to about 3000 BCE (Akkadian personal names in Sumerian texts). It constituted the main language in the ancient Near East for around two thousand years until replaced by Aramaic around the sixth century BCE. The word "Akkadian" derives from the city of Akkad, which was the capital of Sargon's Old Babylonian Empire (end of the third millennium BCE). The location of the city is not known, but it may have been near the modern city of Baghdad.

Alexandria. A city in Egypt founded by Alexander the Great in 331 BCE. The city was famous for its art and science and had the largest library in the world at the time. It became an important center for early Jewish and Christian culture.

allegorical interpretation. A specific way of reading texts that is not interested in the literal or surface meaning, but that looks for the hidden or deep meaning of the text. Allegorical interpretation, which should not be confused with the modern study of allegory in literary studies, was common in antiquity and had a resurgence in the Hellenistic study of Homer. Eventually, it gained ground first in Jewish and later in Christian circles and came to have great significance for reading biblical texts. The most prominent representative for the allegorical method of interpretation in Judaism was Philo of Alexandria, a Greek-speaking Hellenistic Jewish philosopher, who used allegorical biblical interpretation to unite Judaism with Greek philosophy. Later the method was used extensively by some of the church fathers, in particular Clement of Alexandria and Origen, who by interpreting allegorically could read the whole Old Testament as a purely Christian document. Augustine also used the method.

The allegorical method was developed systematically in the Western medieval period, where eventually four levels were identified in textual interpretation: (1) literal, or *sensus literalis*, the original factual meaning; (2) allegorical, also called tropological, the deeper, mystical meaning that teaches what the reader should believe; (3) moral, which teaches how one should live; (4) analogical, which looks ahead to the goal that the Christian believer's life leads to. Partly through the influence from the humanism of the Renaissance and partly in a polemic against the interpretive tradition of the Roman Church, the reformers Calvin, Luther, and Zwingli turned against all forms of allegorical interpretation and recognized only *sensus literalis*, in their belief that the original meaning of the text preserved the word of God in a pure state and protected against the arbitrariness of the various allegorical interpreters. Since the breakthrough of historical-critical biblical studies in the nineteenth century, the allegorical method has played a very modest role.

Ammon. Semitic kingdom situated east of ancient Israel (in present-day Jordan), and often at war with the Israelites. The Ammonite civilization bloomed between 1200 and 500 BCE.

An. The highest god of the Sumerian pantheon. An was the father of Enlil, who was the main god or national god of the Sumerians. The cult of An was mainly in the city of Uruk.

apocalypse. A literary genre in early Judaism and in Christianity that makes extensive use of visions, dreams, departure speeches, cosmic changes, and eschatological expectations of an imminent cataclysm (from Greek *apokalypsis*, which means "revelation"). Examples of apocalypses: the book of Daniel, the book of Revelation, Shepherd of Hermas, *1* and *2 Enoch*, *4 Ezra*, *2* and *3 Baruch*, *Jubilees*, and *Apocalypse of Abraham*.

Apocalypse of Abraham. A Jewish pseudepigraphic book, transmitted only in Slavic. The work, which is based on a Greek translation of an originally Hebrew or Aramaic text, contains a haggadic midrash on Genesis 15:9–17 and covers, among other topics, the youth of Abraham. At the end of the work there are a number of Christian interpolations. It is usually dated to sometime before 100 CE.

Apocrypha. From Greek *apokryphos*, "hidden"; a group of writings not included in the Hebrew canon, but included in a number of early Christian editions of the Old Testament (for example, the Septuagint), In Hebrew these are called *chitsoniyyim*, "the ones on the outside." From the time of Luther the term "Apocrypha" became standard among Protestants. Luther also considered four New Testament writings as apocryphal: the Epistle to the Hebrews, James, Jude, and the book of Revelation. There is no real agreement on which writings should be counted among the Apocrypha, and the selection varies in different contexts. One list consists of Tobit, Wisdom of Solomon, Wisdom of Jesus Son of Sirach, Baruch, Letter of Jeremiah, Additions to the Greek Book of Daniel (Prayer of Azariah, Song of the Three Jews, Susanna, Bel and the Dragon), and Prayer of Manasseh. In the Catholic Church, as part of the canon, they have a higher status than in the Protestant church traditions. In a Catholic context the Pseudepigrapha are often called "apocrypha." A common term for both Apocrypha and Pseudepigrapha is "intertestamental writings," which expresses that these writings belong to neither the Old Testament nor the New Testament, but that they originate in the period between the two Testaments.

Aram. A league of ancient states in the Near East that came to have great significance particularly from around the beginning of the first millennium BCE. The Arameans lived northeast of Palestine, in an area approximately covering present-day Syria, and were continuously at war with the Israelites. The language that we call Aramaic is a West Semitic language closely related to Hebrew. We also know of a number of dialects from later periods. The language is attested from the ninth century BCE all the way to the present. According to biblical traditions, Abraham was of Aramean descent. With the Assyrian king Tiglath-pileser III's conquest of the Aramean states in the eighth century BCE, Aramaic was taken over by the Assyrian Empire as the language of diplomacy and acquired great significance from the eighth to the fourth century BCE. Some Old Testament texts are written in Aramaic rather than in Hebrew (Ezra 4:8–6:18; 7:12–26; Dan. 2:4–7:28).

Asherah. West Semitic fertility and mother goddess. In the past, there was a major discussion about whether this was the name of a goddess or a type of cultic object.

With the discovery of the Ras Shamra texts it became clear that Asherah was indeed the name of a goddess, and it became necessary to reevaluate the understanding of the occurrences of the word *'asherah* in the Bible. Gradually, our knowledge of Asherah has increased markedly. Asherah was worshiped across large parts of the ancient Near East, including Israel. In the latter part of the twentieth century, textual discoveries at Kuntillet Ajrud and Khirbet el-Qom indicate that the God YHWH in ancient Israel was worshiped with the female deity Asherah at his side.

Assyria. Ancient empire in the Near East. The capital was first Ashur, then (from the eighth century BCE) Nineveh. The major part of Assyria covered present-day northern Iraq, by the upper part of the Tigris River. The Assyrian Empire developed in the second millennium BCE (Old Assyrian and Middle Assyrian periods) to an extensive empire. But the Neo-Assyrian Empire became the most significant (around tenth–seventh centuries BCE), developing into the largest empire hitherto known in the ancient Near East. The Assyrians conquered Samaria in 721 BCE and turned the northern kingdom of Israel into an Assyrian province. An attempt to conquer Jerusalem, the capital of Judah, failed. The Neo-Assyrian Empire was taken over by the Babylonians (the Neo-Babylonian Empire) in 612 BCE, when the imperial capital Nineveh fell to the Babylonian armies.

Assyriology. The study of the ancient Babylonian and Assyrian languages, history, religion, and literature.

asylum, right of. Legal provisions guaranteeing a sanctuary, a place of refuge (from Greek *asylia*). Many peoples in antiquity designated specific locations to be secure places of refuge for people who were fleeing for various reasons, including flight as a result of criminal acts. In ancient Israel the festivals and the temple in Jerusalem were times and places for temporary escape from criminal prosecution. In addition, six Levitical towns were appointed as specific towns of refuge for murderers. In this way society attempted to decrease the incidence of blood vengeance.

Atargatis. Head goddess in northern Syria in Hellenistic times, in the Roman period known as Dea Syria.

Attar. A popular war and rain god in ancient South Arabia, also worshiped in other places in the ancient Near East.

Av. The fifth month in the Mesopotamian lunar year. According to Jewish tradition the ninth of Av is the day that both the First and the Second Temple fell. Jewish days of lament and fasting occur during this month.

Baal. Canaanite and Phoenician god of storm and fertility. The common Semitic word *ba'al* means "lord," "owner," "husband," or "head of the household" and was used both as an ordinary noun and as a divine name. Baal was worshiped in a number of local variants. The worship of Baal was widespread in Israel during the monarchic period (and probably also later).

Baba Bathra. "The last gate." The third tractate in the fourth division of the Mishnah (Neziqin, "The Order of Damages"). It contains for the most part rules for buying and selling property.

Babylonia. Ancient empire in the Near East, named for its capital, Babylon. It was located by the lower courses of the rivers Euphrates and Tigris, thus encompassing the southern part of ancient Mesopotamia (earlier Sumer). Settlement in the area is evidenced as early as the sixth millennium BCE. Together with the northern part of central Mesopotamia, Akkad, this area lay within the borders of present-day Iraq. Babylonia gained significance when an Amorite people united southern Sumer and northern Akkad. Because of the lack of sources, we know less about Babylonia than about Assyria. In the first Babylonian dynasty (ca. 1800–1600 BCE) Hammurabi was the most important king. During his reign Babylon became the most prominent city in the kingdom. The most powerful Babylonian empire was the Neo-Babylonian, founded in 625 BCE. It was in this time period that the Babylonian king Nebuchadnezzar conquered Jerusalem and brought the king of Judah and the elite of the people into captivity in Babylonia (586 BCE). The Neo-Babylonian Empire ended its days with the conquest of the Persian king Cyrus in 539 BCE, and would not emerge as an independent empire until the recent past. In 1932 the United Kingdom recognized Iraq as an independent state (a republic from 1958).

Balaam. A seer (prophet) appearing in the book of Numbers and in an inscription from Tell Deir Alla.

Biblia Hebraica Stuttgartensia. The "Stuttgart Bible," abbreviated *BHS*. It is currently the most widely used critical printed edition of the Hebrew Bible, with a set of notes showing textual variants and conjectures where the text is corrupt. *BHS* is a revised edition of *Biblica Hebraica* (abbreviated *BH;* edited by Gerhard Kittel; 3rd edition published in 1937), and was published in Stuttgart in fascicles from 1967 to 1977. *BHS* is based on a medieval masoretic manuscript called Codex Leningradensis B19A (Leningrad Codex), abbreviated L, dated to 1009 CE.

Book of the Covenant. The name given to a collection of laws found in Exodus 20:22–23:33.

Bronze Age. Archaeological period. In the ancient Near East it can be divided into Early Bronze (3200–2200 BCE), Middle Bronze (2200–1550 BCE), and Late Bronze (1550–1200 BCE).

burnt offering. See *'olah.*

Canaan. In ancient times the territory that stretched along the whole eastern coast of the Mediterranean, and that today corresponds to the southern part of Syria, Lebanon, and Palestine west of the Jordan River. In the Old Testament, where the term occurs about eighty times, Canaan is the territory where the ancient Israelites lived, that is, Palestine west of the river Jordan. As early as the fourth millennium BCE Semitic peoples have inhabited this area.

canon. Greek *kanon* means "guideline," "yardstick," and derived from this, "rule" or a "standard." The term for a set of holy scriptures that are seen as authoritative. In Christianity the Bible, with the New and the Old Testaments, makes up the canon. Prior to the canonization of the Old Testament a long and complicated historical process took place of which we have only superficial knowledge today.

chaos. In Greek cosmogony the name of a formless mass that was the beginning of all things, and from which the world came into existence.

chokmah. Hebrew word meaning "skill," "knowledge," "wisdom." The word plays a key role in the Old Testament wisdom literature.

Chroniclers. An authorial group responsible for Ezra, Nehemiah, and 1–2 Chronicles.

codex. From Latin *codex,* "notepad," "writing board." In the medieval period the term for a collection of written manuscripts in the form of a book. During the course of the first three centuries CE, the codices had gradually replaced the earlier use of rolled manuscript scrolls. See also *Biblia Hebraica Stuttgartensia.*

Codex Leningradensis **or Leningrad Codex.** See *Biblia Hebraica Stuttgartensia.*

corrupt. From Latin *corruptus,* "destroyed," not legible. In relation to ancient manuscripts, used of parts of words, words, and sentences that have been destroyed physically or were misinterpreted at an early stage in the textual transmission. Corrupt texts are no longer legible, and the meaning must be reconstructed. The phenomenon occurs often in old biblical manuscripts.

cosmos. From Greek *kosmos,* meaning "world" or "universe." In the Greek world, used in particular of the ordered world, an ordered system, as opposed to chaos.

covenant. A mutually binding agreement between two parties that played a great political, economic, and judicial role in the ancient Near East. Eventually, the concept of covenant, as transferred to the relationship between YHWH and the Israelite people (the people of God), played a significant role, perhaps constituting even the most characteristic theological trait of the Old Testament.

creatio continua. Latin for "continuing creation."

creatio ex nihilo. Latin for "creation out of nothing."

credo. Latin, literally "I believe." A creed, a confession of faith.

D. Abbreviation for the Deuteronomists or the Deuteronomic source.

Day of Atonement. See Yom Kippur.

Day of the LORD. Hebrew *yom yhwh*, literally "day of YHWH." A concept found in the prophets' description of how YHWH will intervene against Israel's enemies. Style and language bear the mark of an original context of war. At first, "the day of YHWH" was seen as something positive to the Israelites, but after a while the tradition developed in a particular way within the prophetic literature. Here it becomes part of the prophetic message of judgment, where "the day of YHWH" entails catastrophe also for the Israelite people. We have to allow that the concept may have had different meanings at different times, and that it has become detached from its original context. There is great disagreement among scholars as to how the concept should be understood. Some think that it has a cultic background. Later, the concept of "the day of YHWH" developed in a more eschatological direction.

Dead Sea Scrolls. See Qumran.

Decalogue. Greek for "ten words." "Ten Commandments." Term denoting a series of commands from YHWH to the chosen people Israel, mediated by Moses. With only a few minor variations, the Decalogue has been transmitted into different contexts in the Old Testament. In Exodus 20:1–17 Moses brings the law down from the mountain, written by the hand of YHWH on two tablets. In Deuteronomy 5:6–21 the Decalogue is part of a speech by Moses, in a retelling of the salvation history of the people.

demonist. Having to do with faith in supernatural powers, often used in a derogatory way.

Deuteronomistic History. A theological-historical work written by the group of authors we call the "Deuteronomists." The Deuteronomistic History is composed of the books of Deuteronomy, Joshua, Judges, Samuel, and Kings.

Deuteronomists. One of the groups of authors (abbreviated D) of the Old Testament responsible for the Deuteronomistic History.

do ut des. Latin for "I give so that you will give." Originally an expression from Roman law referring to a situation in which for one person to give something, the other party must do something in return. In phenomenology of religion it is used of the concept that in order for the gods to react to a request, humans must give something—for example, in the form of a sacrifice.

dragon, myth of the. Ancient Near Eastern myth of a cosmic primordial battle between a god and a mythical, dragonlike creature of chaos. The myth was important in the iconography of the ancient Near East, and sometimes it appears in connection with the creation of the world. In the Old Testament we also encounter this concept a number of times, but only in a fragmentary form (e.g., Ps. 74:13).

dynamistic. An understanding among scholars of religion, widespread in the past, that so-called primitive peoples believed in impersonal, supernatural power in humans and objects.

E. Abbreviation for the Elohist.

Eden. The name of the garden that the first humans occupied, according to the Old Testament. Without coming to any consensus, scholars have alternately explained the name Eden as stemming from Hebrew *'eden*, "charm," "delight," and Sumerian *edin*, meaning "plain," "steppe." According to the account in Genesis (2:8), God planted a garden for humans in Eden and placed Adam and Eve there after creation. When the two of them violated God's prohibition and ate of the tree of knowledge, they were driven out of the garden. A variant of the Eden story is found in Ezekiel 28:11–19. Here Eden is the image of the new Israel that will rise in its greatness after the time of the exile. Countless attempts have been made to localize Eden. The names of the four rivers mentioned in the Eden story have played a particular role in this endeavor. Since we are dealing with ancient mythological motifs (many of which are known also from descriptions of divine dwelling places in Mesopotamian and Canaanite mythology), a closer geographical localization is hardly possible.

Edom. In ancient times a designation of the area south of the Dead Sea, probably settled as far back as about 3000 BCE. The most important way of life was agriculture and trade. Most likely, Edom was an important kingdom already in the eighth century BCE. According to the Old Testament accounts the Edomites were continuously at war with the Israelites. In one period they were ruled by the kingdom of Judah. In the postexilic period parts of ancient Edom was named Idumea. According to the Old Testament the Edomites were descendants of Esau, the brother of the Israelite ancestor Jacob.

Elephantine. An island in the river Nile in Egypt. On this island there was a Jewish military colony, possibly as early as the seventh century BCE. We can read about the life of this colony in a number of papyri written in Aramaic from the fifth century BCE. The Elephantine papyri form one of the most significant extrabiblical sources about ancient Israel before the rise of Judaism. From the papyri it is clear that the religion of the colony did not represent orthodox YHWH religion as we know it from later times. The Jews of Elephantine, among other things, worshiped several gods, both male and female.

Elohim. After YHWH, the most frequent name of Israel's God in the Old Testament. See also YHWH.

Elohist. In classical source criticism, the term for one of the sources of the Pentateuch (abbreviated E). The name "Elohist" was used because this assumed source makes wide use of the divine name Elohim for the God of Israel.

Enoch, First. One of the most important of the pseudepigraphic writings (also called the *Ethiopian Book of Enoch*). *First Enoch* is a complex apocalyptic work, possibly written between 200 BCE and the first century CE. It is transmitted in its complete form only in an Ethiopic manuscript (Ethiopic is a later South Semitic language). It contains five books that can roughly be designated as follows: (1) Book of the Watchers, dealing with Enoch's travels (chaps. 1–36); (2) Book of the Similitudes (chaps. 37–71); (3) Astronomical Book (chaps. 72–82); (4) Book of Dream Visions (chaps. 83–90); (5) Book of the Epistle of Enoch (chaps. 91–107).

Enuma Elish. The great creation epic of the Babylonians. The account takes its name from the opening words, *enuma elish*, which mean "when on high." The account tells of how the god Marduk first kills the chaos creature-goddess Tiamat and then creates heaven and earth out of her body.

eschatology. The part of theology concerned with death and the last things (end times). The term is often used imprecisely about a varied set of religious concepts. Because there is widespread disagreement about the use of the term, and no one can quite agree on what it means, some would like to reduce or abolish the use of the term in Old Testament studies. When the term is used, it is not to denote any real end times, but to characterize specific ways of expression and concepts that we find in the later "authentic" eschatological literature, also with elements of apocalypticism (for example, descriptions of cosmic changes, hope in a distant future). It is important to realize, however, that more specifically eschatological topics such as death, judgment, salvation, or damnation do not belong in the Old Testament. In some instances in the Old Testament one may encounter vague concepts of the place that the dead occupy. The most common term for the netherworld is Sheol (in the LXX rendered by Greek *hadēs*, "hades"). In addition to being a name for the netherworld, the term "hades" is personified as a term for death and the negative forces of death. Compared to, for example, Mesopotamian and Egyptian mythology, these concepts of the afterlife play a surprisingly insignificant role in the Old Testament.

exegesis. The scholarly interpretation of a text (from Greek *exēgēsis*, "explanation," "interpretation"). Academic exegesis is usually historical, that is, it attempts to understand each text as it was meant to be understood in its "original" environment. The text should therefore be read in the original language, and the interpreter should be knowledgeable of the time period, the author, and the purpose of the text. While earlier exegesis tended to be more concerned with the development of the texts, current exegetical practice is more concerned with the texts in their final form.

exile. From Latin *exilium* (Hebrew *golah, galut*; Greek *aichmalōsia*). In the Old Testament, the deportation of the ruling class of Judah into captivity in Babylon, the so-called Babylonian exile of 586 BCE, when the Babylonian king Nebuchadnezzar conquered Jerusalem. From this year, the kingdom of Judah ceased to exist as a sovereign state. The practice of deporting the leading class of a city or country was well known in the ancient Near East and has been documented as early as in the second millennium BCE. Assyrian and Babylonian authorities made frequent use of forced movement as a political tool to prevent upheaval in conquered areas. The time of the exile is an important period in the history of the Old Testament, and it is commonly claimed that most of the Old Testament writings received their final form in this period.

Ezra, Fourth. A pseudepigraphic Jewish book that contains a number of visions; also called the *Apocalypse of Ezra* and *4 Esdras*. It was included in the Vulgate and subsequently combined with two additions in Greek (*5* and *6 Ezra*) to form 2 Esdras in the Apocrypha. Thus several writings under the pseudonymous author Ezra (Esdras) were in circulation in the first centuries CE. *Fourth Ezra* exists in many versions, most complete in a Latin and a Syriac edition. The original version is lost, but it is thought that *4 Ezra* originated in Palestine in the end of the first century CE, and that it was written originally in Hebrew or Aramaic. The coming of the Messiah, the end of the world, and the question of theodicy are topics treated in the book.

Feast of Booths. One of the three annual feasts in ancient Israel, celebrated in the fall.

food offering. See *minchah*.

form criticism. German *Formgeschichte* or *Gattungsgeschichte*, one of the most important methodological approaches in the academic study of the Old Testament. Because the Old Testament is a literary work, we find a number of different literary forms, oral as well as written (also called literary types, literary genres, or in German, *Gattungen*). Examples of such forms are accounts, poetry, hymns, laments, prophetic words of judgment, proverbs, plus many more. Form criticism explores the form and structure of these various literary genres. The purpose is in part to map out where these genres originally belonged in ancient Israelite society (*Sitz im Leben*, "life setting") and in part to study their development and "history."

Gattung. See form criticism.

go'el. Hebrew "redeemer," a term from ancient Israelite family law. A relative had the duty to take care of the members of the family and its property in a situation of hardship. If property had been bought by someone outside the family, the redeemer had to buy it back. Most important was the redemption of indentured family members who had become slaves. Also the honor of the family had to be kept intact, and if a family member was murdered the redeemer became a blood avenger. In the texts of the prophet Deutero-Isaiah the term *go'el* is important and is used figuratively about YHWH as the redeemer of his people after the fall of Judah and Jerusalem in 586 BCE.

Hadad. The god of storm and thunder, worshiped in large areas of the ancient Near East. Hadad is well known from Mesopotamian sources as Adad or Addu, but is most likely of West Semitic origin.

haggadah (plural, haggadot). See midrash.

hakkol. Hebrew, "the all," "everything," "totality."

halakah (plural, halakot). See midrash.

Hammurabi. King in Babylonia 1792–1750 BCE. The sixth and most important ruler in Babylon's First Dynasty. Hammurabi became known particularly as a lawgiver (the Code of Hammurabi). The laws, written in Akkadian (Old Babylonian), are preserved partially on clay tablets and partially on a stone stele now on display at the Louvre in Paris. On the stone stele 282 different legal paragraphs are inscribed, treating the economy, family affairs, criminal law, and civil law. The Code of Hammurabi is a very important document of cultural and legal history, and also plays a significant role for the understanding of ancient Israelite law.

Hatepinu. The female consort of the Hittite god of vegetation, Telipinu.

Hebrew. Hebrew *'ibri* or *'ivri*; Greek *hebraios.* The most common term for the language and culture of the ancient Israelites. In the Old Testament the term is not used very often and denotes the Israelite people, either when it is spoken of by other nations or by the Israelites themselves when they speak of themselves as opposed to other peoples. A possible connection once posited between Hebrew *'ivri* and Akkadian *hapiru* or *habiru*, Egyptian *'prw*, and Ugaritic *'prm*, meaning "outlaw" or "outcast"—a generic term for wandering bands that roamed all over the Near East in the Late Bronze Age—is now considered highly unlikely.

Hebrew Bible. Another term for the Old Testament.

Hellenism. Greek civilization. The Hellenistic period is usually thought to cover the time from the death of Alexander the Great in 323 to the battle of Actium in 31 BCE when the Romans took over Egypt. The length, content, and significance of the so-called Hellenistic period are subject to discussion, but there is agreement that it was of great significance in terms of cultural history. Traditionally, the spread of Greek culture in the Near East has been regarded as a result of Alexander's empire, and primarily through the founding of a number of new Greek/Macedonian cities, particularly in Egypt, Mesopotamia, Syria, and Asia Minor. Through these cities, Greek culture and education spread across all of Alexander's empire in the years after his death. One result of Hellenism was a melding of Greek culture and a number of Near Eastern cultures. However, we know now that this cultural interchange started to take place a few hundred years before Alexander. In terms of the history of religion, the grecizing of Near Eastern cults such as Serapis, Isis, Cybele, Sabazios, and Dea Syria attained great significance. A particularly popular cult was that of Mithras. The rapid spread of Christianity in this period can also be seen as the culmination of the spread of Near Eastern cults. The Jews played a prominent role in this period in several places. One important innovation in Hellenism was the lingua franca Koine Greek (which is also the language of the New Testament). In the city of Alexandria in Egypt, the most hellenized of all the Near Eastern countries, the Old Testament was translated into Greek (see Septuagint) because the Jews no longer understood Hebrew.

hermeneutics. The study of the methodological principles of interpretation; the academic understanding of what it means to interpret and understand texts. The term applies not only to biblical texts, and not just to texts in general, but also, for example, to works of art and music. The term has recently been applied in a number of ways within the humanities, for example, of the methods in the humanities as interpretive rather than explanatory, or of a general science of interpretation.

hieros gamos. Greek "sacred marriage." Originally a term for the marriage between Zeus and Hera in Greek religion. In the study of the history of religion the term is used of all forms of "marriage" or ritual sexual relations between a god and a goddess, particularly well known in Mesopotamian religion. Most scholars have understood that such rites were performed in the cult in order to promote fertility, and that humans participated in them as representatives of the deities. Some thought that humans might have enacted the part of the human in a "sacred marriage" between humans and gods. There is no secure basis for claiming that such rituals took place in ancient Israel.

high priest. Chief religious official. The high priest played an important role in ancient Israel. As a civil servant he was part of the royal administration and had a high level of prestige. He carried the overall responsibility for the sacrificial cult, and was the only one who had access to the inner areas of the temple. This occurred once a year, on Yom Kippur. In early Judaism the high priest had almost unrestricted power and functioned as the de facto head of state in Greco-Roman Palestine. Among other tasks, he was responsible for overseeing the taxation system. He was also the president speaker of the Sanhedrin, the highest governing and judging body of internal affairs in Palestine in this period. See also priest.

Hillel (the Elder). A well-known Pharisaic rabbi active at the time of Herod (37 BCE–4 CE). A number of important Pharisaic rabbinical traditions are presumed to originate with Hillel, and a distinct Hillel school was formed after him.

Hittites. An ancient people of Indo-European origin who forged into Asia Minor at the beginning of the second millennium BCE, and who later developed into a major power. The Hittite Empire lay in the region of present-day Turkey, but the geographic extent of their empire is greatly contested.

Holiness Code. The legal corpus in Leviticus 17–26.

holy war. A problematic term that in recent times has often been used of wars conducted supposedly in defense of a religious cause. In the ancient Near East religion and war belonged much closer together than what most of us can imagine today, and a whole set of cultic rituals had developed around the acts of war. The expression itself does not occur in the Old Testament, where the formula "to sanctify the war" related directly to specific rites to perform as a preparation for war. In the present context "holy war" means simply that the Deity participates actively in warfare on his people's side, and has a say as to the outcome on the battlefield. "Holy war" in the Old Testament is as such a consequence of the ancient Israelite view of salvation history that YHWH is behind everything and decides the outcome of history.

hypostasis. Personification of characteristics or religious concepts so that these appear as an independent, divine being.

hyssop. A plant that in ancient Israel was attributed the power to cleanse and that was used in rites of purification. It is unclear which plant it refers to, but it could possibly be *Majorana syriaca.*

Ibn Ezra. Abraham Ben Meir Ibn Ezra (1090–1164), famous Jewish author, biblical commentator, grammarian, and philosopher, born in Spain. He is known in particular for his extensive biblical commentaries, in which he greatly emphasizes the study of Hebrew grammar and the "simple sense of the text," while not avoiding using the texts as point of departure for philosophical principles.

idealistic. In the social sciences, failure to account adequately for the economic factors in the development of cultures.

idiographic. Pertains to the study of the specific (for example, specific events, specific persons) as opposed to the general. Used in particular of the historical sciences as opposed to the natural sciences. Historical incidents do not happen as a result of natural laws, but each one happens only once.

Iron Age. Archaeological period from about 1200 BCE to 586 BCE. The end of the period is usually set at the fall of Jerusalem in 586 BCE. In recent archaeological debate this has been questioned. Archaeology has shown a clear continuity in material culture from preexilic to postexilic times. With the Persian king Cyrus's takeover of the Babylonian Empire in 539 BCE, Persian culture became dominant. Archaeologically, it is more accurate to say that the Iron Age in Palestine lasts until the Persian period.

Ishtar. Sumerian Inanna; the most important goddess in Mesopotamian religion. The goddess of war, love, and fertility, worshiped all over the ancient Near East in countless variations as the original theology often dissolved completely into local cults. Her symbol was the planet Venus. Particularly famous was the myth of Ishtar and the god Tammuz, which involves Ishtar's descent into the netherworld. Even though Ishtar was worshiped from the earliest times down to the Common Era, it is hard to make out a satisfying impression of her, due to the extremely complex picture that the sources provide.

Isis. The sister and consort of the god Osiris, and mother of the god Horus. Isis was worshiped in ancient Egypt as a nature goddess. As the cult became very popular it absorbed a number of local cults. In late times the cult of Isis developed as part of the myth of Osiris, with Osiris as the dying and resurrected deity, and became one of the most important mystery religions. Eventually the cult of Isis spread across the whole Roman Empire. "Mystery religions" is a fairly imprecise designation for various religions in Greco-Roman times that were extremely popular. These cults, often of Middle Eastern origin, had secret membership and secret rituals, and attracted numerous followers. Apparently, the phenomenon disappeared during the 5th century CE.

Israel. Name used in a number of different ways in the Old Testament. (1) Another name for the patriarch Jacob as the ancestor of the Israelite people. (2) A term for the people who are the subject of the Old Testament. (3) A term for the northern kingdom of the divided monarchy as opposed to the southern kingdom of Judah. (4) A term for the southern kingdom of Judah after the fall of the northern kingdom in 721 BCE.

J. An abbreviation for the Yahwist or Yahwist source.

Jerome. Church father (ca. 342–420 CE) and skilled exegete who knew several languages. He spent a few years as a monk in Bethlehem. He is best known for the Vulgate, the translation of the Bible into Latin. See also Vulgate.

Josephus, Flavius. Most important Jewish historiographer in the Roman period (37–100 CE). He was of priestly descent. Among his most important works are the *Jewish War* and *Jewish Antiquities*. Although discussion of the reliability of Josephus as a historical source has been hot at times, more recent research has proven him to be far more reliable than what was thought earlier.

Jubilee. The fiftieth year came after a cycle of seven Sabbath years, each lasting seven years. In the Jubilee, all land should be returned to its rightful owners and all slaves be freed. In the Jubilee, land was not farmed, but rested. The name "Jubilee" comes from the Hebrew *yobel*, which is the name of the ram's horn used to proclaim the Jubilee. This happened on Yom Kippur, the great Day of Atonement.

Jubilees. Important pseudepigraphon, possibly written around 100 BCE. The book represents an expansion of the biblical material, with a rewriting of Genesis and the beginning of Exodus, presented as the revelation of an angel to Moses. The purpose was to make the biblical patriarchs more "Jewish." The tone is highly conservative in terms of Judaism, with great emphasis on the law and the Sabbath. The name *Jubilees* comes from the fact that history is divided into periods of "jubilees," or seven times seven years. In many ways the number seven plays a big role in the book. *Jubilees* constitutes a significant source of knowledge about Judaism in this early period.

kerygmatic. Relating to a message of salvation. The term is used by German scholars in particular to emphasize the nature of the texts as a proclamation of the faith of the ancient Israelite community of faith.

Ketuvim. Hebrew "writings"; in the Hebrew Bible, the term for the third part of the canon, also called the Hagiographa, from a Greek word meaning "holy scriptures." Psalms, Job, Proverbs, Ruth, Song of Songs, Ecclesiastes, Lamentations, Esther, Daniel, Ezra, Nehemiah, and Chronicles belong to the Ketuvim.

Law. See Torah.

Leningrad Codex. See *Biblia Hebraica Stuttgartensia.*

Leviathan. A mythical creature. In Ugaritic mythology Leviathan (Lothan) appears in the cosmic divine battle as a sea creature who fights against the god Baal on the side of the god Mot, and who is finally vanquished. Similar ideas can be found in the Old Testament and reflect the fact that such cosmic and mythical concepts must have been known also in ancient Israel, but that they gradually became marginalized within the YHWH religion.

levirate marriage. In ancient Israelite marriage law, the rule that if a man dies without having any sons, the man's brother must marry the widow. The first son born in the new marriage is counted as the dead man's son.

Levites. A group of temple servants or lower priesthood, named after their ancestor Levi. Moses belonged to the tribe of Levi.

Lex talionis. Latin for "law of retaliation"; the juridical principle that the one who has wrought another person injury should suffer to the same degree as the victim ("An eye for an eye, a tooth for a tooth").

LXX. The roman numeral 70, used for the Greek translation of the Bible. See Septuagint.

Maccabees, books of. Four apocryphal writings with varied content from various periods. Mainly authored in the first century BCE, they tell the story of the Maccabees' struggle of liberation. The Maccabees, or Hasmoneans, were a Jewish priestly family who spearheaded a revolt against the Seleucid rulers of Palestine in the second century BCE.

Marduk. The main god in the Babylonian pantheon. The cult of Marduk went through major developments over the centuries. From a minor Sumerian god in the third millennium BCE, Marduk came to be the head god of the Babylonians. His female consort was the goddess Sarpanitum. Together they had a son, Nabu, who became a central god for the Assyrians in particular. The cult of Marduk is attested down to Hellenistic times.

Mari. Powerful city-state in ancient times, by the Euphrates River in present-day Syria. It was settled from the mid-third millennium to the eighteenth century

BCE, when the Babylonian ruler Hammurabi destroyed it, and it never rose again. Through excavations by French archaeologists from the 1930s, great monumental buildings and many thousands of clay tablets inscribed with religious, judicial, and administrative texts came to light. The Mari texts have significantly increased our knowledge of Syrian and Mesopotamian culture in ancient times.

mashiach. See messiah.

Masoretes. Rabbis from the sixth to tenth centuries CE who had as their special task to secure the correct pronunciation and transmission of the Biblical Hebrew text; the name comes from Hebrew *massorah*, "transmission," really a collection of textual readings for the Hebrew Bible. By adding vowels and accents to the texts (which originally only had consonants), the Masoretes wanted to make sure that the unvocalized consonantal text was pronounced and understood correctly in a time when many people no longer understood Hebrew. The Masoretic Text, abbreviated MT, can also be found in a printed version. See *Biblia Hebraica Stuttgartensia.*

Media. An ancient empire in the northwestern part of present-day Iran (from ca. 900 BCE). It was incorporated into the Persian Empire by Cyrus in 550 BCE.

Mesopotamia. Greek, literally "between the rivers." The area between the rivers Euphrates and Tigris in ancient times, corresponding to present-day Iraq. In ancient times it was the place of Sumer, Babylonia, and Assyria.

messiah. From Hebrew *mashiach*, "anointed." The term is used in the Old Testament of kings and high priests who were anointed to their positions. It is worth noting that *mashiach* in the Old Testament is never used of a future figure of salvation, and that the eschatological expectation of the Messiah as a savior who is coming is a later development.

midrash (plural: midrashim). Biblical Hebrew word for "interpretation"; in early Judaism originally a term for the biblical interpretation (exegesis) of the rabbis. The term was used both of the interpretation of individual biblical books and of collections of these. There are two types of midrash, midrash halakah and midrash haggadah. Halakah (plural halakot) deals with the legal material, and haggadah (plural haggadot) deals with the narrative parts of the Bible and is therefore more homiletic in character. Haggadah came to include also the legendary material that had developed in connection to the biblical accounts. Eventually, "midrash" was used not only of rabbinical literature, but also of biblical interpretation in this period in general, including that within the New Testament.

minchah. Hebrew for "gift." Food offering, a common form of sacrifice in the Old Testament.

Mishnah. See Talmud.

Moab. In antiquity a territory and a people who inhabited the area east of the Dead Sea. Moab was, like ancient Israel, one of several small kingdoms that developed in the Near East at the beginning of the Iron Age. Even though, according to the Old Testament accounts, there were blood relations between the Israelites and the Moabites, the two kingdoms were constantly at war with each other. Moab's time of greatness was probably under King Mesha in the ninth century BCE. The famous Mesha Stela or Moabite Stone comes from this time. Except for a few fragmentary inscriptions, this is the only text that has survived from ancient Moab, though archaeological excavations have been carried out in the area. Moab's national god was Chemosh. In the eighth century BCE Moab became part of the Assyrian Empire.

Moses. Prophet and lawmaker, leader of the Israelites in the exodus from Egypt and through the desert on the way to the promised land of Canaan. What might lay behind the figure of Moses historically is very difficult to determine, but there is no foundation for claiming that he is a purely fictional character.

Moses, books of. See Torah.

Mot. From Semitic *mawt, mot,* meaning "death." The god of death, infertility, and the netherworld, known in particular from ancient Ugarit. In Ugaritic myth the divine battle of life and death between the gods Baal and Mot seems to have some connection to the change of the seasons.

MT. Abbreviation of Masoretic Text.

myth. A problematic term that has been used in a number of different ways in the study of religion. "Myth" was used in the past to denote stories about gods and divine beings and their interaction with humans. Later it became common to see a myth as representing an important "primordial event" that has significance in the present. Some would also connect the concept of myth to the cultic reenactment of such mythical past events. Others would claim that myth, through a story, seeks to portray an extrasensory reality in a form that is accessible to humans.

Nahar. A dragonlike creature in West Semitic mythology, perhaps mentioned in the Old Testament (e.g., "streams," Ps. 74:15; cf. vv. 13–14; "floods," 93:3; "rivers," Hab. 3:8).

Near East. Now commonly referred to as the Middle East, referring to the countries between present-day Egypt in the southwest, Turkey in the north, South Arabia in the southeast, and Iran in the east. The expression "the ancient Near East" usually refers, in terms of time, to the period from the earliest times to the fall of the western Roman Empire around 476 CE. In this period a whole range of significant cultures bloomed in the Eastern Mediterranean. Western civilization is far more influenced by the Near Eastern heritage than is commonly recognized. Important lands in the Middle East of ancient times were Sumer, Assyria, Babylonia, Elam, and Egypt. In the Syro-Palestinian area the Canaanite, Aramean, Phoenician (our alphabet originated with the Phoenicians), and Ugaritic cultures blossomed, in addition to ancient Israel. Other examples of highly developed cultures are the Hittites, pre-Islamic South Arabians, Nabateans, and Persians.

Nevi'im. Hebrew "prophets"; term used of the second part of the Hebrew canon that follows the Torah. In addition to the Deuteronomistic History (Joshua, Judges, Samuel, and Kings), Nevi'im includes the prophetic books Isaiah, Jeremiah, Ezekiel, and the Twelve Prophets. From the medieval period the Nevi'im was divided, and the historical material was called "Former Prophets" and the prophetic books were called "Latter Prophets."

nomothetic. Relating to, involving, or dealing with abstract, general, or universal statements or laws; often used of the natural sciences as opposed to historical sciences, which are characterized as "idiographic."

'olah. Hebrew for "burnt offering," "holocaust."

'olam. Hebrew for "a long period of time," "long duration," sometimes translated "eternity," although this must not be understood in the Greek, philosophical meaning of the word.

Osiris. Egyptian god of sun and vegetation, the most famous among the ancient Egyptian gods. In late antiquity (ca. 300–500 CE), the cult of Osiris spread all across the Mediterranean. See also Isis.

P. Abbreviation of the authors of the Priestly writings and the writings themselves. See Priestly History.

Palestine. A term used in different ways for an area in the Near East. In the Old Testament the term *peleshet,* which is the origin of the name "Palestine," can refer to the territory of Philistia, southwest of Canaan, and to the people who lived in the area, the Philistines. Later, "Palestine" became a term for the whole area in the Eastern Mediterranean that in the Old Testament is called Canaan.

parallelismus membrorum. Latin for "parallelism of the parts"; poetic compositional technique in which the content of one line (or phrase) is repeated (or expanded) in the next line (or phrase) through the use of other words or expressions. The technique is probably the best known and most used technique in Hebrew poetry. For an example see Psalm 64:3.

particularistic. In archaeology a concern with one's own scholarly tradition; less universal and cross-disciplinary.

Passover. A major feast in the Old Testament, celebrated in memory of the exodus from Egypt.

patriarch. From Greek *patriarchēs*, "original father"; used of the ancestors of the Israelites, Abraham, Isaac, and Jacob.

peace offering. See *shelamim.*

Pentateuch. The first five books of the Bible, the books of the Law. See also Torah.

Persian Empire. Ancient Near Eastern state to the east of Mesopotamia, roughly located where Iran is today. This vast area has an ancient culture with Elamite civilization attested as early as 2900 BCE. Around the mid-sixth century BCE, a hitherto unknown people emerged on the political arena in the Near East: the Achaemenids. Under the leadership of King Cyrus the Achaemenid Empire grew rapidly. Soon great states such as Egypt, Babylonia, and Media were part of this vast Persian Empire. The growth of the Persian Empire had consequences also for Judah, in that the Judeans who had been taken away captive by Nebuchadnezzar after the fall of Jerusalem in 586 BCE were allowed to return to their homeland. The return of some of the families probably began in 538 BCE and took place over a long period of time. These events are reflected in the books of Ezra and Nehemiah. The Achaemenid Empire fell in 330 BCE when it was incorporated into the great Hellenistic Empire of the Macedonian conqueror, Alexander the Great.

Pharisaism. An important religious movement in Judaism at the time of Jesus. The significance of the movement and its place in relation to mainstream contemporary Judaism is difficult to grasp clearly because of conflicting source material. Pharisaism is alternately described as a culturally liberal, centrally oriented, mass movement, or as a smaller sect that was exclusive, conservative, and fanatical. The description of Pharisaism in the New Testament is highly tendentious. Many influential Jews belonged to the Pharisees. Among their characteristics was the importance placed on the Oral Torah as just as important as the Written Torah (Pentateuch), the belief in angels, and certain eschatological concepts (e.g., the belief in the resurrection of the dead). Before his conversion Paul was a Pharisee. Even though Pharisaism seems to be a term that is difficult to define, there is little doubt about the great significance of the movement. Pharisaism grew in extent and came to play an important role in the consolidation of Judaism after the fall of Jerusalem in 70 CE. There seem to be clear connections between the early Pharisaic movement and the later rabbinical circles that created the Mishnah and the Talmud.

Phoenicia. A nation in the coastal area of Syria (present-day Lebanon) in the first millennium BCE. The Phoenicians were a Semitic people, perhaps descended from the ancient Canaanites. They were seemingly on good terms with the ancient Israelites. The Phoenicians produced crafted products such as glass, metals, woodwork, and carved ivory, and primarily made themselves known as a wealthy merchant nation. In connection with their extensive trade, they managed a shipping business that was impressive for its time and colonized large areas of the Mediterranean (Cyprus, Sicilia, Sardinia, coastal areas of present-day Spain and France). Famous cities in Phoenicia included Tyre, Sidon, Byblos, and Berytus. The most famous colony was

Carthage in North Africa, founded as early as the ninth century BCE. In the western colonies Phoenician was called Punic. Our alphabet is from the Phoenicians.

Pirqe Avot. Hebrew for "chapters of the fathers"; one of the 63 tractates of the Mishnah, also called simply "Avot." Contains collections of wisdom sayings and educational sayings, mostly of ethical and haggadic character, often set out in "sentences" or in the form of aphorisms. Avot has enjoyed enormous popularity in Judaism and has been highly influential.

Priestly History. Also called the "Priestly writings" or the "Priestly work." The authorial group responsible for the Tetrateuch, the first four books of the Bible (Genesis, Exodus, Leviticus, and Numbers), were priests. The Priestly History was not written as a new work in the sixth century BCE (or later), but was based on old Priestly sources that were reworked, expanded, and given a new framework. "P" is the abbreviation for both the authors behind the final work of Genesis through Numbers, and for the sources or traditions that this work is based on.

proselyte. From Greek *prosēlytos,* used in the Septuagint to translate Hebrew *ger,* "resident alien"; common term for non-Jew who through circumcision and other rites has joined Judaism. Today the term is used in general of a person who converts from one religion to another.

Pseudepigrapha. Greek for "writings with false titles," that is, works that have been falsely attributed to biblical characters. These works stand even more distant from the Jewish and Christian canons than the Apocrypha. The term is problematic for several reasons. First, the term seems somewhat demeaning today. The purpose of using fictitious authorial labels was to show respect and honor for the Old Testament models rather than to try to trick anyone. Further, the distinction between "apocryphal" and "pseudepigraphic" seems fairly arbitrary. It is not really possible to set down criteria to distinguish between them. As with the Apocrypha, the Pseudepigrapha were known in their Greek form. Most of them were probably originally written in Greek, or translated to Greek from a Hebrew or Aramaic original. Sometimes the Greek original has been lost, and we know the texts only through translations into more distant languages of the church in antiquity: Ethiopic, Syriac, Armenian, or Coptic. A number of new, hitherto unknown pseudepigrapha in Hebrew and Aramaic have been discovered at Qumran. All in all, this amounts to a significant group of literature. These texts are almost impossible to date individually, but scholars estimate that they have been composed in the period from about 200 BCE to around 50 CE. In other words, these writings represent an invaluable source of knowledge about Judaism in the period around the beginning of the Common Era.

Purim. One of the lesser feasts in the Jewish calendar, based on the account in the book of Esther. The celebration of Purim, which takes place on 14–15 Adar, is not prescribed in the Law, and the origin of the feast is unknown.

Q. Conventional abbreviation for manuscripts from Qumran. For example, 4QJer^a is the first manuscript (^{a}) of Jeremiah (Jer) found in Qumran Cave 4 (4Q).

qinah **(plural,** *qinot***).** Hebrew term for a lament for the dead, a dirge.

Qohelet. The Hebrew name for Ecclesiastes.

Qumran. Site of ruins by the northwestern shore of the Dead Sea where a number of handwritten manuscripts from about 200 BCE to 70 CE were found in eleven caves from 1947 to 1956. The discovery of these scrolls (aptly called the Dead Sea Scrolls) caused quite a stir when it turned out that they included biblical writings. Eventually, more and more texts came to light, and today the number of manuscripts has increased to a whole library. Most scholars agree that the texts come from a sectarian Jewish community that lived in the area at the beginning of the Common Era.

In addition to biblical writings the Dead Sea Scrolls also include a number of other types of texts. Some manuscripts have been found in complete form, many only in pieces and fragments. The Dead Sea Scrolls have revolutionized Old Testament research in textual criticism. Also in terms of history of religion, these texts have had great significance in that they have illuminated both Judaism and Christianity of this early period.

rabbi. Jewish scholar and teacher of the law, also the religious leader of a Jewish congregation. Rabbinism refers to the distinct culture emphasizing devotion to law and learning that developed in particular after the destruction of the Jerusalem temple in 70 CE, the period when the Oral Torah was collected and written down. The primary works of rabbinism or rabbinic Judaism are the Mishnah and the Talmud.

Ras Shamra. See Ugarit.

Rashi. Acronym for Rabbi Shelomo (Solomon) ben Isaac from Troyes (1040–1105), famous French rabbi. Rashi wrote a commentary on almost all parts of the Talmud. As the prime Talmud scholar of the medieval period Rashi came to have great and lasting influence on later Jewish thought.

redaction criticism. An approach to texts primarily to discern how an author uses the source material (oral and/or written) that he or she has access to. The authorial process itself involves modifying, presenting, and ideologically or theologically reworking already existing material. Redaction criticism seeks to understand this process. The redaction-critical method should not be used in isolation from other methodological approaches to texts.

Rig-Veda. In Vedic religion, a collection of hymns written in ancient Sanskrit, probably in the last half of the second millennium BCE. The hymns were used by the priest responsible for the acts of sacrifice.

Rosh Hashanah. Hebrew for "New Year." The Old Testament has no real indication of when the year began or ended, and there are indications that the New Year may have been celebrated both during the spring and the fall. We must also count the possibility that changes may have occurred in the ancient Israelite calendar. Some scholars have claimed that the New Year was celebrated in the fall in the preexilic period, and that the celebration was changed to the spring in postexilic times; but this is uncertain.

Sabbath. The last day of the week in the Jewish calendar. In ancient Israel the Sabbath seems to have been celebrated somewhat differently in different time periods, and it is difficult to reconstruct the Sabbath celebration in detail using the biblical sources. A Sabbath year was celebrated every seven years.

saga. Short fictional accounts, claiming to be historical, transmitted in oral tradition. There may have been an original, historical core in the saga, but over the course of the transmission process so much has been added that it is no longer possible to distinguish what that core might have been. There are different types of sagas; some of the major categories are: etiological sagas, to explain how something has come to be; historical sagas, perhaps originally had ties to persons or events; legendary sagas deal with supernatural experiences.

salvation history. From German *Heilsgeschichte;* a theological interpretation of history that focuses on God's saving activity. It is important to be aware that the overall perspective in the Old Testament is "salvation-historical" rather than "historical." For the Old Testament authors the course of history is a result of YHWH's interference in the world and his interactions with his people. There is a divine plan behind everything that happens. The central salvation-historical events in the Old Testament are creation, election, exodus, covenant making, desert wanderings, conquest, settlement in the promised land, exile.

Samaritans. In the Old Testament this term is used only as a designation of the population of Samaria and its surroundings. Only later do the Samaritans appear as a distinct sect with ties to Mount Gerizim. The negative view that we find in the New Testament is confirmed also by other sources. In Josephus we read about how the Samaritans were excluded from temple worship in Jerusalem through a public edict. When this schism between Jews and Samaritans began is a subject of much discussion. Some claim it started during the Persian period, but there are no sources to support this. The Samaritans live on in the present time as a small religious minority, most of them in the area around Mount Gerizim, not far from the city of Nablus.

Semitic. Common term for people and languages of a number of related ancient Near Eastern cultures. The term derives from the name of Noah's oldest son, Shem— "Semites" are descendants of Shem. The following languages are counted among the Semitic languages: Akkadian, Amorite, Ugaritic, Phoenician, Hebrew, Aramaic, Syriac, Arabic, and Ethiopic.

Septuagint. A Jewish translation of the Hebrew Bible into Greek, carried out for the most part in Alexandria. The naming of the Septuagint (abbreviated LXX, the roman numeral 70) stems from a legend found in the pseudepigraphic *Letter of Aristeas*. It tells the story of how 72 scholars were separated into closed cells to translate the Pentateuch. When they were released from their isolation, it turned out that they had miraculously translated the Law identically. In later tradition the understanding developed that the whole of the Bible had been translated in this way. In reality the translation of the Septuagint was complicated and went on for an extended period of time. The Pentateuch was translated in the third century BCE, while it most likely took about two hundred years before the whole of the Hebrew Bible had been translated. Many translators were involved, and translations were made from several different manuscript traditions. The Septuagint has played an important role in textual criticism. Today it is perhaps even more important as an example of early exegesis and because there are many quotes from it in the New Testament.

Shamash. From a generic Semitic word for "sun"; name of the Babylonian sun god, who played a significant role in ancient Mesopotamian religion. The sun was the natural symbol of the sun god. But it is important to note the dual role of the sun in this part of the world. The sun is not only life giving but may also kill. The harsh summer sun that came and singed all vegetation was not connected to Shamash. This death-bringing sun was tied to the god Nergal of the netherworld, or the fire god Gibil. Shamash was, among other things, responsible for law and order. As the deity that saw everything, he was also responsible for giving oracles. His female consort was the goddess Aya, one of the oldest Semitic deities known from Mesopotamia. Shamash had major sanctuaries in Sippar in northern Babylonia and in Larsa in the south. In Ashur Shamash had a famous temple together with his father, the moon god Sin.

Shammai. A famous rabbi, contemporary with Hillel. Together they were the most prominent Jewish learned men around the end of the first century BCE. Their influence was so great that in later Judaism two schools of thought formed: that of Hillel and that of Shammai. According to tradition Hillel was kind and Shammai was strict. The debate between the two movements significantly influenced the development of Judaism.

shelamim. Hebrew for "peace offering," "offering of thanksgiving."

Shema. Hebrew for "Hear!" after the opening words in Deuteronomy 6:4. This text became the creed of Judaism: "Hear Israel! YHWH is our God, YHWH alone." This difficult Hebrew text can also be translated in other ways, such as, "YHWH our God is one YHWH," or "YHWH is our God, YHWH is one," or "YHWH our God, YHWH is one."

Sitz im Leben. German for "place in life," "life setting." See form criticism.

source. Controversial term, traditionally used in historical research of all traces from the past that witness to human activity. Historical sources include both the material culture that is the field of archaeology and all forms of written documents, from the very short inscriptions of perhaps only one word to more complex literary compositions.

source criticism. A more recent term for literary criticism. With the increasing awareness in the eighteenth and nineteenth centuries that the Pentateuch was a complex document, the drive to identify the various sources of the final written document grew. The high point of the classical literary criticism was the source hypothesis of Julius Wellhausen, who identified four sources in the Pentateuch: the Yahwist, Elohist, Deuteronomy, and the Priestly source (J, E, D, and P). He claimed that, against the background of these sources, he could reconstruct the history of Israel and the history of its religion at various points in time. Classical literary criticism understood these sources as pure historical sources. In more recent research the word "source" is used in a completely different way as a term for the various documents that have been used by the authors of the Pentateuch (and the rest of the Old Testament writings). A "source" today is understood more as records or data. Literary criticism is also an important method in the study of the New Testament.

stratigraphy. The study of layers (strata), the most important principle of archaeological work and the cornerstone for interpreting an excavation. Explained simply, the principle, taken from geology, is that where one finds several compressed layers of ruins on top of one another, the upper layer must be younger than the ones beneath it. From studies of the wall in the excavated area (texture, content, color), the archaeologist will separate different layers from one another so that each of them can be studied carefully. See also tell.

Sumer. Ancient empire in the southern part of modern Iraq, between Baghdad and the Persian Gulf. The Sumerians, who settled in this area around 3300 BCE (there had been an earlier settlement in the area back to around the seventh millennium BCE), developed one of humanity's first advanced cultures, which initially consisted of a number of city-states. As a consequence of the many archaeological excavations in the area our knowledge of ancient Sumer is extensive. The most important gods were the four gods of creation: An, the god of the sky; Ki or Ninhursag, the goddess of earth; Enlil, the god of air (eventually the head of the pantheon); and Ea or Enki, the god of water and wisdom. The Sumerians were not Semitic, but their language is structurally similar to Turkish, Hungarian, Finnish, and a number of Caucasian dialects. But we have no idea where the Sumerians came from. Among their "inventions" we may count cuneiform (the writing system using wedge shapes), the mathematical sexagesimal system (based on the number 60, which we still use today in our division of units of time, and angles in minutes and degrees), monetary economy, city-state administration and bureaucracy, the development of legal codes, and systems for the division of labor. When the Babylonians took over power in this area sometime after 2000 BCE, they inherited Sumerian civilization. Through Babylonian influence, what was originally Sumerian religion, literature, and art spread across the whole Near East. In this way the Sumerians exercised their influence long after they had succumbed to and had been swallowed up by the Babylonians; for example, a number of biblical literary genres have their prototypes in Sumerian literature and religion. One of the most important cities in Sumer was Ur, which according to the biblical traditions was the birthplace of the patriarch Abraham.

Talmud. Hebrew for "teaching," "learning"; compilation of rabbinic interpretation of the Mishnah. The Mishnah received an almost canonical status soon after it was written, and became a norm for the interpretation of law in Judaism. The scholars who worked on interpreting the laws of the Mishnah were called Amoraim. Because some lived in Palestine and some in Babylonia, two separate traditions developed. The Talmud consists largely of halakot (legal material), but also has a number of haggadot (homiletical narratives). (See midrash.) The Talmud therefore has two parts: the Mishnah and an interpretation of the Mishnah. The interpretation, which is by far the larger part, is called Gemara (meaning "completion"). The Mishnah was written in Hebrew (a later Hebrew than that which we find in the Bible), and the "completion," the Gemara, is written in Aramaic. The Palestinian Talmud was completed around 400 CE and the Babylonian Talmud around 500 CE. When speaking of the Talmud in general, it is usually the Babylonian edition that is meant.

Tanak. Acronym for the Hebrew Bible based on the initial letter of the three divisions (Torah, Nevi'im, Ketuvim).

Tannin. Mythical, dragonlike creature mentioned in the Old Testament (e.g., Isa. 27:1).

Tehillim. The Hebrew title of the book of Psalms.

tehom. Hebrew for "deep (sea)." In the Priestly creation narrative, a term for the primordial waters or "deep" (Gen. 1:2).

Telipinu. A central god of vegetation in Hittite religion, son of the weather god Taru.

tell. Arabic word for a natural or artificial mound (Hebrew *tel*). Normally used in archaeological contexts of an artificially created mound, a mound of ruins. These tells are very common all across the Middle East, and hide earlier settlements of villages or cities. Many have been excavated, and it is the study of the content of these tells that has provided most of the knowledge we have about the ancient Near East today. The word also appears in place names, such as Tell el-Hesi or Tell Dan. See also stratigraphy.

temple. The temple in Jerusalem played a central role in ancient Israelite, Old Testament, Jewish, and New Testament traditions. Over time, Jerusalem had not one but three different temples. The temple of Solomon was built in the tenth century BCE. We do not know much about this temple except that it was destroyed by the Babylonians in 586 BCE. A new temple was built between 520 and 515 BCE. Eventually various renovations became necessary. King Herod built a completely new temple. Herod's temple, begun in 20 BCE, was the grandest of the three temples, but it was also the one to exist for the shortest period of time. In 70 CE Herod's temple was destroyed by the Roman legions of Titus. There is a fair amount of information available today about Herod's temple, due to extensive excavations, in particular in the last years.

Tetrateuch. Name given to the first four books of the Bible: Genesis, Exodus, Leviticus, Numbers.

textual criticism. The study of ancient manuscripts and old translations of the Bible in order to achieve the best biblical text that for various reasons is not intelligible or is in other ways problematic. At first, textual criticism understood its task as attempting to reconstruct the "original text." More recent scholars are not so confident that this is possible. Further, the term "original text" is itself methodologically questionable.

theophany. A visible manifestation of the divine to humans, a limited visualization of God in the world that can be grasped by the senses. For example, YHWH shows himself to Moses on Mount Sinai in Exodus 19–20.

Tiamat. In Babylonian mythology the name of the sea creature-goddess that is vanquished by the god Marduk. In the creation account *Enuma Elish*, we read about how the creation god Marduk parts the dead body of Tiamat in two and creates the sky and earth of the two parts. The name Tiamat is the feminine form of the Akkadian word for "sea," *tamtu*.

Torah. Hebrew for "instruction," "teaching," "law"; also called the "Written Torah" as opposed to the Oral Torah. *Torah*, or "Law," is the Hebrew term for the first part of the Bible, the Pentateuch. Contrary to popular belief, one cannot equate the Torah and Judaism. The five books of Moses play a significant role in Judaism, but are not the expression of Jewish faith in the way that many might think. The content of the Talmud treats the Pentateuch only to a modest extent. Similar to Christianity, Judaism found its shape *after* the time of the Hebrew Bible. In the formative period of Judaism, torah (with lowercase *t*) became something much more important. In the course of the first centuries CE, when Judaism, like Christianity, found its shape, Torah went from being a name for the first five books of Moses to become torah, a symbol of a complete rabbinic system, practically identical to "Judaism" in the true sense of the word.

Torah, Oral. A generic term for the Jewish religious traditions that circulated in the Second Temple period (515–20 BCE), and in the following centuries. Eventually, these oral traditions were written down and make up what we today know as the "rabbinic writings." The Mishnah and Talmud belong to the Oral Torah. Gradually, the idea developed that the Oral Torah had also been transmitted to Moses on Mount Sinai, together with the Written Torah (the Pentateuch).

tradition criticism. One of the classical historical-critical methods in biblical research (in New Testament research, the term "redaction criticism" is often used of the same method). Tradition criticism posits that oral and written traditions predate the texts in their present form. Tradition criticism, or tradition history, is the practice of identifying these traditions, and the study of their origin and development. Normally, tradition criticism also employs other methods, such as source criticism or form criticism. Even though tradition criticism is a result, in many ways, of literary criticism and form criticism, one might also see a contradiction between these approaches. A comparison of German tradition criticism (von Rad, Noth) and the Scandinavian (Mowinckel and, in particular, Engnell) shows further that there are major differences between the ways that the method has been practiced. It is, in this case, important to be aware that the classical, so-called methods of biblical research are not as clear as one might expect when the term "method" is used. Rather, these are specific approaches, sometimes almost an expression of what one wishes to emphasize.

Twelve Prophets, Book of. The collection of "minor" (i.e., shorter) prophetic books: Hosea, Joel, Amos, Obadiah, Jonah, Micah, Nahum, Habakkuk, Zephaniah, Haggai, Zechariah, and Malachi.

Ugarit. Port city in northern Syria in antiquity, with settlement going back to the Paleolithic. In Modern Arabic the place is called Ras Shamra; it lies at the same latitude as the northern tip of Cyprus. The site has been excavated by French archaeologists since 1929, and excavations are ongoing. The city of Ugarit was the capital of a small kingdom and was completely destroyed around 1200 BCE. From the Late Bronze period temples, palaces, and richly decorated private homes have been excavated. In this period the city was a flowering trade metropolis. A particularly spectacular find was several thousand clay tablets with texts in a number of Semitic languages, including a hitherto unknown alphabetic language clearly related to Hebrew and Phoenician, subsequently called Ugaritic. From the many texts much has been learned about the history, religion, economy, and social situation of this city. In a number of areas, Ugaritology has cast light also on the study of the Old Testament. This is true in particular for language and religion. The main gods of ancient Ugarit were El and Baal, known from the Old Testament, and the goddess Anat.

Urash. In ancient Sumerian religion, the consort of the god An, and mother of Nininsina, the god of salvation. The name of the goddess means "earth."

Urim. Object of divination used to answer inquiries about the will of YHWH. Probably the answers were usually yes or no to this type of inquiry. "Urim" usually occurs with "Thummim"; both were placed in a pocket of the ephod (garment worn by the high priest). We do not really know what they were, how they were used, or how widespread their use was.

verbal inspiration. The idea that the whole Bible has been inspired directly, word for word, by the Holy Spirit and is therefore infallible. In Judaism a similar view of the Law was found in earlier times.

Vulgate. From Latin for "the common"; Jerome's translation of the Bible, undertaken in 382–405 CE, later became the authorized Bible translation of the Roman Catholic Church. The Vulgate was printed was the first time in the Gutenberg Bible of 1456. It has been seen as particularly valuable because Jerome knew Hebrew and was able to translate (with the help of Jewish scholars) almost the whole Old Testament from the primary text, and relied less on the Septuagint.

Writings. See Ketuvim.

Yahweh. See YHWH.

Yahwist. In classical source criticism the Yahwist (abbreviated J, from German "Jahwist") was one of the four main sources. More recently there has been much disagreement about the Yahwist, and few scholars who work within this field today think that it is possible to distinguish the Yahwist as a distinct source in the same way as in the past. See also source criticism.

Yam. From West Semitic for "sea"; a sea god, known from Ugaritic religion.

YHWH. The most important name for Israel's God in the Old Testament, occurring almost seven thousand times. It is this divine name that in our Bibles is translated as "the LORD." But this is really an incorrect rendering. YHWH is a proper noun and cannot be translated. The name YHWH is made up of four consonants (hence also called the Tetragrammaton) and is not vocalized, so we cannot know how it was pronounced. Scholars assume that the correct pronunciation may have been "Yahweh." Another pronunciation, "Jehovah," is not probable, but comes from the vowels of 'adonay, the word Jews read when they encountered the Tetragrammaton in the text, because God's name is too holy to be uttered.

Yom Kippur. The great Day of Atonement, a grave day of fasting celebrated in ancient Israel ten days after the New Year in the fall. On this day the sins of the people were symbolically transferred to a scapegoat that was chased out into the wilderness.

Index of Hebrew Bible Texts

Index of Subjects

King (*continued*)
  of Tyre, 59
  YHWH as, 35, 95, 138, 142, 143
  See also Israel; royal
kingdom, in Israel. *See* Israel
Kittel, Gerhard, 178
Knoppers, Gary, 79
knowledge, in wisdom tradition, 158, 162, 166, 180
Koine Greek, 183
Korah, 47
Korahite psalms, 136
Kuenen, Abraham, 50
Kugel, James, 133
Kuntillet Ajrud, 76, 77, 177

Laban, 58
Lachish, 66
Lady Folly, 159
Lady Wisdom, 159
Laish, 66
lament
  Akkadian city lament, 157
  city lament, 154, 156
  communal, 126, 136, 141, 149, 150, 155
  of the destruction, 156, 157, 177
  funerary, 7, 154, 155, 189
  individual, 7, 104, 123, 136, 140, 155, 160
  lament literature, 154
  lament psalms, 139, 140, 141, 144, 145, 146
  Laments of Jeremiah, 123
land
  allotment of, 45
  conquest of, 14, 32, 51, 54, 56, 60, 62, 63, 66, 67, 190
  of Israel, 3, 4, 48, 56, 89, 90, 116, 117, 130, 155
  possession of, 57, 60, 117
  promise of, 29, 30, 33
  promised, 11, 21, 31, 32, 54, 56, 58, 60, 71, 117, 186, 190
  restoration of, 80
  settle in, 21, 32, 61, 62, 63, 65, 66, 71, 74, 110, 117, 190
language
  Akkadian, 6, 59, 175, 182, 191
  Ammonite, 47
  Amorite, 191
  Arabic, 191
  Aramaic, 5, 6, 47, 59, 81, 84, 85, 87, 132, 175, 176, 180, 189, 191, 193
  Armenian, 189
  Assyrian, 6, 175, 177
  Babylonian, 6, 156, 175, 177, 182
  Biblical Hebrew, 5, 18, 81, 84, 183, 193
  Coptic, 189
  Deuteronomistic, 57, 92, 101, 123
  of diplomacy, 87, 176

  Ethiopic, 180, 189, 191
  Hebrew, 5, 6, 9, 13, 18, 47, 76, 81, 84, 176, 182, 183, 189, 191, 193, 194
  Old Babylonian, 156, 182
  Phoenician, 5, 191, 194
  prophetic, 114, 133, 179
  Sanskrit, 190
  Semitic, 6, 175, 191, 194
  South Semitic, 180
  Sumerian, 192
  Syriac, 189, 191
  and the Tower of Babel, 27
  Ugaritic, 191, 194
  of war, 61, 179
  West Semitic, 5, 26, 47, 176
Larsa, 191
Late Bronze Age, 62, 63, 66, 178, 182, 194
Latter Prophets, 6, 98, 187
law
  Book of the Covenant, 178
  in the Deuteronomistic History, 54, 57, 67, 70, 71, 72
  and *go'el*, 182
  in the history of biblical research, 50, 99, 102, 105
  in Jeremiah, 123
  in Joshua, 60
  lawbook and Deuteronomy, 60, 73
  levirate marriage, 172
  of Moses in Nehemiah, 84
  natural laws, 19, 158, 161, 169
  origin of law in Semitic cultures, 16
  in the Priestly History, 14, 15, 32, 33, 39, 40–44
  purity laws, 43–44
  of retaliation (*see* lex talionis)
  Roman, 16, 179
  and Sabbath, 39
  and Shamash, 191
  See also Torah
lawgiver, 33, 57, 182
leader, 17, 29, 60, 61, 67, 68, 87, 117, 118, 121, 123, 124, 144, 186
Leah, 29
learning, in wisdom tradition, 158, 162
leavened dough, 42
Lebanon, 149, 162, 178, 188
legend, 26, 27, 28, 31, 32, 46, 51, 60, 61, 67, 108, 109, 110, 171, 174, 190, 191
legitimize, 28, 57, 60, 73, 90, 131
Lemaire, André, 76, 77
Leningrad Codex, 8, 9, 178, 185
Letter of Aristeas, 191
Letter of Jeremiah, 176
Levant, 80
Levi, 185
Leviathan, 24, 25, 185
levirate marriage, 172, 185

theophany of, 129, 143, 193
trust in, 61, 144
turn to, 113, 114, 126, 140, 146
unfaithful against, 71, 123, 125
and war, 56, 60, 61, 183
will of, 83, 195
word of, 15, 22, 118
worship of, 36, 44, 47, 58, 70, 74, 77, 94, 99, 113, 127, 177
wrath of, 69, 126, 148, 150
YHWH psalms, 136
YHWH religion, 74, 75–78, 82, 90, 118–20, 180, 185
YHWH's Anat, 76
YHWH's enthronement, feast of, 138, 142

YHWH's feast, 35
yield, 147, 148. *See also* agriculture; crop; harvest
Yom Kippur, 35, 36, 183, 185, 195. *See also* Day of Atonement

Zedekiah, 115
Zerubbabel, 85, 87, 88
Zeus, 27, 183
ziggurat, 28
Zion, 143, 148
Zion hymns, 143
Zionism, 30
Zvi, Ehud Ben, 110
Zwingli, Huldrych, 175